Best Wishes,

Ray Williams

2001

ENDORSEMENTS

This motivational book on Bill Veeck is right on the mark
Jim Murray (deceased)
Former Sportswriter, *Los Angeles Times*

A new and revealing look at Bill Veeck. Pat Williams and Michael Weinreb have done a masterful job. This book is almost as much fun as being at one of Bill Veeck's promotions.
Terry Pluto
***Akron Beacon Journal* Sports Writer**

I am really happy that Pat Williams wrote this great book about Bill Veeck. There was no finer man than Bill. He was a man who would try anything. If all baseball owners could be like him, then we would all be in for a treat.
Roy Sievers
Former Major League Baseball Player

Pat Williams, a junior-grade Bill Veeck, has the time of his life—and ours—with this accurate, amusing account of baseball's one-and-only Bill Veeck. You will love this happy, pleasant, inspiring book about an inspiring guy.
Bob Broeg
***St. Louis Post-Dispatch* Hall of Fame writer, 1979**

Bill Veeck brought his philosophy of life to the game of baseball, and the result was professional sports' greatest 20th Century entrepreneur. In *Marketing Your Dreams*, Pat Williams convincingly argues that we all can gain inspiration and valuable lessons from Veeck's genius.
Dr. Andrew Zimbalist
Department of Economics, Smith College

Bill Veeck and P.T. Barnum have been integral topics in my sport marketing classes because of the way they understood human nature and consumer behavior. In *Marketing Your Dreams*, Pat Williams portrays Veeck as a lifetime learner who loved people and went out of his way to understand their likes and dislikes and to interact with them. This book is an inspirational examination of a great human being who happened to be a great sport marketer and of the legacy of enjoyment and entertainment he left for sports fans everywhere.
Dr. Bill Sutton
Graduate Program Director, University of Massachusetts Sport Management Program
Principal, Audience Analysis Consulting Group

Bill Veeck was one of the most inspirational individuals there has ever been in the game of baseball. He not only motivated you professionally but personally as well. Bill's messages and guidelines can help anyone who reads this book.

David Dombrowski
President, Florida Marlins

I loved Bill Veeck, and I love that Pat Williams has given us a book to make sure Bill's life can be accurately remembered.

Ned Garver
Former MajorLeague Pitcher

If memories are made to last forever, mine will be of Bill Veeck and the St. Louis Browns. This book will give you the opportunity to share in many of those same memories.

Marty Marion
Former Major League Shortstop and Manager

Aside from some pompous fat cats and stuffed shirts, Bill Veeck was an inspiration to all who were lucky enough to know him. In this entertaining book, Pat Williams, Bill's protégé, shows us why.

Larry Ritter
Author of *The Glory of Their Times*

A telegram I received from Bill Veeck prior to the 1981 season highlights a few of his many wonderful qualities that you'll read about in Pat Williams' terrific book. Bill wrote: 'For the first time, you have a chance to win. Do your best and have fun doing it!' ''

Tony La Russa
Manager, St. Louis Cardinals

When you read this great book about Bill Veeck, you'll learn about courage, intelligence, devotion to family, plus respect for people, all wrapped around a gigantic sense of humor. Everything you would hope for in a man, you found in Bill Veeck.

Chuck Thompson
Hall of Fame Baseball Announcer

Most people judged Bill Veeck as an entertainer. However, Bill was as good as anyone with his knowledge of baseball, his players and the fans. Bill found ways to make the game entertaining for all of us in or around the ballpark. You'll read all about it in this book.

Lou Boudreau
Former Cleveland Indians Manager

There has been only one Bill Veeck. He was the original Internet. Ideas galore! His craving for knowledge was boundless. Always thinking, always musing, always inquiring. And always for the fans—his people—sharing a common love: BASEBALL. This giant leprechaun left everyone who knew him with a lasting memory of graciousness, warmth and generosity. How fortunate, we who called him "friend" have had our lives enriched. This wonderful book captures the Bill Veeck I admired and remember.

Al Rosen
Former Cleveland Indians player

A top sports promoter's homage to the greatest of all sports promoters; heartfelt and instructive.
Leonard Koppett
Author and Hall of Fame Sportswriter

Bill Veeck was one of the most positive men I have ever had the honor of knowing. He felt you could be or do anything you wanted in life. He had three simple rules for me: #1 was never quit; #2 was really important: that was never, *never* quit; but #3 was the most important of all: it was never, never, *never* quit. This is how you reach your dreams. He helped me reach mine and also many others. This book will help you reach yours.
Chuck Tanner
Manager, '79 World Series Champs—Pittsburgh Pirates

Pat Williams delivers an excellent piece of writing and truly captures the spirit of Bill Veeck.
Art Modell
Owner, Baltimore Ravens

Each day working with Bill Veeck brought adventure, humor, knowledge, creativity, spontaneity, achievement, wisdom, vision and much more. This book captures all of that plus more.
Roland Hemond
Senior Executive Vice President of Baseball Operations for the Arizona Diamondbacks

This powerful book brought Bill Veeck back to life for me. Reading this book is the next best thing to a six-hour dinner with Bill at Toots Shor's in New York City.
Buzzie Bavasi
Former Los Angeles Dodgers and San Diego Padres Executive

Pat Williams treats his subject with the same fearless passion, energy and enthusiasm that was so characteristic of Bill Veeck's life. A helpful and fun book.
Andy McPhail
President, Chicago Cubs

What a great book. Each chapter is more interesting than the previous one. There was no one like Bill Veeck, and there is nothing like this book anywhere.
Bob Feller
Hall of Fame Pitcher, Cleveland Indians

In a rarity, Pat Williams pitches a winning doubleheader. Not only does he tell you the story of one of the most fascinating and successful promoters in the history of baseball—if not all of sports—Bill Veeck, but also shows you how to apply his successful formula for your own success.
Bert Randolph Sugar
Author, *The 100 Greatest Athletes of All Time*

Pat Williams' book provided me with wonderful memories of Bill Veeck. Bill loved baseball almost as much as he loved life. You had to be there to appreciate the joy he got from making people laugh. To him, it was all about having fun. He believed it was his job to entertain the fans until game time, then it was up to the team. What a job he did!
Don Kessinger
Former Major League Shortstop and Manager

This book captures the story of our American legend, Bill Veeck. It is full of anecdotes and penetrating insights about a great man! It is a significant addition to any library.
Ray Meyer
Former DePaul University Basketball Coach

Bill Veeck, who once owned three different major-league baseball teams, was a man who knew how to make money and have fun doing it. The Pied Piper of Joy, as he was called, had a young disciple, Pat Williams, who learned many valuable lessons from the master. Pat never sent a midget up to the plate but, like Veeck, has been an inspiration to everyone he has ever met. This is a rare opportunity to get to know them both.
Peter Golenbock
Sports Author

People always ask me what Bill was like. No mystery. Whatever you saw that was the real Bill Veeck.
Ed Linn (deceased)
Bill Veeck's Biographer

Pat Williams is one of the most insightful observers of the human experience. His work once again brings out so much about someone you thought you knew but really didn't.
Jerry Reinsdorf
Chairman, Chicago White Sox and Chicago Bulls

Bill Veeck was more than the best business mind in professional sports during the 20th Century. Bill also was a warm, generous, inspiring person who deeply touched his friends and associates. This book, like no other, fills in this second part of Bill's portrait, so that generations of readers to come can be inspired by his example as those of us fortunate enough to know him were inspired during his life.
Roger Noll
Economist and Author

Bill Veeck was the essence of fun, and Pat Williams never loses sight of the importance of Veeck and fun as we live our daily lives.
Bud Collins
***Boston Globe*/NBC**

Marketing Your Dreams is a primer for entrepreneurs, a textbook for sports-team executives, and a manual for the curious fan interested in big-time athletics. Inspirational? Certainly. But Pat Williams doubles the reader's pleasure by penning a paean to Bill Veeck, the premier sports promoter of the recent millennium. Veeck would teach anyone who would listen to him how to have fun in the baseball business. Bill became Pat's icon, his guru, his role model. In time, Williams found success…and fun…in pro baseball and pro basketball. Veeck, the master, would have enjoyed *Marketing Your Dreams*. "Great fun," he would say—his ultimate compliment for work well done.
Jim Brosnan
Former Major League Pitcher and Best-Selling Author

Bill Veeck was one of the most memorable characters I met in my long baseball career. I'm so pleased that you can now get to know him in Pat Williams' fabulous new book.

Billy Pierce
Former White Sox Pitching Great

I knew Bill Veeck for many years as a player and manager. We had a great time together, and I always felt a book like this should be written about him. I'm so glad Pat Williams did it.

Bob Lemon (deceased)
Baseball Hall of Fame Pitcher

An interesting and inspiring book by Pat Williams, with the great innovator Bill Veeck looking over his shoulder—great reading!

Ernie Harwell
Baseball Hall of Fame Broadcaster

Bill Veeck always wanted you to leave the ballpark with a memory. Pat Williams has captured enough Veeck memories to last a lifetime (not just ours, our grandchildren's!). It is like having lunch at Bill's favorite spot in Chicago—the Vernon Parkway Tap on the Southside of Chicago—all over again.

Milo Hamilton
Baseball Hall of Fame Broadcaster

Marketing Your Dreams contains a message for everyone who has a vision and a drive for success, and is essential reading for those seeking an understanding of Bill Veeck's unique contribution to sport and society. The book provides an opportunity for everyone to know and understand one of the greatest personalities of our time and to capitalize on his providence to enrich our own lives. If you are looking to rekindle your passion for people and life, read this book. Pat Williams was able to successfully capture the spirit of Bill Veeck and convey Veeck's passion for life. *Marketing Your Dreams* can reawaken the passion in all of us.

David K. Stotlar
Professor, Sport Marketing - University of Northern Colorado

Pat Williams has written the classic book on sports marketing from the life of my hero Bill Veeck. I'll be recommending this book a lot.

Jon Spoelstra
Sports Marketer and Author of *Ice to the Eskimos*

This book is the story of courage in the face of disabilities; conviction in the face of resistance to progress; and complexity in the face of simple-mindedness. Veeck is fascinating because the lessons of his life and the truth of his beliefs are timeless and applicable. This is good stuff!

Fay Vincent
Former Commissioner, Major League Baseball

Bill Veeck was one of the most interesting, controversial and exciting characters in the history of baseball. And who better to tell the story than Pat Williams.

Lee MacPhail
Former President of the American League

When it comes to marketing, no one's more qualified to document Bill Veeck's accomplishments than Pat Williams, the Bill Veeck of minor-league baseball and pro basketball.
Rudy Martzke
USA Today, **Television Sports Columnist and the ghost writer for Bill Veeck at the 1982 World Series**

Bill Veeck was the most fascinating man I met during the many years of my baseball broadcasting career. Pat Williams, quite a promoter himself, has certainly captured the savvy personality and flair of this intriguing genius.
Curt Gowdy
Hall of Fame Sportscaster

Bill Veeck was a good guy. Billy Martin and I would go visit him upstairs at Comiskey Park. He was a lot of fun and a terrific promoter.
Yogi Berra
Baseball Hall of Famer

Bill Veeck made baseball fun for the fan. The fans were his main interest—fun plus fans. I always admired him.
Andy Pafko
Former National League Outfielder

I was with Bill Veeck during the 1976 season in Chicago. He was a free spirit and taught me the importance of having fun every day. I never met anyone else like him in baseball. He really made an impact on my life.
Rich "Goose" Gossage
Former Major League Pitcher

Bill Veeck was a baseball visionary whose unique combination of intellect and showmanship made him a legendary man of the game. Pat Williams captures the indelible essence of the man as well as the many lives he touched.
Steve Stone
Chicago Cubs Broadcaster

Pat Williams teaches us what Bill Veeck taught him—Be goofy whenever possible!
Dave Kindred
The Sporting News

Pat Williams' book about Bill Veeck is wonderful! A real labor of love that you will enjoy.
Jerome Holtzman
Official Baseball Historian, Major League Baseball

Bill Veeck was a fine man. He was a great promoter and worked very hard. This book by Pat Williams details what you can achieve by working hard, just like Bill Veeck did.
Al Lopez
Baseball Hall of Fame Catcher and Manager

Bill Veeck was a happy person, a good guy. He loved life and was always on the go.
Phil Cavaretta
Former Chicago Cubs Great

Bill Veeck could motivate anyone who would listen with an open mind. Unfortunately, his contemporaries in baseball ownership did not hear him because their minds were closed. Long after Bill's death, baseball continues to suffer. Read this book and be motivated!
Bill Gleason
Sportswriter & Television Personality

Boy, Bill Veeck could promote anything! A great guy.
Ted Williams
Baseball Hall of Famer

Bill Veeck's enthusiasm for fun and games and life was infectious Pat Williams caught it and in this book spreads it. Lucky us.
Larry Merchant
Sportswriter and Broadcaster

Bill Veeck's simple messages endure: Live. Laugh. Enjoy. Never forget that the best thing about sports is the fun we all have playing them, watching them, or, better still, working in them.
Gary Bettman
Commissioner, National Hockey League

Bill Veeck is one of my heroes. Pat Williams is one of my favorite people. What a winning exacta this is!
Larry King
Talk Show Host

Pat Williams, an innovative promoter in his own right, is the proper guy to do a book about Bill Veeck.
Tim McCarver
Baseball Broadcaster

I played for Bill Veeck in Cleveland in 1949. He was the most unusual owner I ever knew. A great promoter, very friendly and always taking care of the fans.
Mickey Vernon
Two-time American League Batting Champion

In this game of life, there are some people who are simply so unique, so very special, that no words can do them justice. To me, Bill Veeck was such a person. I cannot say enough about him. Bill respected me—not just as a ballplayer—but as a human being. He is someone I have never forgotten, and I never will as long as there is a breath of life in me.
Minnie Minoso
Former Major-League Outfielder

Bill Veeck was my friend and encourager. I loved him and you will too after you read this book.
Early Wynn (deceased)
Hall of Fame Pitcher

Pat Williams is the perfect person to write a motivational book on Bill Veeck. I felt honored to contribute to this project.
Jack Brickhouse (deceased)
Hall of Fame Broadcaster

Bill Veeck was the most memorable baseball executive in baseball history. This book will inspire you no matter your field of endeavor.
Harry Caray (deceased)
Hall of Fame Broadcaster

Marketing Your Dreams

Business and Life Lessons from Bill Veeck
Baseball's Marketing Genius

by
Pat Williams
with Michael Weinreb

Director of production: Susan M. McKinney
Dust jacket design: Todd Lauer
Editor: Christopher Stolle

ISBN:1-58261-182-3

Sports Publishing Inc.
804 N. Neil
Champaign, IL 61820
www.SportsPublishingInc.com

Printed in the United States of America.

To my son Bobby, who aspires to a career in baseball, just like Bill Veeck. I hope your dreams are as vast as his.
—Pat Williams

To my mother and father.
—Michael Weinreb

Contents

Acknowledgments .... *vii*

William the Unconquerable by Roger Kahn .... *viii*

Foreword by Mike Lupica .... *xi*

Bill Veeck's 12 Commandments .... *xiv*

Bill Veeck: A Biography .... *xv*

Introduction 2

1 Tomorrow Never Comes 14
   On Veeck's coddling of life's every moment.

2 Attack The Camera 32
   On Veeck's unbridled passion and enthusiasm.

3 Now That Causes Some Thought 48
   On Veeck's prolific imagination and creativity.

4 That Sounds Like Great Fun 62
   On Veeck's zest for fun and humor.

5 Who Do You Think You Are, Bill Veeck? 78
   On Veeck's striking penchant for individuality.

6 Keep The Change And Buy A House 90
   On Veeck's remarkable penchant for dealing with people.

7 A Ph.D. In Veeck 106
   On Veeck's influence and empowerment.

8 Spoken Like A True Bum 122
   On Veeck's unwavering humility.

9 A Little Pizza Smell In A Crowded Car 132
   On Veeck and family.

10 That First Fine Careless Rapture 148
   On Veeck as a reader and writer and the value of acquired wisdom.

11 Speaking In A Coal Mine 162
On Veeck as a public speaker.

12 A Pest, A Salesman 176
On Veeck as a salesman.

13 Fifty Thousand Bolts And A Bunch Of Nuts 188
On Veeck as a promoter.

14 One Will Do It 208
On Veeck's work ethic.

15 A One-Legged Man Playing Tennis 218
On Veeck's competitive nature.

16 The Last Honest Used-Car Salesman 228
On Veeck's notions of honesty and integrity.

17 The Razor Edge Of Disaster 238
On Veeck's confidence and courage and willingness to take risks.

18 Can't Beat The Mileage 250
On Veeck's ability to transform handicaps into strengths.

19 You Can't Beat A Man Who Won't Be Beat 260
On Veeck's perseverance.

20 The Incidental Leader 272
On Veeck's leadership abilities.

EPILOGUE: If You Don't Have A Dream 286
On Veeck and the fulfillment of dreams.

Afterword by Michael Weinreb 296

Appendices 299

Acknowledgments

I would like to thank Bob Vander Weide, president and CEO of RDV Sports, and the RDV Sports family; Melinda Ethington, my assistant; Leslie Boucher and Hank Martens of the mailroom at RDV Sports; Ken Hussar, Roland Hemond, Dr. Bill Sutton and Bert Randolph Sugar, for their thorough proofreading of this book; Michael Weinreb, a skilled young writer who has organized this material brilliantly; and my wife Ruth and our children, who have been so supportive of this all-encompassing project.

William the Unconquerable

by Roger Kahn

Some millennia backwards in time, the citizenry of Rome maintained that Julius Caesar could do seven things simultaneously. (Sadly, at least for the illustrious general, sniffing out a murderous conspiracy was not one of them). Bill Veeck, when he was between ballclubs and living a squire's life in the rolling green countryside of Maryland's eastern shore, could only do, say, five or six things at once. But he was better than Caesar on conspiracies. He knew that the lords of baseball plotted consistently to keep the greatest promoter since Barnum unemployed. "Their opposition to me begins with one fact," he said. "I think baseball is supposed to be fun."

I visited him often during his Maryland years. He and Mary Frances had contributed enthusiastically to the population explosion, and there were always Veeck children about for mine to play with. Plus swings, Frisbees, a trampoline and a broad, calm estuary called Peachblossom Creek that was a gentle place until the jellyfish moved in. On arriving at Chateau Veeck, I usually saw something like this: Veeck was sitting on a couch in shorts and a polo shirt, baring what he called his "wooden leg." He was reading a novel, but in case he wanted a change of pace, a biography sat open on the cocktail table. Some sort of talk show barked from the television set. Above that sound, Veeck was explaining to one of the children that

Roger Kahn (Courtesy of Roger Kahn)

certainly, he would drive to the Washington airport to pick up the new pet armadillo, but the animal would not arrive until tomorrow. And, oh, yes, hi, to all of us and did I know that if the establishment kept barring him from baseball, he might open a bookshop or run for the Senate or even pass the bar exam and sue them all. He was drinking beer. He was always drinking beer. And smoking mentholated cigarettes. No one ever accused Bill Veeck of running a health club.

What happened next would be a renaissance weekend centered about a one-man renaissance. As you might know, Veeck lost a leg after a grievous injury in the South Pacific during World War II. Something like jungle rot attacked open bone, and he had to undergo a series of amputations. "I'm not handicapped," he liked to say. "I'm crippled. If I couldn't say I was crippled, then I'd be handicapped." He must have suffered a lot, but he never let on. Indeed, his life was a defiance of suffering.

"Let's play some tennis," he suggested one Saturday morning. Have you ever played tennis against someone who moved about on an artificial leg? I believe you would remember if you had. Veeck had mighty arms, and a shot into his power zone came back as a fuzzy yellow missile. You could obviate that with lobs and drop shots—running him. But then you would be running a one-legged opponent. Ty Cobb would surely do that, but I chose to cope with the missiles. When we were done, Veeck said only, "Work on your backhand." (I have been doing that ever since with little effect).

Then, we gathered the children for a swim. Veeck, in khaki shorts, unhooked the artificial limb and headed toward one of my boys who was five. He swam a strong butterfly, spouted water and called, "I'm coming after you. I'm a sea monster."

"Try and get me, sea monster," the child called. "Try and get me, you one-legged sea monster."

I made some sort of apology later. "Wonderful thing about small children is that they're truthful," Veeck said. "I was trying to look like a sea monster and I am one-legged. The boy just called out what he saw. You ought to apologize to me for apologizing."

We'd talk politics in the evening. He was an old one liberal—we were all liberals in those days—although not dazzled by the glitter of FDR. "Roosevelt bailed out the country," he said, "but there was nothing original in his campaigns. He simply stole the 1920 Socialist Party platform and gave it a new name: The New Deal." Veeck disliked obscenity. He had a soft spot for hoodlums. "Probably," he said, "because when my father was dying, it was during Prohibition. He wanted one last drink of great French brandy. Al Capone came through and got it for him."

He remembered two of his favorite ideas from when he was running the Milwaukee Brewers in the American Association, circa 1940. He had some sort of metal tracks installed in the outfield so the fences could be moved in or out. Milwaukee up—in come the fences. Visitors at bat—the fences move out toward the county line. After a riotous day or two, authorities pulled up the tracks. "They sent in troops to do it," Bill said, grinning. His second idea was to hire black ball players. The Baseball commissioner then, Kenesaw Mountain Landis, had many merits but an apartheid soul. "Hire one of them," Landis raged through dentures, "and I'll bar you from baseball for life." Bill had to wait, but in 1947, when he was running the Cleveland Indians, he integrated the American League with Larry Doby and later Satchel Paige. In 1948, the Indians won the World Series from the Boston Braves. Paige was one of Cleveland's most effective pitchers. Doby was one of Cleveland's better hitters at .301.

Veeck had a run with the St. Louis Browns, who went under, and another with the Chicago White Sox, who won the pennant in 1959. Bad health forced him to pull out about 1961. When he finally came back to baseball, with the White Sox again during the 1970s, I saluted him with a chapter in my book: *A Season in the Sun*. By way of thanking me, Bill held a Comiskey Park night in my name during 1977; first 5,000 fans got the book in paperback free. The team was flawed, and with the paranoia that is an endemic disease of writers, I began to imagine a crowd of 1,100 and subsequent newspapers accounts suggesting that you couldn't even give my book away.

My paranoia underestimated Veeck. He picked a Friday night Yankee game, the place was sold-out and fans grabbed *A Season in the Sun*, as if it were a cut-rate beer. The scoreboard blinked my name in outsized letters. Bill invited some principle characters in the book—Early Wynn, Wally Moon, Hank Greenberg—to fly in at his expense for a surprise party. Not a bad night; not bad at all.

I'm pleased my friend Pat Williams is here celebrating my friend Bill Veeck, who, above all things, celebrated sports, friendship and the glory of being alive.

Roger Kahn
Croton-on-Hudson, N.Y.

Foreword

by Mike Lupica

This was before the 1983 World Series in Philadelphia, which turned out to be a quite forgettable Series, the Orioles thumping the Phillies in five games. But not forgettable for me because I got to spend a little more time with Bill Veeck. My relationship with Veeck had begun long before I ever met him, with a paperback version of what is still the best sports autobiography ever written: *Veeck—as in Wreck.* Bill's coauthor was Ed Linn. And all I would find out later, when I was lucky enough to get to know Bill Veeck, was that Linn had gotten it exactly right. The remarkable man. His remarkable life. I was a teenager when I bought the book and knew hardly anything about the swashbuckling path Veeck had cut through Cleveland and St. Louis and Chicago, laughing at and with baseball the whole way.

But all I knew as a kid in Nashua, New Hampshire, was that I had never heard about an owner, in any sport, who thought this way or acted this way, one who seemed to be having such a marvelous time.

He answered his own phone. Fans would call him in St. Louis when the Browns

*Mike Lupica (Courtesy of the **New York Daily News**)*

weren't drawing and say, "What time does the game start?" Veeck would say, "What time would you like it to start?"

I knew I had to meet him someday, and, finally as a sports columnist for the *New York Daily News*, I did one afternoon in Chicago. I was there to write about a Mets-Cubs game, and by then, I had at least struck up a phone relationship with Veeck. He always said, "If you're ever in town . . . " I was in town. He told me to meet him at his favorite joint, Miller's.

Lunch nearly turned into dinner that day. He was retired by then, on his way out to sit in the bleachers at Wrigley. He told stories about his friend Hank Greenberg and the White Sox of '59 and his fights with all the baseball commissioners and made fun of George Steinbrenner, which became one of his favorite hobbies late in life.

We laughed a lot.

So now it was the Series of '83, and Veeck was there writing a column for the *Chicago Tribune,* and we were both staying at the same hotel. We met in the lobby checking in. Then, Veeck made the following statement, full of both fun and terror, for anyone who ever knew him: "I'll meet you in the bar."

These were the days before I learned that drinking wasn't as much a part of the newspaper business as deadlines and room service and my old Olivetti-Lettera typewriter. So, I met Veeck in the bar, and before long, we had a whole group of new friends with us, and before much longer, the bartender was begging us to go to bed. But Bill Veeck, who still had a lot of life in him, never wanted to go to bed. He might miss a story, or a good line, or miss out on a chance to make another memory for himself or somebody else.

We took the party out into the lobby, and finally, we went to bed. When I woke up, I knew it was more than a hangover sitting on my chest. The hotel doctor was summoned and told me I had about a 102 degree temperature and some flu that was going around Philly at the time.

He told me to stay in bed until the game started, and I didn't require a second opinion on that.

Of course Veeck called from his room directly below mine about noon and wanted to know where I wanted to have lunch.

"I'm sick," I said.

He asked for my symptoms, and I told him that it was only a mild case of malaria or something.

"Oh," he said, "come right down. I've got something that will fix you right up."

I dragged myself down the stairs and knocked on his door. There he was, wooden leg stuck out from his chair, pecking away at his own manual typewriter, smoking away. In the middle of the room, like a centerpiece, was what looked like the world's largest bucket of ice, mostly featuring fruit and bottles of beer.

Bill Veeck came over to me, handed me a cold pill and a bottle of ice-cold beer and said, "Take these."

That was his idea of a house call.

For the next couple of hours, he read aloud from the column he was writing, told more stories, drank beer himself.

And gave me another memory.

I don't want to spoil this wonderful book—this marvelous tribute to Bill's memory and spirit—Pat Williams has written. I will just say that the '83 World Series ended for me with poetry from Bill Veeck; like the poetry he always carried around in his heart and soul.

I still have that copy of *Veeck—as in Wreck*, by the way. Signed by the great man himself.

Enjoy.

Mike Lupica
New York City
April, 2000

Bill Veeck's 12 Commandments

---

1. Take your work very seriously. Go for broke, and give it your all.

2. Never, ever take yourself seriously.

3. Find yourself an alter ego and bond with him for the rest of your professional life.

4. Surround yourself with similarly dedicated soulmates—free spirits of whom you can ask why and why not. And who can ask the same thing of you.

5. In your hiring, be color blind, gender blind, age and experience blind. You never work for Bill Veeck. You work with him.

6. If you're a president, owner, or operator, attend every home game and never leave until the last out.

7. Answer all your mail; you might learn something.

8. Listen and be available to your fans.

9. Enjoy and respect the members of the media, the stimulation and the challenge. The "them against us" mentality should only exist between the two teams on the field.

10. Create an aura in your city. Make people understand that unless they come to the ballpark, they will miss something.

11. If you don't think a promotion is fun, don't do it. Never insult your fans.

12. Don't miss the essence of what is happening at the moment. Let it happen. Cherish the moment, and commit it to your memory.

(By Mary Frances Veeck)

Bill Veeck: A Biography

His day began in the idyllic silence of dawn, in a bathtub the stump of his amputated right leg soaking in a therapeutic bath. And his day began with a book. Every morning, there was a book, and every morning, Bill Veeck read mercilessly, and fully and with alarming speed, the passages radiating into the immense labyrinth of his own photographic memory.

At its heart, this book is the story of a baseball man. And yet that is a woefully incomplete incapsulization of Bill Veeck. This is the story of a baseball man, of a skilled author, of a passionate collector, of an emotive humanitarian, of a respected leader, of a rapturous speaker, of a doting father, of a diligent promoter, of an encyclopedic expert in virtually every subject. This could be the story of a dozen men. This could be the story of the most influential executive in sports history. His days were a blur of handshakes and speeches and phone calls and toothy grins and elaborate discussions that burgeoned deep into the night in local taverns. His days were a blessing. His nights were a blessing. His sleep was rare and halting because he lived in paralyzing fear of missing a singular moment.

So, how do you begin to describe a man like this—a man with oddly kinked pinkish hair and a rubbery Halloween mask of a face and a stubborn wooden leg—a man who lived so earnestly, so unabashedly, who bowed to no one's will and yet was so eager to please?

Here's a start:

Born Feb. 9, 1914. Chicago, Illinois.
Died Jan. 2, 1986. Chicago, Illinois.

Simple math tells us 71 years, which is somewhere near the median life expectancy of the average American male. But here is where the calendar lies. Because Veeck's life was so replete with experience, and the path of his career so disparate from that of the average American male, that sometimes it seems almost mythical. And given that he spent most of his life immersed in myth, of midgets in baseball uniforms and spacesuits, of live lobster giveaways, of lush fireworks displays and tightrope walkers and flagpole sitters and exploding scoreboards, that only seems a fitting epitaph.

Except that Bill Veeck was anything but mythical. Except that he was the closest baseball has come to placing the everyman in charge. He was the one the populace could relate to, the one who was never too busy, never too important, never unapproachable, never unavailable for comment. And here is the paradox, and here is what elucidated his character: He had the intelligence to become whoever he wanted, and yet he chose to be with the rest of us.

He was born in Chicago. He was a determined boy, a troublemaker, his incisive energy bubbling over into interminable fights with bullies who wanted nothing to do with him. He began his baseball career working for his father, William, a sportswriter who later became

Young Bill Veeck (right) and Cubs manager Joe McCarthy in 1929 (Brace Photo)

president of the Chicago Cubs, mailing out tickets, running errands, manning the concession stands, emptying trash cans, spreading the tarp across the field. He went away to Kenyon College in Ohio, where he nearly died after falling four-and-a-half stories from a dorm window, and returned to Chicago to help with the Cubs after his father, a man he called "Daddy" his entire life, died in 1933.

He became the club's treasurer. At night, he studied accounting and business law. By day, he devised an array of promotions, including the ivy-covered walls at Wrigley Field, but most of his ideas were stymied by the tradition-

Bill Veeck (left) learned the game at the grassroots level. Here he mans the phones in the Wrigley Field Box Office. (Brace Photo)

bound thoughts of Cubs' owner Phil Wrigley. So, after begging and pleading investors for support, in 1941, at the age of 28, on a drizzling and gray Saturday afternoon, with $11 in his pocket, Veeck rode the train toward Milwaukee to become the owner of the Triple-A Milwaukee Brewers.

He commanded attention, of course. He brought along a charismatic manager named Charlie Grimm and gave away lobsters, pigs, horses, geese, white mice, eels and a 200-pound block of ice. He hired cleaning ladies to scour the ballpark, used hydraulics to move the fences in when the Brewers were batting and garnered national attention for his show, for the curiosity and incongruity and the unprecedented laughability of his ideas. He lifted a team on the verge of bankruptcy to immediate success and was named *The Sporting News* Executive of the Year in 1942. "Veeck is running the greatest baseball show on earth," wrote *Esquire* magazine.

Charlie Grimm (Brace Photo)

And here, it was only the beginning.

Feeling he'd earned a shot at running a major-league club, Veeck attempted to buy the Philadelphia Phillies and stock them with Negro League players. His attempt was barred by baseball's governance. So he left Milwaukee after the 1943 season; left for the South Pacific, for the Marines and World War II. He spent two years there in places like Guadalcanal and Bougainville. Half of that time was spent in military hospitals. In 1944, an anti-aircraft gun recoiled and shattered Veeck's foot. A year-and-a-half later, the leg, a victim of jungle rot, would be amputated below the knee, and for the rest of his life, it would antagonize him, landing him in hospitals for surgery and repeated amputations as it continued its slow deterioration.

He spent the remainder of his life in combat with his physicality. His lifestyle was relentless: a collage of beer and cigarettes and interminable nighttime talk sessions. His body couldn't keep up. His hearing dimmed, and he had an itchy fungus in his ear, and he soaked in the bathtub to alleviate the irritation of his leg's stump. He refused to acquiesce, to bow to circumstance. When his leg was amputated, first thing he did when he got out of the hospital was throw a post-amputation party. He joked continuously about his infirmities. It became some of his best material: the ashtray he hollowed out in his wooden leg: the ice pick he thrust into it to shock unsuspecting children.

In 1946, back from the war, yearning for an entry into major league baseball, Veeck purchased the Cleveland Indians for $2.2 million. "But of course," American League president Will Harridge chided him, "you're going to cut out the gags."

It was typical—that attitude. Throughout his career, the establishment of the game distrusted him, censored him, and dismissed his philosophy as childish and disgraceful. And he didn't care what they thought. In Cleveland, he drew massive crowds by luring people to the ballpark with a parade of gimmicks, putting loose-limbed clown prince Max Patkin in the first base coaches' box and acrobatic ex-Brewer Jackie Price on the field to entertain before games. He gave away hard-to-find nylon stockings, hired flagpole sitters, held a night for an "average" fan named Joe Earley, and spoke to any group that would invite him, averaging two or three talks a day in the off-season, disseminating a buzz that helped the Indians draw more than 2.6 million fans in 1948. That same year, not coincidentally, the Indians also won a World Series.

They won it, in part, due to the contributions of two players. One was Larry Doby. Weeks after Jackie Robinson became the first black player in the major leagues, Doby became the second. Veeck harbored Doby from the epithets; from the criticism. Later, he signed aging black pitcher Satchel Paige, and, amid criticism of the signing as a publicity stunt, Paige went 6-1 in the final months of the season.

And yet despite his success, Veeck's personal life had crumbled. His first wife, Eleanor, an equestrian performer for Ringling Brothers and Barnum and Bailey Circus, had grown weary of his constant movement. They'd met in childhood, and had three children. They were divorced in 1949. A short time later, Veeck met Mary Frances Ackerman, a publicity agent for the Ice Capades. A week after they met, Veeck proposed. They were married until Veeck's death and had six children, including the oldest, Mike, who owns a series of minor-league franchises.

Amid confusion and wonder at his interest in a downtrodden organization, Veeck bought the St. Louis Browns for $2 million in 1951. No one seemed to understand what he was doing there. The Browns had drawn less than 250,000 fans in 1950. Wrote

Bill Veeck signs papers (left) with Bill DeWitt, making him the owner of the St. Louis Browns (AP/Wide World Photos)

sportswriter John Lardner: "Many critics were surprised to know that the Browns could be bought because they didn't know the Browns were owned."

There was a reason, of course. The reason was that Veeck relished the chase of lost causes—resurrecting both individual careers and franchises; nurturing them back to health. He threw himself into competition against the St. Louis Cardinals, moved his family into an apartment inside Sportsman's Park and on August 19, 1951, produced the most recognized stunt in baseball history.

The midget's name was Eddie Gaedel. Veeck had surreptitiously signed him to a $100 contract then told him if he so much as dared to swing a bat, he'd tear him in half all by himself. So in the second game of a meaningless doubleheader, Gaedel came to the plate wearing the number 1/8 on his uniform. He walked on four pitches. The next day, baseball's contentious and horrified establishment banned midgets from the game.

There were other promotions in St. Louis. There was Grandstand Managers Night, in which a thousand fans sitting behind home plate held up "YES" or "NO" signs in response to questions of strategy posed by the St. Louis coaches, while manager Zack Taylor reclined in a rocking chair with a pipe in his mouth and a pair of bedroom slippers on his feet. There was the first Bat Day, a promotion (like so many others of Veeck's) replicated today by virtually every major league team. Attendance more than doubled in Veeck's first season in St. Louis, but it was too hard, and there were too many obstacles presented by his rivals, and in the end, muddled in debt, Veeck's only option was to move the team to Baltimore. Except that baseball's establishment wouldn't even let him do that.

So Veeck sold the Browns. And then the team moved to Baltimore. And it wasn't until six years later, after failed attempts to buy teams in 1954 and 1956, and a stint running a minor-league club in Miami, that he was able to squeeze back through the slats of baseball's picket fence, back into the game and back to his hometown of Chicago. He bought the White Sox, refurbished aging Comiskey Park, became the first owner to introduce names on the back of uniforms and introduced the first exploding scoreboard, replete with Roman candles, strobe lights and background music.

Bill Veeck directs the Go-Go Sox of '59 (Courtesy of Jim Prohaska)

Again, the fans were magnetized. The White Sox broke the franchise's all-time attendance record, and Veeck was rewarded with a pennant by Luis Aparicio and Nellie Fox and the Go-Go Sox in 1959.

Yet his health had once again deteriorated. He suffered through headaches; through vicious coughing spells that led to blackouts that eventually led Veeck to the Mayo Clinic, where he was convinced he had a brain tumor. Turned out, it was merely a chronic concussion, but Veeck was ordered away from baseball; toward a life of rest. He sold the White Sox. He moved to an estate in Easton, Md., raised dogs, entertained a melange of visitors, played quiz games with his children, and danced unabashedly with Mary Frances in the kitchen. And he read books, in the bathtub, on the front porch, as many as five in one week. He often reviewed books for newspapers, and eventually wrote three of his own with coauthor Ed Linn, including his 1962 autobiography, *Veeck—As In Wreck*, widely considered one of the seminal sports books of the 20th Century.

Veeck lectured. He spent a year as a commentator on ABC's Wide World of Sports. He testified for Curt Flood during the fight against baseball's reserve clause. In 1969, his restlessness overcoming him, he became the president of Suffolk Downs Race Track in Massachusetts. Among other things, he staged a chariot race, importing Hollywood props from *Ben Hur*, and after losing his rapport with the track's owners in 1971, wrote a book, *Thirty Tons a Day*, based on his experience.

But it was still baseball he craved. And in 1975, he found it again, buying the White Sox, saving them from a move to Seattle. He and his general manager, Roland Hemond, immediately set up in the lobby of a Hollywood, Florida, hotel during baseball's winter meetings, with a phone rigged to ring constantly and a sign that read:

OPEN FOR BUSINESS:
BY APPOINTMENT ONLY

Veeck removed the door to his office, replaced the artificial turf infield with natural

Bill Veeck and his protege, Roland Hemond (Courtesy of David Dombrowski)

grass, dressed his players in short pants and installed a shower in the bleachers. He convinced reluctant announcer Harry Caray to sing "Take Me Out to the Ballgame" during the 7th-inning stretch in what became a piece of Chicago baseball lore. The White Sox again broke the franchise attendance record in 1977 and were credited with inventing such traditions as the post-home run curtain call, and a team picked to finish last wound up with the most wins by a White Sox club since 1965.

But the game and its evolution would prove to be too much for Veeck to withstand. July 12, 1979, at Comiskey Park, Disco Demolition Night would serve as Veeck's most glaring promotional failure, even though today it is considered a treasured—albeit disastrous—moment ("Looking at it objectively as possible," Veeck said, "it was both.") in White Sox history. The Sox were forced to forfeit the second game of a doubleheader versus Detroit after fans overwhelmed the field, destroyed batting cages and set fires. That, along with the continued pressures of negotiation with free agents and the interminable failing of his health, led to Veeck's sale of the team in 1980.

He didn't want it to end there. He continued to attempt to buy into baseball teams, even pursuing the Cleveland Indians the week of his death. He died in Chicago, the second day of January 1986, from an embolism in his lung.

The legacy of Veeck endures through the hand-me-downs of his promotions; through the spirit of his son, Mike, who served a short tenure as senior vice president of the Tampa Bay Devil Rays before returning to the minor leagues, and directs his teams in unabashed tribute to his father. But the lasting beauty of Bill Veeck is that he could never be replicated. In this, there is simply no dispute.

"At what Bill Veeck did," wrote Ed Linn in the afterword to *Veeck—As In Wreck*, "he wasn't only the first, and he wasn't only the best. He was the only."

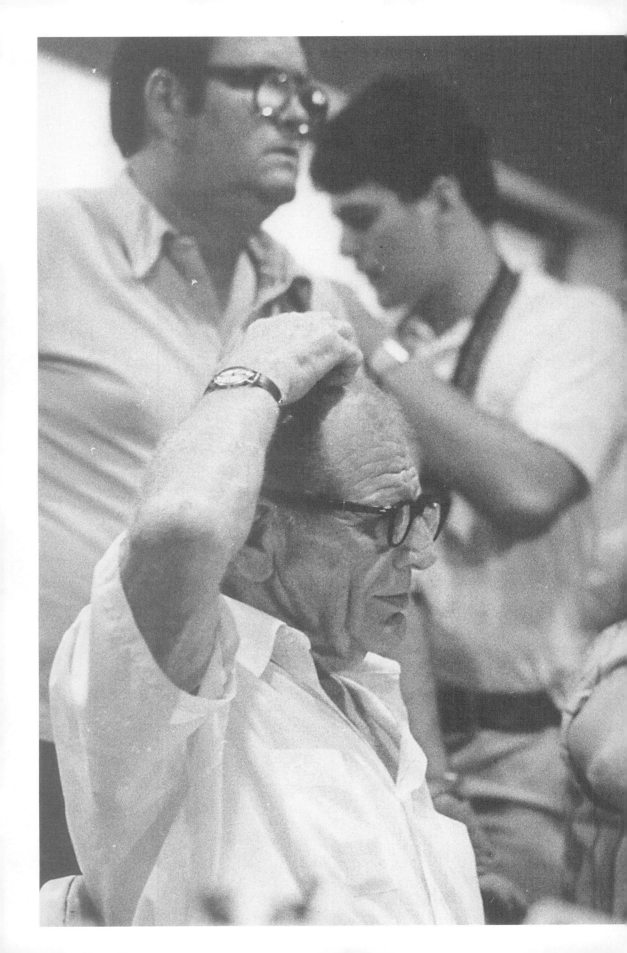

"To me, a ballpark filled with people is a beautiful thing. It's an epitome, a work of art. I guess I have seen everything in the country: Yosemite, Old Faithful, the Grand Canyon, and the most beautiful thing is a ballpark filled with people. Ballparks should be happy places."

Introduction

I met him at Tranquility, a sprawling 20-room country house that sloped toward the banks of Peachblossom Creek. He was on the porch, wearing a pair of khaki shorts, reveling in the warmth of a September sun. He was reading a volume of Civil War poetry. He was not wearing a shirt. He was not wearing one of his legs.

I was driving a 1958 Chevy. It was 1962, the year my father died. I was 22 years old. I wasn't sure what I was doing there, except that I wanted to meet him, that I was determined to see him, that I'd called him on the phone, that he'd invited me to his estate in Easton, Maryland, to the house with chocolate-brown shingles and white shutters and a screened-in porch.

Bill Veeck was in retirement. Doctor's orders. Two years before this, he'd sold the White Sox after checking into the Mayo Clinic. He'd had coughing spells, had inexplicable blackouts. He'd lost 50 pounds in a year. Turned out he was fine, that what he needed

Twenty-two-year-old Pat Williams.
(Author's collection)

was merely a rest; a space of relative quiet in an otherwise frenetic life. So he'd nicknamed the house "Tranquility."

And this was how he rested: by inviting visitors to his home, by reading with his wooden leg propped next to him, by gardening, by refinishing early American furniture, raising his five (soon to be six) children, along with a dozen dogs, a horse, multiple fish tanks, gerbils, guinea pigs and an armadillo. He had a guesthouse that held a dozen people, had a beer tap connected to a keg in the wall, had a game room in an adjacent building, had a massive Seeburg automatic jukebox.

I approached him on the porch. He shut the book and smiled a broad and unassuming grin.

I opened my mouth. For a moment, no words came out.

I'd gotten Veeck's number from Bill Durney, his traveling secretary with the St. Louis Browns, my general manager when I played catcher for the Miami Marlins of the Class D Florida State League

I'd hit .295 that first summer in Miami. I'd been given a $500 signing bonus and made $400 a month. I'd been playing as much for my father as for myself. I'd graduated from Wake Forest that spring, soon after my father died in a car accident, and I was headed for graduate school at Indiana University in the fall, but I wanted one last push at baseball.

My best friend from home in Wilmington, Delaware, was Ruly Carpenter. His father, Bob Carpenter, owned the Philadelphia Phillies. I called Bob Carpenter a few days after my father's funeral, told him

Miami Marlin rookie Pat Williams. (Author's collection)

I wanted to play baseball, assured him that I would play anywhere.

He told me about Miami. He told me to keep my senses awake; to keep them alive, on and off the field. He understood my future better than I did.

Former Philadelphia Phillies owner Bob Carpenter. (Courtesy of the Philadelphia Phillies)

The greatest sports book I have ever read begins with the story of the midget. It begins with this sentence: "In 1951, in a moment of madness, I became owner and operator of a collection of old rags and tags known to baseball historians as the St. Louis Browns." *Veeck—As In Wreck* sprawls forth from there, into the life of Veeck, his stories, his theories, his philosophies. I picked up the book in Miami that summer at a Burdine's department store. I'd been spending my spare time at bookstores, picking up baseball books by sportswriters like Arthur Daley of the *New York Times* and Shirley Povich of *The Washington Post* and by baseball historians like Lee Allen. None of them had a cover like this, of a self-assured and grizzled man, his artificial leg propped on the seat of a ballpark, a cigarette smoldering in his hand.

I read the first chapter at the bookstore. I read this passage:

> Eddie Gaedel remained up in the office between games, under the care of big Bill Durney. Between games, Durney was to bring him down under the stands, in full uniform, and put him into a huge seven-foot birthday cake we had stashed under the ramp . . .
>
> "Gee," I could hear (Gaedel) saying, "I don't feel so good." And then, after a second or two: "I don't think I'm going to do it."
>
> Now, Bill Durney is 6'4", and in those days, he weighed 250 pounds. "Listen, Eddie," he said. "There are eighteen thousand people in this park, and there's one I know I can lick. You. Dead or alive, you're going in there."

I read the rest at home. I still read it once every year, and it is still the funniest, the liveliest, the most influential sports book I have ever found. A few days later, I walked into the office of my boss, Big Bill Durney. I was a rookie asking a favor from the general manager. I didn't care. I started to seek him out, to spend time with him.

That summer, I told Bill Durney I wanted to meet Bill Veeck.

I had a respectable batting average for a rookie, but that first season in Miami was fraught with an inevitability. This was the season I first accepted the end of a sustained and improbable dream. I would never play major league baseball. The luster had faded. (My only claim to fame was being Ferguson Jenkins' first catcher in organized baseball.)

The dream had begun when my father took me to Shibe Park, 21st and Lehigh in Philadelphia, to see the Philadelphia Athletics play the Cleveland Indians. It was a doubleheader between two teams mired near the bottom of the

Former Miami teammates Ferguson Jenkins (left) and Pat Williams hooked up again in an old-timers game in Kissimmee, Florida in 1992. (Author's collection)

standings trying to move up. It was June 15, 1947, the year after Bill Veeck had bought the Indians. I was seven years old.

Seven-year-old Pat Williams shows off his first uniform. (Author's collection)

A boy's first baseball game is so often bookmarked by its sensory cues. Everything takes on a shimmering hue—the grass, the players, the architecture of the park itself. What I remember are the lyrical cries of the vendors, the whistles of police officers directing traffic, the cavernous size of the ballpark, the luminescent glow of the A's uniforms. I remember sitting with my father and sister, eating hot dogs and popcorn, watching the grounds crew lay down the chalk baselines, watching a tractor drag a brown mat to smooth the infield dirt. There were half a dozen men handling a giant hose to settle the dust.

I woke up the next day, and I wanted baseball. It was my first crush. I stood in front of the mirror and tinkered with my swing. I carried around a bat and ball and a glove, searching for a game of catch.

In the summer of 1948, Bill Veeck had produced a championship team in Cleveland. The Indians won the pennant. They drew 2.6 million fans. They won the World Series. It was the last world championship team in Cleveland for half a century and counting. It was the summer of Lou Boudreau and Satchel Paige and Larry Doby and Gene Bearden at Municipal Stadium, the summer that Bill Veeck's promotional acumen first flourished on a national stage.

I was lying on the floor of our house in Wilmington when the Indians won the World Series over the Boston Braves in six games. I was listening to the broadcast and the crowd noise crackle through our radio—an old wooden Philco. When you're young, you tend to hoard your experiences, and to view them as singular to yourself. Listening to that World Series, to the steady rumble of those Cleveland

Bill Veeck and friend. (Courtesy of Russell Schneider)

crowds, there was the realization that baseball did not belong to me—that it was a game that belonged to our people; to our nation.

I was obsessed with baseball. I pored over the boxscores in the *Wilmington Evening Journal.* My parents subscribed to the *New York Times*, which is how I learned to read, hands on knees, scanning the sports pages. I bought *The Sporting News* every week. My mother took me to Shibe Park virtually every weekend, to watch the A's, to watch the Phillies. She also took me to The Smoke Shop in Wilmington to stock up on packs of baseball bubble gum cards, which I still have to this day.

That summer, 1951, Bill Veeck sent the midget, Eddie Gaedel, to bat. (Actually, to walk on four pitches, which was the plan, and which is what happened.) I remember opening the newspaper, seeing the picture of Gaedel perched at home plate like a porcelain doll, the number 1/8 jersey loose around his shoulders, the catcher on his knees behind him, the umpire hunched down in the background.

You have to understand what it meant for an 11-year-old to see this: a grown man throwing a cream pie in the face of convention, turning his back on the establishment, injecting such absurdity into the solemn nature of his sport. I suppose kids don't expect adults to act like kids. And I suppose that's why baseball never really accepted Veeck because he didn't think like the rest of them.

One summer afternoon, when I was 11, a package arrived in the mail. I'd been expecting it. I'd been writing to every baseball team that summer, mostly the same letter, beginning with the same ingratiating salute. "I'm a very serious Chicago Cubs fan." Or "I really like the Boston Red Sox." Most of the clubs had written back. Some sent gifts, like the black-and-white publicity photos the A's had sent, which then hung on my wall.

So, this time, the package in the mail was from the St. Louis Browns; from Bill Veeck. There were two decals inside, both of an animated cartoon character, a "Brownie," with a bat slung over his shoulder. I peeled off the decals and stuck them to my bedroom window, where they remained through my teenage years, through college and as my baseball career ended. It was Bill Veeck's first lesson in promotion for me.

Bill Veeck opens up his office at Sportsman's Park in December of 1952. (Courtesy of Jim Dyck)

"Call him," Bill Durney had said. "He's expecting your call."

I had left Miami in September and gone back to Wilmington. In a few weeks, I'd leave for Indiana University, to start graduate school in health and physical education.

I can still recite Bill Veeck's phone number: (301)-TA-24545.

I had called numerous times and stopped dialing in the middle. It was like calling for a date, all awkward nerves and shyness. I still had that crush on baseball, and Bill Veeck was baseball, and when I finally called, and Veeck answered, I was, for a moment, startled by the gentility of his voice.

"Bill Durney told me about you," he said.

I told him I wanted to meet him. He suggested a date. It was a Wednesday. I paused for a moment as if scanning an appointment book that didn't exist. "Sounds fine," I said.

His house was two hours from Wilmington. He gave me directions. And on a Wednesday in September, in 1962, I drove to Easton. And Bill Veeck was smiling at me, and Bill Veeck was shaking my hand, and Bill Veeck was insisting that I sit down.

There was an air of informality, of gregariousness. We shook hands. Now, we were friends. This was Veeck's way. He asked about my season in Miami. He asked about the league, about attendance, about the players in the league. The conversation meandered. I still hadn't asked a question. I could tell that the time away had cleared his head. He was vibrant, dynamic. He was the Veeck I'd read about, the Veeck I'd heard about.

I mentioned his book. I told him how much I enjoyed it. Next thing I knew, it was lunchtime. "Mr. Veeck," I said, "I don't want to take any more of your time …"

He nearly forced me back into my seat.

"Please," he said. "Bill Durney would never forgive me if I had you down here and you didn't stay for lunch."

So I sat. "And call me Bill," he said. "I don't know who Mr. Veeck is."

We ate lunch. Mary Frances served bacon, lettuce and tomato sandwiches. The day wore on. It was almost one by the time we finished, and another car bounded along the dirt driveway toward the porch. It was Mark Kram, the *Sports Illustrated* writer, one of dozens of frequent visitors to Veeck's home.

 I followed them to the backyard. We stood on a dock overlooking Peachblossom Creek, and I listened while they talked, discussing *Veeck—As In Wreck,* jousting quite jovially about who would play the lead if the book were made into a movie.

And then it was 4:30. And I'd been there for five hours.

"I've got to go," I said.

I shook hands with Veeck again. I started the Chevy and pulled out of the driveway and headed back to Wilmington, to a 6:30 touch football game with my friends we'd scheduled. I met them at our old high school and attempted to explain what I'd just done. They didn't grasp the moment like I did.

There was a moment in the midst of that day when I told Bill Veeck I didn't think my future was as a baseball player.

"Why?" he said. "You hit .295, didn't you?"

That's true, I told him. But I was starting to think my future was in the front office. So I asked for his advice.

"The most important thing is to know somebody," he said.

I told him I grew up with Ruly Carpenter, whose father owned the Phillies.

Ruly Carpenter. (Courtesy of the Philadelphia Phillies)

"Ah," he said. "You did that well. Good move."

He told me to learn to type, to take classes in advertising, to train myself in book-keeping and economics. I realize now that I did everything he told me to do. Everything, that is, except the bookkeeping. And I'll be honest about that, Bill: It couldn't keep me awake.

I wrote a letter to the editor of *The Sporting News* about that day. It was my way of thanking Veeck. The letter was published in October 1962, while I was at graduate school, broadcasting Indiana football and basketball games for the student radio station that originated the statewide network.

I went back to Miami the next summer to play baseball again. It wasn't something I wanted anymore, and I began to play like it, and halfway through the season, I began working in the front office. I went back to Indiana for a year, finished my Master's degree, worked as Durney's apprentice in Miami the next summer and spent six months in the army fulfilling my military commitment. I got out in January 1965,

President-General Manager Pat Williams (right) and the 1967 Western Carolinas League Champion Spartanburg Phillies. John Gordon, longtime Minnesota Twins broadcaster, is standing at the left, middle row. (Author's collection)

and Clay Dennis, the Phillies' farm director, called.

He offered me a job as the general manager of the Spartanburg Phillies in Spartanburg, S.C. I was 24 years old and a general manager.

All this time, I'd kept up correspondence with Bill Veeck, writing notes to him, keeping him apprised of my whereabouts. I'd mailed him newspaper clippings. I hadn't talked to him, but he knew where I was. As soon as I accepted the general manager's job, I called him. Asked if I could come see him. He said fine. And so, a month after I started in Spartanburg, I flew back to Baltimore, rented a car and drove to the house again.

It was March. It was snowing. Bill Veeck was in the living room. This time, it was a business meeting. I brought a pad and paper. Veeck lectured. I listened. I scribbled. I asked questions about *what* promotions worked and what didn't; about *how* promotions worked and why they didn't. I sat on one end of a wide couch. Veeck sat on the other. There were books, spines spread open, and manuscripts of newspaper columns he'd written scattered across the coffee table. He chain-smoked unfiltered cigarettes, and drank beer, one after the other, like a luxury car guzzling hi-test. It was the only time he showed me one thing, and I did the opposite. Those habits I left with him.

We had these meetings regularly after that. I would go to the house, we'd sit in the living room, and Veeck would expound, and I would digest. "I always thought you were another Veeck kid," Bill's son Mike kidded me, years later.

Once I came in and Veeck ignored me for a half hour. Didn't say anything to me. Didn't even look up. He was in the dining room, helping one of his daughters fashion a papier-mâché re-creation of Teddy Roosevelt and the Rough Riders storming San Juan Hill. He was gluing. He was cutting. He was irretrievably lost in the moment.

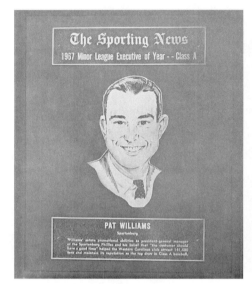

Pat Williams' first big award.
(Author's collection)

When he was finished, he stood. "Pat," he said, "Let's talk. I'm ready now."

And then it was about me.

I earned national recognition in Spartanburg because of him. Our franchise was honored by *The Sporting News*. We drew the largest crowds in the history of the city; of the league. We sold and promoted and marketed, but none of it belonged to me. All of it was overseen and advised and tweaked by Bill Veeck, by the calls I'd make to him once a week, every Sunday, with a list of questions; of ideas. A checklist. What should I do? How should I do it?

We held an "Impress Bill Veeck Night" once at Duncan Park in Spartanburg, and Bill Veeck spoke at our luncheon and later wrote about it in his syndicated column. "He has just added something extra to try to make baseball entertaining even when the Phillies get shellacked," Veeck wrote. "And if you think the little extras haven't worked, last year with a seventh place club, and not a good seventh at that, Williams set a league attendance record."

The NBA's Philadelphia 76ers hired me in 1968, and by then, I didn't have to talk to Veeck every week. But everything I did was with him in mind. I even held another "Impress Bill Veeck Night" when I worked for the Chicago Bulls, and whenever I saw he was giving a speech, I'd try to make it. He endorsed my first book when it was published in 1974. He was my friend until he died.

Sometimes people ask me if I worked for Bill Veeck. I tell them I didn't. I tell them I didn't have to.

And so, I was asked to speak at a Sports Career Day in Miami in 1994 to 200 young people interested in sports management careers. I was brainstorming, attempting to formulate an idea, and I kept thinking of Veeck, and I began to list the ways he's affected my life and my career. My list began with seven or eight numbers. The speech went well.

When it was over, the list swelled. I was up to 11, to 12, to 15 and 20. I started thinking I could make a book about this. I wrote other people who had known Bill well, former players, ex-employees, writers, broadcasters, childhood friends. I sent them my ideas and asked them to add their own—whatever they could remember. I began to solicit comments from fans.

Some of the people I talked to are no longer living. The people of Bill Veeck's generation are elderly now, and memories grow cloudy. But it seemed like they all had a moment. Even as this book was being completed, the memories continued to trickle through.

Bill Veeck doesn't need another biography because he wrote his own, because he and his coauthor, Ed Linn, did it as well as it could have been done. But that's not the objective of this book. This is a book about success. This is a book about one of the most relentless and fascinating personalities in the history of modern sport. It's about a man without prejudice, a man who allowed a midget to bat and an African-American to bat, who promoted and who laughed and who read like a scholar and who had a vision unique to himself. This book is an attempt to extract those traits—to present them in their purest form—so that you can pull the same sort of inspiration from Bill Veeck that I did.

Sports marketing has become a buzzword for this generation. Professional sports are expanding, and women's sports are burgeoning, and media coverage is layering and replicating. And yet in so many ways, professional sports are flatter than they've ever been—attendance slipping, ticket prices soaring, the fun of the sport overwhelmed by the spiraling salary, the multi-million dollar television contract, the holdout and the lockout and the strike.

This is why we need Bill Veeck. This is why we need him today perhaps more than we ever did.

This is a book for the baseball fan, for those who have fallen in love like I did. It is a book for the sports fan, for the businessman who sells and promotes, for the student who hopes to make his living that way. It is a book as diverse as Bill Veeck himself, who worked and laughed and loved and treasured like no one else—freely, unconditionally.

He taught that to me. He can do the same for you.

"Today isn't so bad. It could be a lot worse, but tomorrow is going to be great. You know? And tomorrow never comes, you see, because by the time tomorrow comes, it's today … In other words, I've had enough problems physically to recognize it's just great to be around."

Chapter 1

Tomorrow Never Comes

"The anecdotes go on. You beg him to stop. Not another beer. Will Bill Veeck ever wind down? Does he ever go to bed? Does he ever work?"

William Brashler, writer

P lease forgive the man for his overzealous nature. He could not help himself. He could not avoid a conversation, could not help but keep the drinks coming until closing time, could not bring himself to go home, striking match after match on his wooden leg, poking the end of his cigarette into the ashtray built into a knothole in his artificial leg for dramatic effect. He could not help his habits of listening to music until four in the morning and reading a novel cover-to-cover in the bathtub and tending his garden for an entire afternoon and harnessing the sea of ideas careening through his head and weaving it all into a series of compelling stories. He had so many stories that it made your head begin to hurt, so many stories that it seemed almost like he'd spent his life stockpiling them.

And that's because he had.

Bill Veeck did not sleep because he could not sleep, because sleeping was a solitary act, and he was not a solitary man.

He would talk to his friends, to sportswriters, to baseball executives, to anyone who was willing to listen. He stayed up all night tapping a cigarette into that ashtray, for it was as much a part of the show as he was. He would broach subject after subject, some appropriated from baseball, others notched on his vote for a dead socialist for president in 1972 or the tedium of a James Joyce novel. There was the time at the World Series when Veeck dropped thousands of dollars into massive meals for the press and fountains that dripped with streams of wine until late into the night. There was the time he and a Chicago-area sportswriter, Rob Gallas, began a conversation over lunch and kept talking, and kept talking …

And then it was 11 at night.

"If you observe a really happy man, you will find him building a boat, writing a symphony, educating his son, growing double dahlias, or looking for dinosaur eggs in the Gobi desert. He will not be searching for happiness as if it were a collar button that had rolled under the radiator, striving for it as the goal itself. He will have become aware that he is happy in the course of living life 24 crowded hours of each day."

W. Beran Wolfe, educator

He had a passion for so many things. His days were so crowded that he had to push away hours of rest just to find the room. He explained it to me once, saying: "I guess I'm just not bright enough to stop." And Bill's acumen for conversation and remembrance was aided by his photographic memory. "There are a lot of people I've met who have a knowledge on all subjects," Chicago sportswriter Bill Gleason once said. "But it's very shallow. But Veeck knows everything about the subject. And the reason is because he reads so much and can retain it."

Bill Gleason. (Courtesy of Bill Gleason)

"Try to learn something about everything and everything about something."

Thomas H. Huxley, English Biologist

He was an expert on tropical fish, on horticulture, on the law, on the plight of the Native American. He restored secondhand furniture and worked in his garden and had a penchant for animals. He owned thousands of books, from every genre, and he hosted a television show, and he wrote hundreds of newspaper columns, and he was a gifted speaker, and he could fold a $100 bill and toss it so that it would stick to the ceiling.

"In fact," said his longtime friend, Hank Greenberg, "I don't know what he wasn't."

"When I retire, I want to turn to my wife and say, 'My dance card was full. I lived life to the fullest.'"

George W. Bush

There are people who complain constantly about time; who say they don't have enough time to take care of everything. But look at what Veeck did. And think about what you can do with time. You have exactly the same number of hours per day as William Shakespeare, as Marie Curie, as Thomas Jefferson, as Bill Veeck. You have the time to do anything, to be anything. All you have to do is use it.

"I would rather be ashes, than dust! The proper function of man is to live, not to exist. I shall not spend my days trying to prolong them. I shall use them."

Jack London, author

To call Veeck a conversationalist was to make the gravest of understatements. There were times when you couldn't stop him. Once he started, he was like a train rolling downhill, and the momentum carried him. Roland Hemond, general manager of the White Sox, used to sneak into his room after dinner during spring training whenever he needed sleep. He wouldn't even turn on the light. If Veeck saw the light, he saw an open door for an all-night conversation.

"Did I ever tell you about the time I …" he'd start. And then he would just go.

Or he'd say, "Let's suppose…" and 10 hours later, you were still supposing. It's why Lee McPhail, once president of the American League, would haul his son, Andy, to the press box anytime he visited the Bard's Room in Chicago, so that Andy could announce, in the midst of these late-night forums, that he had to go to bed, and his father would slip out.

Bill Brashler, the writer, had no way out, however, and Veeck turned an attempt at a magazine profile into the New York City Marathon, leaving him gasping for air, for sleep, wondering if Veeck would indeed *ever wind down.*

Brashler was not the first to attempt to follow Bill Veeck for a day trying to keep up with the most chaotic schedule in baseball. Joe Goddard of the *Chicago Sun-Times* began his day with Veeck at 6 a.m., standing in Veeck's doorway as he emerged from the bathroom in a ragged old robe. "With you in a minute," he said.

From there, the day was a blur. Breakfast with the cab driver who picked them up. A Girl Scouts luncheon in his honor. A barbecued rib dinner with his drinking buddies. And everywhere Veeck went, he was recognized. And everywhere he went, he sparked such intense feeling, such good will, that it couldn't help but brighten the day.

"Seize the moment. Remember all those women on the Titanic who waved off the dessert cart."
Erma Bombeck, newspaper columnist

Left in this man's wake was a stream of kinetic energy, and in that stream, one of the most crucial messages we can extract from our life. And one of its simplest doorways to happiness.

Because there is a reason why Veeck went to bed in the middle of the night. And a reason why he woke up four hours later. And a reason why he was never dulled by routine, why every day became an opportunity, and every hour, every moment of his 71 years, was gilded and precious.

He did not sleep because he could not sleep. He could not sleep because he was afraid to sleep. He was afraid to sleep because sleeping meant missing something. He was so caught up in the basest virtues of each day that his mind couldn't let go.

Said Washington writer Tom Boswell after Veeck's passed away in 1986, "Cause of death: Life."

"With the amount of sleep he didn't get," says longtime Chicago White Sox organist Nancy Faust, "Bill probably died at 85 instead of 71."

Nancy Faust. (Brace Photo)

"Make use of time. Let not advantage slip."
William Shakespeare, playwright

I had lunch a few years ago with a man named Max Jacobs. Max is the former owner of the NBA franchise in Cincinnati. Back then they were the Royals. Now they're the Sacramento Kings.

Max's family knew Bill Veeck; knew him for years. They ran Sports Service, the concession company. They'd invested money in Veeck's teams. They'd known Bill, all his quirks and idiosyncracies, everything that made him unique.

I told Max I wanted to write a book. I told Max I wanted to capture the essence of Bill Veeck. Max did it in one sentence.

"More than any man I've ever known," he said, "Bill Veeck was present in his own life."

Sure, we say it all the time. We repeat it to ourselves. We hear it everywhere. People tell us to maximize our lives. To make every day count. *Carpe diem.* Seize the day.

And how many of us do it?

I've thought about what Max Jacobs told me. I've turned those words about in my head as the years passed. It's an easy thing to preach, isn't it?

To be present in your own life. To live for the now. To postpone nothing. To refuse to acknowledge that someday your life will begin, and that today is the prelude, and everything up to now has just been dress rehearsal. To barge past the excuses.

It takes a passion to live that way. It takes perspective. It takes a certain sense of urgency.

"I believe the fires of greatness in our hearts can be kept aglow only after we develop a sense of urgency and importance of what we are doing. I mean a sense of urgency to the extent that we feel it is a matter of life or death … A sense of urgency is that feeling that lets you know yesterday is gone forever; tomorrow never comes."

Charlie "Tremendous" Jones, motivational speaker

This, I think, is what kept Veeck awake at night. This is what kept him dreaming. This is what kept him embroiled in debate until the lights went up for last call in so many bars and nightclubs. This is the tonic that enabled him to brim with ideas, with innovations. This is what separated him from the people around him and helped him become one of the greatest innovators in baseball history.

"He had so much energy," says longtime *Chicago Tribune* columnist Bob Verdi. "I never heard him say, 'I'm tired. I'm going to bed.' I never saw him yawn. I don't know how he did it. He had such a fertile mind and was so curious, I don't think he could sleep."

*Bob Verdi. (Courtesy of the **Chicago Tribune**)*

"Life is something to do when you can't get to sleep."
Fran Lebowitz, author

He was chaotic, even as a child. In grammar school in Hinsdale, Illinois, Veeck was a terror, antagonizing teachers, earning failing grades for conduct, throwing himself into fights. One Halloween, he painted a section of the sidewalk red. No one ever caught him.

In high school math class one spring afternoon, he and his friend, Scott Jones, waited until their teacher had his back turned. Then they crawled out the window and went to the Chicago Cubs game. "A high-school rowdy," Veeck called himself in his autobiography.

So he was hyperactive, unable to submit to authority, unable to restrain himself. He was a fighter, a troublemaker, a teacher's nightmare. When he played football, he did so without a helmet and still wound up at the bottom of every pile, his kinked hair spilling out from underneath.

All of which tells you that even then he had this endless surge of unrestrained energy. Even then, Veeck was just a boy trying to live it all.

I saw a Dennis the Menace cartoon, appropriately enough, that reminded me of Veeck. I could see him like this. It's nighttime, and Dennis' father is carrying him up the stairs to bed. His mother is standing at the foot of the stairs. And Dennis asks, "Why is tomorrow always getting here before I'm through with today?"

"Life is truly a ride. We're all strapped in, and no one can stop it. I think the most you can hope for at the end of life is that your hair's messed up, you're out of breath, and you didn't throw up."
Jerry Seinfeld, comedian

The energy. The passion. That sense of urgency. The realization that life could end tomorrow. It was Veeck's legacy. It was not nullified by sickness or heartbreak or failure. There was always room for a smile, always a place for a joke, even in the darkest moments.

Veeck had more than 30 operations in his life, so many that he lost track. It was his most noticeable imperfection, a body that continued to quit on him. He had leg surgery, ear operations, back operations, a lung-tumor removal. He had to soak in that bathtub for hours to assuage his leg pain. No one had more right to bemoan his circumstances, to curse his own luck, to damn the events that brought him to that point.

The thing is, no one can ever remember him doing it.

Of course, he could not avoid small bouts with depression. It is, after all, part of being human. One of his closest friends, Hank Greenberg, only once caught a glimpse of that dimension of Veeck. It was when he accompanied Veeck to the doctor, who told Veeck they'd have to cut off his leg above the knee to prevent a bone infection from spreading. Veeck could move around relatively well with the knee, but without it, his way of maneuvering would change drastically.

So Veeck turned to Greenberg and said, straight-faced, "I want you to have all my tennis shoes."

Bill Veeck (right) and Detroit Tigers Hall of Famers Charlie Gehringer and Hank Greenberg. (Courtesy of Bob Broeg)

> *"It is not the experiences of today that drive people to distraction. It is the remorse or bitterness for something that happened yesterday…"*
>
> ## Glenn Kerfoot, philosopher

And that's the first step to securing such a vibrant present. Dealing with our past. It is accepting the deeds of our past as complete; as irrevocable. So many people look backward. So many people remember the "good old days" and accept those days as the quintessential experience of their lives, and never allow room for the present and what might lie ahead. And maybe the good old days weren't even that good. Maybe it's just memory that lends such comfort. Maybe it's a way to shield ourselves from uncertainty.

This is not to say you should forget everything. Memories can be a pleasant diversion, as long as they are just that, and not the focus of your attention. I wrote the foreword to a book that Robin Roberts, the Hall-of-Fame pitcher, authored on the 1950 National League champion Philadelphia Phillies. When the book was published, Robin, a good friend of mine since childhood, signed it, mailed it to me and enclosed a note that I've kept over the years.

This is what it said: "Life goes on. But great memories keep us smiling."

Robin Roberts. (Author's collection)

This is not to say there won't always be pains. There will, just as there will always be burdens, whether physical, like those Veeck faced, or mental, like those we all face. And the only thing that separates one of us from the others is the way we let those burdens affect us.

You shouldn't have time to stop and think. Harry Truman didn't. The story is that when he was president, he made a decision. And then he let it go. He hadn't the time nor the inclination to look back, to second guess himself. If he made a mistake in a decision, he corrected it by making another decision.

Your time is too valuable. Your present is too important to be viewed through the magnified lens of the past. A former coach with the NBA's Orlando Magic, Chuck Daly, had what he called the Midnight Rule: At midnight, forget everything and start over again. Just let it all pass.

I remember a quote from the book *Tuesdays with Morrie,* by sportswriter Mitch Albom. In it, Albom spends time with his old college professor, Morrie Schwartz, who's dying of Lou Gehrig's disease. And Schwartz tells him, "If you haven't reached your goals, don't assume that it's too late to get involved. Accept the past as the past without denying it or discussing it. Learn to forgive yourself and forgive others."

So let it go. Forgive yourself. And look ahead.

"Don't let yesterday take up too much of today."
Will Rogers, humorist

I was driving past a church in Winter Park, Florida, near my home, when I saw a quote on the marquee that still resonates. This is what it said: "Heal the Past. Live the Present. Dream the Future."

And that's what's left once you've healed your past, once you've inspired yourself to enjoy the present: The Future.

It stands before you, arms crossed, glaring. It terrifies you. It glows with uncertainty. It is an intimidator. It is why so many people live in fear. Why they avoid change. Why they tell themselves, "When I finish college …" or "When I get married…" or "When I have children…" They establish boundaries so that they can prolong the moment of change. And until that moment, they are unsatisified. Unfulfilled. They long for something better, but they lack the courage to dive into new experience. So they become mired in the present, in their dreams, in their own lack of action.

"People sort of live in the dark about things. A lot of young people think the future is closed to them; that everything has been done. This is not so. There are still plenty of avenues to be explored."

Walt Disney

The first step is to accept today for what it is: the only moment in which you can truly affect change. The only moment you can control. We have a women's basketball coach in Orlando named Carolyn Peck. She took a job as coach of our WNBA franchise, the Miracle, the summer before her final season as coach at Purdue. But when reporters asked her about the Orlando job, she refused to answer them. She refused to think about it. Purdue plays a game tonight, she told them. That's all I'll think about.

Carolyn Peck. (Courtesy of Orlando Miracle)

And that's all she did think about. And that season, in 1999, Purdue won the national championship.

Take care of today, and you'll better your tomorrow.

"My interest is in the future because I am going to spend the rest of my life there."
Charles F. Kettering, business leader

Veeck bought the Milwaukee Brewers of the American Association in 1941, when he was 27 years old. He borrowed $25,000 to buy the team. On the day Veeck assumed control, there were 22 fans at Borchert Field. Three of them were members of the Boy Scouts' honor guard celebrating Boy Scout Day.

Veeck took a massive chance, stepping away from the Cubs, the franchise he'd been a part of for more than two-thirds of his life. But he yearned for his own identity. He had sweeping ideas, brilliant, innovative thoughts that would revolutionize the game.

Bill Veeck, circa 1943. (Courtesy of **The Sporting News***)*

He yearned for a conduit. Once he had his forum, his own team, those ideas bubbled to the surface. He turned around a franchise that was mired in the depths of indifference.

He was a success.

And he might never have found out by staying in Chicago, where he had trouble gaining acceptance for his radical ideas, where his role in the organization had been restrained. He did not wait for an opportunity. He borrowed the money, bought the team, and created his own. He sold it in 1945 for $250,000, after the team had won three straight American Association pennants.

"Here's a test to find out whether your mission on earth is finished: If you're alive, it isn't."

Richard Bach, author

Veeck could never wait to win a pennant. He wanted it now. He didn't want to build a five-year plan or develop a team over time. He was, in that sense, fervid, unyielding, willing to give up anything, to trade anyone, to win. The best promotion, he knew, was winning. And winning right away.

In 1947, he nearly traded Lou Boudreau, his manager and shortstop, the best player on his team, because he thought the deal would bring him a pennant. Turned out, after Veeck was besieged by angry Cleveland fans, that Boudreau stayed, and the Indians still won the 1948 World Series. And when it happened, Veeck admonished himself and called it the best trade he'd never made.

When the White Sox lost the 1959 World Series, Veeck wanted desperately to get back the next season. He traded for veterans Minnie Minoso, Gene Freese and Roy Sievers, and traded away some of his most promising prospects. He knew that the fans didn't want to wait, that he couldn't afford to wait, that success was imperative. So he took chances. Some worked; some didn't. So be it. He'd thrown everything at his goal.

"Really, that's what the sports world is coming to: let's provide a team now. Very few teams want to get involved in that whole rebuilding process, so everybody's looking to be champions this year."

Phil Jackson, NBA coach

These stories become legends after a while. For all his energy, for all of his boundless enthusiasm, Veeck was still just one man. He switched off sometimes. His energy could not translate to 24-hour days.

When Veeck owned the Indians from 1946-49, he was in constant motion. He would stand on street corners and shake hands and sit in bars like the Theatrical Grill on St. Vincent Avenue, buying drinks for whoever wandered in, stirring up conversation until closing time. And he was in the office early the next morning, conjuring up new promotions, answering his own phone, chatting endlessly with customers and employees.

Sometimes he wouldn't even go home. He'd close up a bar, go back to the stadium, sleep for a few hours on the trainer's table and, at 8 a.m., shower, shave and go back up to the office.

So here's one more day-in-the-life story by one more frustrated writer.

Hal Lebovitz, a longtime Cleveland sportswriter, decided that he would do the ultimate, incisive, introspective piece on Veeck. He offered to drive Veeck to a speaking engagement in central Ohio. It was two hours from Cleveland, but that was Veeck, willing to go anywhere to sell tickets. The way Lebovitz saw it, two hours would be enough. They'd talk. He'd listen. Then he'd write.

Lebovitz picked up Veeck at his Cleveland Stadium office. Veeck smiled, a broad grin through a jutted jaw. His smile was like a whispered secret in a crowded room and before long, it had spread.

"Do you mind if I take a nap?" he asked.

Lebovitz, of course, said no, and Veeck fell asleep. Two hours later, they arrived. Lebovitz woke him up. Veeck wiped the weariness from his eyes, straightened his clothes, walked into the small party room and became himself again. He shook hands with everyone. He told jokes, and the room shook with laughter.

When it was over, they got back into Lebovitz's car. Veeck fell asleep again. When they returned to Cleveland, at about one in the morning, Lebovitz dropped him off at the Theatrical Grill. Veeck stayed there until the place closed down.

"So much," Lebovitz said, "for the myth of the man who never slept."

"Since it is not granted us to live long, let us transmit to posterity some memorial that we have at least lived."

**Pliny the Younger,
Latin historical figure**

The aura of happiness and potency and durability was no myth. This was just Bill Veeck. Every moment, every situation, carried such value. Even the simplest trips were enriched by his presence.

Jeffrey Loebl, a young White Sox employee, drove Veeck home after work one night in the mid-1970s. Veeck's wife, Mary Frances, had asked him to stop and buy a watermelon. So they stopped at one stand and picked out a watermelon. And they stopped at another stand. And Veeck picked out another watermelon. And they stopped at a third stand. And Veeck picked out another watermelon.

"I wonder," Loebl said, "what Mary Frances did with all those watermelons."

Chances are, she was used to it. Veeck always had more of everything than he knew what to do with. He always had more of today than the rest of us.

"How much money can you pay a tulip to bloom?

How much more can you pay a song to hum?

So I wonder what relationship money has to being happy, to enjoy-

ing your world, your life? I think very little."

Chapter 2

Attack the Camera

"If you worked for Bill Veeck, the greatest thing that happened to you was that you had more fun than you ever imagined. You came in a fan, and you were able to leave a fan."

Mike Veeck

Ten days before his death, Bill Veeck was in a hospital bed and working the phone. This was nothing new. His hospital stays were never trying enough to quench his yearning for people. And here it was at the tail end of 1985, and Veeck was attempting to convince Art Modell, the owner of the Cleveland Browns, to join his ownership group that would attempt to buy the Cleveland Indians. Modell agreed. The deal was coming together.

The Monday before Veeck died, Hank Greenberg, his close friend, called Veeck's hospital room. "You know," Veeck said, "I think I can get the Cleveland club."

Veeck hadn't owned a team since he sold the White Sox in 1980. He was hopelessly broke because he never felt a need to stockpile money, because everything he took in, he spent just as readily. He was 71 years old, his body ravaged by years of pain and surgery. And now he was in a hospital bed, drawing forth support to buy a baseball team in a league full of people he had alienated with his complete disregard for their binding rules.

"You're crazy," Greenberg said. "Why don't you go someplace where you have a chance to make some money? Why don't you go into the stock market or some other business? With your talents, you can make a lot of money at anything."

Hank Greenberg. (Brace Photo)

Perhaps it was his last delusion. Perhaps it was just Veeck being Veeck, always caught up in a dream. Perhaps it was the pure simplicity of his philosophy, surfacing one last time.

But he was serious about this. He could do this.

"Wouldn't it be great," he said, "to get the old gang together again?"

Money meant nothing to him. You could have the stock market. You could have the Armani suits and the business lunches. He had found his life's love long ago. It was baseball.

His last conversation with his son, Mike, was about buying a team. He wanted to upset baseball's entrenched inner circle once more. But more than that, he yearned for the joy that ownership brought him and the joy he could elicit.

Greenberg shook his head. He said, "You still want to sell peanuts at the ballpark, don't you?"

"Yeah," Veeck said. "I do."

When he realized that it couldn't be done, that the dream was over, that baseball had ostracized him for good, he died.

"I loved the game. I didn't worry about the 1st and the 15th, when they gave out paychecks. I was the first in the clubhouse and the last to leave. I liked to rub dirt on my hands, wrists and forearms, on hot days, to soak up the sweat. I loved the Wrigley Field dirt."

Ron Santo,
Cubs third baseman

Stop what you're doing for a moment. Stop and think about your life, about your career. Stop and think about how you feel when you wake up in the morning, how you feel when you come home in the afternoon, how you talk when you tell people what you do. Stop, and ask yourself this: Do you love it? Does passion burst from your voice?

Simple question. But how many people ever stop to think about it? How many people assume their career, their job, is supposed to carry some semblance of drudgery and blandness?

Ron Santo. (Brace Photo)

No job can be perfect. There are always burdens in working; in thinking and creating and selling and molding a lasting legacy. But there is no reason for it to be shrouded in misery.

In the end, there are two qualities that matter, two qualities that go hand-in-hand which should carry you through your day, the highs, the lows.

Enthusiasm: Lively, absorbing, keen interest.

Passion: Strong affection.

Ask yourself if you carry these through life. Ask yourself if you approach your workday like this, if, like Bill Veeck, you are so eager to leap from bed that you have trouble sleeping, if you burst headlong into everything you do, if you believe that what you are doing is what you were meant to be doing.

Perhaps you hedge here. Perhaps you have excuses. Perhaps you console yourself by saying that the money is good, and the benefits are strong, and you are nestled in security. But in the end, the money and benefits and security can only take you so far. They are not guarantees. If anything, success without enthusiasm breeds a sort of emptiness and carries you farther from everything you yearn for: the chance to contribute something meaningful and transcendent before your life is complete.

Here's how writer William Barry Furlong put it: "Bill Veeck is full of the humor that springs from the unsuppressed human being. To Veeck, baseball is not an ultraconstitutional mission, a crusade, a holy jousting for men's minds, souls and pocketbooks, but simply an exhilarating way to make a living. His approach to the game is seasoned with an almost visceral irreverence, a wit that is sometimes droll, sometimes wry or macabre."

"Like the chicken and the egg, we suspect that enthusiasm and success seem to go together. We suspect, however, that enthusiasm comes first. If you hope to succeed at anything in this world, polish up your enthusiasm, and hang onto it."

John Luther, philosopher

There is an image of Veeck, bent over, on his knees, inspecting the grass like he'd just dropped a contact lens. He knew enough, had read enough, had spent enough time in his garden to be able to discuss some of the intracacies of ballpark surfaces with reasonable intelligence. So there were mornings at Comiskey Park, when he owned the White Sox, when Veeck would hobble out of the dugout and inspect the condition of the field like he was a groundskeeper. This is how much he loved baseball. This is the affair he had with baseball. Every blade of grass was precious.

"Bill knows everything there is to know about running a baseball team," Roland Hemond observed. "He can count a big stack of tickets just by rifling through them with his thumb. He can tell you what kind of grass you ought to have in the outfield. He can tell you what pitch a pitcher is having trouble with. I've never worked as hard in my life trying to keep up with him, and I've never enjoyed myself more."

"He was a pied piper of joy," says reporter Stan Isaacs. And that's the way it looked, so often in public, with Veeck leading and a train following. He would talk baseball anywhere. He would walk to the ballpark, fans straggling alongside him, walking with him, listening to stories, shaking hands. In Chicago, after his retirement, he sat in the bleachers at Wrigley Field with his shirt off, the sun drenching his wrinkled skin, a beer in one hand, a cigarette in the other, a picnic basket of homemade pork chops at his feet,

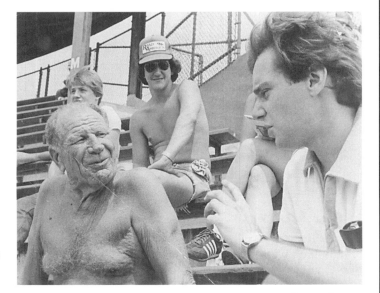

Bill Veeck is interviewed in the center field bleachers by George Castle. (right) (Courtesy of George Castle)

the smile dripping from his face and stories careening from his mouth. When Veeck owned the Brewers during the World War II years, he started games at 8:30 in the morning to help accommodate the late-shift workers at the factories, and he stood at the gates, handing out Corn Flakes and coffee for breakfast. He was visible because he wanted to be visible, because if someone wanted to talk baseball, he was more than willing to talk back.

He loved his job so much that he couldn't imagine doing anything else. He started law school once but never finished. And it wasn't that he didn't have other interests. He read so much, he had so many hobbies, so many subjects on the periphery that he could explore in depth. But baseball was his job. And the way he saw it, how could a man hate a job like that? How could anyone transform the greatest game ever played into an exercise in routine?

Bill put it this way: "I was in the game for love. After all, where else can an old-timer with one leg, who can't hear or see, live like a king while doing the only thing I wanted to do?"

So in St. Louis, Veeck sat in the clubhouse in his shorts and sport shirt, playing hearts with the players. At other times, he just sat around, in the dugout, in the press room, waiting for people to approach him. He was always at an open table, never in his office, because how could you spread your passion when you've locked yourself in an office?

"I have no pride. I'll do anything that's necessary to get people involved. I am a dispenser of enthusiasm."

Benjamin Zander, conductor

It's something that I take pride in. It's the way I try to approach each day, unleashing enthusiasm and zest for life on those who come into contact with me on a daily basis. It's something Veeck taught me early on, when I was in Spartanburg, running a Class A Phillies minor-league franchise. I invited Veeck to visit once. This is what he wrote about that visit in his syndicated column:

First, there's a fellow named Pat Williams, who among other things, is general manager, business manager, assistant concessions manager, public relations director and part-time broadcaster.

He's a fellow who dares. He'll try anything once. And if it doesn't work? Well, then he'll try something else.

I wasn't asking for the credit (although I will admit it was flattering to be recognized like that at my age). I did all those things because I enjoyed them, because I yearned to generate the enthusiasm of the man who had tutored me in the game. And it's something that I recognize in the people around me. There was a night in the early 1980s, when I was general manager of the Philadelphia 76ers, that I invited a well-known preacher, Dr. Stephen Olford, to speak to the Phillies at a Sunday evening chapel service before a game. After the service, Dr. Olford and Mike Schmidt had a pleasant conversation.

That night, we were at the game, eating a picnic supper, sitting beside the Phillies dugout, and in the first inning, the Phillies

Mike Schmidt. (Courtesy of the Philadelphia Phillies)

loaded the bases. Up came Schmidt. He hit a ball into the left-field seats. Forty thousand people stood as Schmidt rounded the bases, and up went Dr. Olford, this distinguished preacher, out of his seat, down the aisle, trying to work his way into the Phillies dugout to shake Schmidt's hand.

I had to explain to him that it didn't work that way. But I couldn't help but smile. It was the enthusiasm that erupted in him, that drove him out of his seat before he'd known what happened. And isn't it better to live this way, to let the joy of life carry us, than to meander through flat-footed and straight-faced?

Lady Mary Clayton, 82-year-old niece of the 100-year-old Queen Mother, in August 2000 said, "Her secret is her joy in life." That reminds me of a bumper sticker I saw one day when I was out running: DON'T POSTPONE JOY.

A man named Rich DeVos and his family bought the Orlando Magic in 1991, and one night that season, late in a tight game, the Magic called time-out. And Rich stood up, and hurried down the aisle, and slipped into the huddle. Of course, who was going to tell the owner of the team that this wasn't exactly within the boundaries of NBA rules?

Orlando Magic owner Rich DeVos and Pat Williams. (Author's collection)

"People who never get carried away should be."
Malcolm Forbes,
financier and publisher

It can be a cynical world. I should know. I have children. Nineteen of them, to be exact. Fourteen are adopted—from four different countries. Sixteen of them were teenagers at one time. In a sense, I consider myself the world's foremost researcher on teenage behavior. So, you ask, what is the most common and universal characteristic among teenagers?

The Pat Williams clan. (Author's collection)

It's this: Everything in their life is directly relative in importance to how cool it is. Well, not cool. They don't say cool anymore. Now they say, "phat." Which apparently stands for "pretty hot and tempting." Which doesn't make any sense to me but makes perfect sense to them. So who am I to argue?

"On with the dance; let joy be unconfined, is my motto, whether there's a dance to dance or any joy to unconfine."

Mark Twain, author

So everything in the life of my teenagers revolves around coolness or its proportion of "phat" in the eyes of the gang. Yet whenever I come home and ask what's going on, they say, "We're chilling." Or "We're vegging." Or "We're chilling and vegging."

Then they tell me, "I'm bored." (If I hear the word "bored" one more time, I might go completely insane.) Which tells me that nothing in this world is apparently cool enough, or "phat" enough, in the eyes of a teenager, to take seriously. Because the most un-"phat" thing in the eyes of a teenager is to think that anything is too "phat." So nothing is ever phat. So there's never anything to do. (Which explains my teetering on the brink of insanity).

This is why we're thankful when they either a.) go to college; b.) go into the military; or c.) dive headlong into the workforce. Because by then, they have no choice. And they'd better uncover a passion in a hurry because they're paying their own way.

"If you are not fired with enthusiasm, you will be fired with enthusiasm."

Vince Lombardi, football coach

All that mattered to Veeck about baseball was that people have a good time. The rest became simply a means to that end, a way to ensure that the people at the park felt the same way he did, that they left feeling they had witnessed something unique; something special. So if you engaged him, he would engage you back. He would never push you away. Said the late *Los Angeles Times* sports columnist Jim Murray, "I think Bill was the first one I ever heard say of baseball: 'It ain't high Mass. It's a game, for cripe's sake!' "

And isn't it easier to accept our careers if we view them that way; not as life and death, not as a constant battle to tread water, to survive but simply a way of carrying through by doing something we love? Won't it make us better at what we do? Won't success flow that much easier?

The inventor of the self-starting engine, Charles Kettering, worked for General Motors. By the time he approached retirement age, he was a wealthy man. He didn't need the work, didn't need to put in more hours. But he approached GM with a proposal: he would work for $150,000 a year from the age of 70 to 75. For the next five years, from 75 to 80, he would work for nothing. And for the five years after that, from 80 to 85, he would pay GM $150,000 a year to keep working.

*Jim Murray. (Courtesy of the **Los Angeles Times**)*

There is no record his proposal was officially accepted, but Kettering retired at the age of 82.

It is the attitude of every great businessman and scientist and politician and writer and athlete and promoter. I met a man at a convention who'd once played golf with NHL Hall of Famer Gordie Howe. Howe shot a 74, and the man asked him, "Gordie, have you ever thought about playing golf professionally?"

"No," Howe said. "I love to skate too much."

Someone once asked Thomas Edison, the inventor, when he planned to retire. He told them he'd retire the day before his funeral.

"I don't care what you do for a living. If you love it, you are a success."

George Burns, comedian

A couple of years ago, I went to a dinner for Ted Williams, one of the greatest hitters of all time. Williams was 77 at the time, and his health

Ted Williams. (Author's collection)

was already failing, and yet at the dinner, there unfolded this remarkable scene. Three perennial All-Stars, Mark McGwire, Gary Sheffield and Mike Piazza, were huddled around Williams in his wheelchair. And Ted was wringing his hands around an imaginary bat, demonstrating the mechanics of the swing. His eyes danced. He still brimmed with the same ardor for hitting as he had in 1941, the year he became the last player to hit .400.

Sometimes it will take an effort to find what's right, where your passion lies. But when you discover it, either by tripping over it or being led to it, you will know. Back when she was 15, Jim Lynam's daughter, Dei, was lost and lacking spirit. She was in a new school, her father having just become an assistant coach with the Portland Trail Blazers under Jack Ramsay. So Ramsay got her a job working for the TV crew at Blazers games, holding the boom mike near the huddles at time-outs.

As time went on, Dei held the boom mike closer and closer, until one night she held the mike in the middle of

Jack Ramsay. (SPI Archives)

the huddle. A furious Ramsay turned to her and shouted, "Get that thing out of here."

Dei pointed to Ramsay and said, "You do your job, I'll do mine!"

Dei is now in her 30s. And she's one of the top female sportscasters in the country.

"Unless the people you meet with are fun-loving kids out for a romp, tossing ideas like confetti and letting the damn bits fall where they may, no spirit will ever rouse, no notion will ever birth, no love will be mentioned, no climax reached. You must swim at your meeting. You must jump for baskets. You must take hefty swings for great or missed drives. You must run and dive. You must fall and roll and, when the fun stops, get the hell out."

Ray Bradbury, author

In meetings, Veeck encouraged imaginations to wander deep into the realm of impossibility. You could propose any idea, and he would let you know whether it would work, whether it could be embellished to become even more dynamic.

He did not let you sleep because he rarely slept. But you didn't need as much sleep because your working hours were so stimulating; so relentless and replete with ideas. "This made you feel," says one of his ex-employees, Roland Hemond, "that sleep was a valuable waste of time."

"I go to bed at 1 a.m. and get up at 5. I don't like the first five minutes, but that's life. Those people still sleeping, they're the ones missing out."

Dennis Connor, sailor

Our games, like our corporate lives, have become over-whelmed by the spectre of big busi-ness. So often, in pursuit of contract extensions and lucra-tive endorsements, of big-budget accounts and promotions, the fun is wrung from what we do. But Veeck lived a life of uninterrupted and

Bill and Mary Frances Veeck operated as a team wherever they went. (Courtesy of Jim Dyck)

unadulterated fun. He danced and partied. At times, before he married Mary Frances, he flew from Cleveland to New York for the night, stopped in at the nightclubs, and flew back in the morning.

For a time, Bill and Mary Frances lived in an apartment inside St. Louis' Sportsman's Park. The place had its own jukebox, and Veeck would invite people over, and they would delight in his music collection. He listened to Louis Armstrong, and had a remarkable affinity for jazz. And then he went to work. And he figured, why should work be any different?

"I don't want to get to the end of my life and find that I just lived the length of it. I want to have lived the width of it as well."

Diane Ackerman, author

He was an ambassador. And certainly, there were days when he didn't feel like he had the energy, when his leg stump was sore or his body ached or his energy was ravaged, but he did it nevertheless. "It's hard work," he said, "but the best way to promote the team."

Hard work is to be expected. No reason, though, for it to be dreaded.

Bill Bradley, the former NBA player and senator, has told a story, time and again, of a conversation he had with a man at a postgame reception.

"Do you really like to play basketball?" the man asked.

"More than anything I could be doing right now," Bradley said.

"That's great," the man said. "You know, I once played the trumpet. I think I know what you feel. I played in a little band. We were good. We played on weekends at colleges. In my last year, we had an offer to tour and make records. Everyone wanted to. Except me."

"Why didn't you?"

"My father thought it wasn't secure enough."

"What about you?" Bradley asked.

"Well," the man said, "I didn't know. I guess I agreed. The life is so transient. You're always on the road. No sureness that you'll get your next job. It just doesn't fit into a life plan. So I went to law school. I quit playing the trumpet, except every once in a while. Now I don't have time."

"Do you like the law?" Bradley asked.

"It's okay," the man said. "But it's nothing like playing the trumpet."

"I can't quite explain it, but I don't believe one can ever be unhappy for long, provided one does just exactly what one wants to and when one wants to."

Evelyn Waugh, author

I had my picture taken a couple of years ago for a story in the *Orlando Sentinel.* The photographer wasn't getting the excitement in the shot he wanted. He told me to "attack the camera." So I did. He got what he wanted, and I kept those words with me since then. That's how you define success. Attack the camera.

His whole life, Bill Veeck dove headlong into the camera. When he was a kid, he went sledding with his friends, and they attached a bobsled to the back of a car. He got to the front of the sled as the car was drifting along a snowy road at about 40 miles per hour, and he lifted the front of the sled. Just to put on a show, which, eventually, became his intent in life.

He could have been killed that day. But Veeck was never one to think of things like that. Too much living going on to become intimidated by the bottom line. Too many passions to satisfy. Too much entertaining to do.

"There's nothing to giving everyone in a ballpark an Eskimo Pie. But to give one person 30,000 Eskimo Pies ... now that causes some thought. What are they going to do with them? What happens when they start to melt? How fast are they going to pass them around? Are they going to eat them all themselves?"

Chapter 3

Now That Causes
Some Thought

"We used to have fire drills in our house, and in the fire drill, one of the kids would grab the wooden box with the file cards of ideas. So I grew up in a household where respect for ideas was paramount. That leaves a huge impression on you. It just means, 'Try everything.'"

Mike Veeck

A lifetime of ideas was gathered in that box, more than 1,500 of them, typed on yellow index cards and filed under various headings: One-Shot Gags, Concessions, Special Nites and Days, Ticket Sales, Civic Contributions, Parking, Far-Out Ideas. Bill Veeck wouldn't disclose the ideas publicly, because there is no copyright on ideas, and as much as the establishment of baseball had ostracized him, he wasn't about to reveal his innovations so they could adopt them as their own.

Veeck once hinted to a reporter about a Far-Out Idea: Play a baseball game in Havana. This was in the mid-1970s. Today, 25 years later, this is not so far-out. In fact, it's reality! In the spring of 1999, long after Bill Veeck had died, long after baseball's inner circle had forced him from the game, a major-league team, the Baltimore Orioles, played the Cuban national team in Havana.

He fought for interleague play and for night baseball in Wrigley Field, years before either happened. The day after he was admitted back into baseball, in 1976 with the Chicago White Sox, Veeck pulled a card from the idea box. On it were the words: "Trade in the open like an honest man." So with the help of his general manager, Roland Hemond, Veeck set up a table in the lobby of the Diplomat Hotel in Hollywood, Florida, where baseball's owners were meeting. He hooked up a telephone to a nearby jack and told the White Sox' publicist to call him every half-hour, just to make it look like business was brisk. He hung a sign that read: "OPEN FOR BUSINESS: BY APPOINTMENT ONLY," and for 14 hours, amid the gawking mouths of onlookers and the angry grumblings of some of his fellow owners, Veeck completed four different deals, one only a few minutes before the midnight trade deadline.

Ideas were his resource. He cherished them more than material belongings and more than money. He nurtured them like they were his own children. He walked through the stands during games, shaking hands and talking and gathering ideas from fans, from reporters, from the hot dog vendors and the cab drivers, from anyone with a thought to share.

"Curiosity is one of the permanent, certain characteristics of a vigorous intellect."

Samuel Johnson, author

What separates a genius from the rest of us?

Certainly, the reputation is not built through pure intelligence. That's the stereotype, of Einstein and Michaelangelo and Da Vinci. But if that were the case, we would all be subservient to our computers, to hard drives and modems and megabytes of RAM with IQs twice that of any human. And what computers lack is where our advantage lies. A computer cannot generate something original; something unfettered by the rigidity of preexisting principles. A computer is subservient to the power of imagination. And even Einstein admitted as much. "Imagination," he once said, "is more important than knowledge."

Here are two distinctly human concepts:

Imagination: The act ... of believing or supposing.

Creativity: Resulting from originality of thought or expression.

With these traits, we believe what computers cannot. We have faith in the impossible. We have the ability to try anything. Or to try everything.

"Sometimes, I've believed as many as six impossible things before breakfast."

Lewis Carroll, author

Names on uniforms. Bat day. Fireworks night. West Coast expansion. The circus. The Harlem Globetrotters. Tightrope walkers. Flagpole sitters. Jugglers. The exploding scoreboard. A blackboard in the men's room. A shower in the park. A night for the trainer. A night for the average fan. Grandstand Managers day. A pregame garden party. A midget at the bat ...

We could go on. We could fill this book with Veeck's thoughts; with the scraps of notions that he generated in his head like so much confetti. We are dealing with the most

Jim Rivera and Bill Veeck pose to publicize one of Bill's least successful ideas: summer baseball uniforms. (AP/Wide World Photos)

"To stay ahead, you must have your next idea waiting in the wings."

Rosabeth Moss Kanter, author

fertile imagination in baseball, if not sports, history. We are dealing with baseball's Da Vinci, baseball's Einstein, with "the most innovative thinker the game has ever known," says Cubs broadcaster Steve Stone.

He gave away a swaybacked horse, 1,000 pounds of chicken feed and 500 jars of iguana meat. Nothing was too ridiculous. The more incongruous, the greater the unthinkability, the more Veeck's buoyant spirit took pleasure in it. "It hasn't been done, or it can't be done," says his old friend, Max Jacobs, "had no meaning to him."

Baseball could never catch up to Veeck. Until the end, he remained a step ahead, consistently flirting with trouble, with potential disaster, yet continuing to pull ideas from his Idea Box and implementing them and delighting in the spark of result. "Baseball has always been a straitjacket for the imagination," says writer Mark Kram, "but Bill Veeck squirmed and squirmed out of it repeatedly to make his view count."

"Nothing limits achievement like small thinking; nothing expands possibilities like unleashed imagination."

William A. Ward, author and poet

When I was a young general manager in Spartanburg, enthused and awed by the responsibilities of my job, Bill Veeck was my sounding board. I visited him in the off-season. I called him on the phone every

Sunday night. I called if I had the wisp of an idea or the germ of a notion. It starts with that; with the kindling of imagination. Veeck refined my ideas. He streamlined them; shaped them into something that could work at more than just an imaginary level. He lent his creativity. He caused them to happen.

This is how the process went.

It was 1966. We were coming out of spring training. The Phillies assigned two minor league pitchers to Spartanburg. One was named John Parker. The other was named John Penn. Of course, what came next was a natural. "Parker Pen Night," I said. Give away thousands of Parker pens. Promote our newest pitchers. Promote the pens. Everyone wins.

I ran it by Veeck. It was like dropping a match into an open gas tank. The pleasure of possibility exploded through his gravelly voice. And we were off.

"I can never stand still. I must explore and experiment. I am never satisfied with my work. I resent the limitations of my own imagination."

Walt Disney

Let's pause here to tell a story of another creative force. Walt Disney, like Veeck, was unrestrained by the trappings of his imagination. Disney never intruded on his animators during the day. He understood the fragility of the creative process, the solitary nature it required. But there was nothing to stop him from coming in at night, after everyone had gone home. The animators learned to expect this, and often centered their best work on their desks before they left.

Walt Disney. (AP/Wide World Photos)

But sometimes, they arrived the next day with crumpled pieces of paper taped to their storyboards. Seems that Disney had gone through the trash baskets, pulled out discarded sketches, and, in his unmistakably majestic handwriting, had written, "Quit throwing the good stuff away."

"I believe that dreams—daydreams, you know, with your eyes wide-open and brain machinery whizzing—are likely to lead to the betterment of the world."

L. Frank Baum, author

Veeck knew what the good stuff was. The Parker-Penn idea, he liked. It had potential. So he said, "The first thing you need to do is get hold of the Parker Pen Company." Then he started spewing information, that they were in Janesville, Wisconsin, that he'd spoken to people there in the past, that he knew the person I should call. Which shouldn't have surprised me, because Veeck had contact with virtually everyone in the free world at one point or another.

So I called the Parker Pen Company. They came through. Bushels of pens would be provided. Enough to transcribe the Dead Sea scrolls a thousand times.

"But how will you give them away?" Veeck asked.

There were possibilities. We could give a pen to each fan. We could give them to people sitting in certain lucky seats. We could give them all to one fan. We could give them out if a player hit a grand-slam home run.

"And what will you do about entertainment?" Veeck said.

I shrugged. Hadn't thought that far ahead.

"Only one thing you can do," he said. "The Inkspots."

The Inkspots were a popular musical group at the time, suitable entertainment for Parker Pen Night. So I tracked them down through an agent. Turned out they were booked that night. Strangely enough, they were playing at Mickey Mantle's Holiday Inn in Joplin, Missouri. But this is how it worked. You threw out ideas. Some came through. Some fell through. Nothing was ever lost.

So we threw Parker Pen Night without the Inkspots. We anticipated a huge Saturday night crowd. And then the whole thing collapsed in our laps. The day before the game, John Parker was called into the army. The morning of the game, John Penn's wife gave birth to their first child. He had to leave town.

So now we had Parker Pen Night with thousands of Parker pens. But without Parker. And without Penn. Our gimmick had been shattered. And the night of the game, the skies opened up like never before, and the most intense thunderstorm in the history of Spartanburg dumped buckets of rain onto picturesque Duncan Park.

Parker Pen Night was rescheduled. John Parker got a pass from the army to come to the game. John Penn's son was a month old. You roll with disaster. In the end, the power of imagination comes through. It's just a matter of weathering the storm that comes with it.

"The most important thing I learned, from big companies, is that creativity gets stifled when everyone's got to follow the rules."

David Kelley, founder, IDEO product development

When Veeck took over the White Sox, he told Roland Hemond, his general manager, "Let your imagination run rampant." In his meetings, no thought was taboo. You lobbed it out there, without fear of repercussion, of looking stupid, of bending the rules. There were no rules. And that's the only way for a business to keep from running itself into the ground. It must take risks. It must imagine and create and innovate constantly. It must encourage free thinking.

Back to Walt Disney for a moment. The following comes from a message board at Epcot Center. I think it fits here.

1. ***How to Improve Your Imagination: Use it.*** Ask questions. Take risks. Take a picture. Take a vacation without leaving home. Be

curious. Expect the unexpected. Invent your own language. Think backwards. Doodle. Build a model…without the instructions. Look at the world from a different angle.

2. ***Exercises for Your Imagination: Stretch your mind.*** Play "What if?" Pick up a camera, and see what develops. Stay up all night. Write with your opposite hand. Take a blank piece of paper… then, do something with it. Make believe. REMEMBER: Things aren't always what they seem.

3. ***How to Jumpstart Your Imagination: Think about something else.*** Talk to yourself. Talk to the animals. Look at the BIG picture. Look to nature for inspiration. Play. Be playful. Look at the world … through the eyes of a child.

4. ***How to Come Up With an Idea: Brainstorm.*** Don't procrastinate. Turn your thinking inside out. Notice the little things. Get in touch with your inner child. Loosen up. Stay focused. Daydream. Paint something. Use all the colors of your imagination. Imagination comes in many colors.

5. ***THE FIRST RULE OF IMAGINATION: THERE ARE NO RULES!***

"Creativity is allowing yourself to make mistakes. Art is knowing which ones to keep."

Scott Adams, cartoonist

Don't fear the labels. Don't fear the unsafe path. In a room of suits, of stale ideas, there is nothing worse than another conformist. You should, says Thomas Watson, the first president of IBM, be more wary of the label of conformist than of the label "crackpot."

I've heard people say they lack creativity. They have this notion that creativity is an exclusive concept, belonging to Thoreau and Robert Frost and Picasso. Not true. If you've ever bent your paycheck to last until the next one, if you've ever come up with a new twist for an age-old sales technique, you've utilized it. If you've ever watched a four-year-old make a peanut butter and jelly sandwich, you've seen it. Because we all have it. It's just that some of us forget to use it. Part of it is our own fault. Part of it is the fault of a society that suppresses it. "In my day, it was okay to enjoy childhood, to believe in Santa Claus and bask in the sun," says a man named Robert Keeshan, more well-known as childhood TV show host Captain Kangaroo. "Today, we stage a full-force attack against creativity in childhood."

The best businessmen know how to avoid this. When Charles Kettering was head of research at General Motors and needed a problem solved, he'd call a meeting. Then he'd set up a table outside with a sign: LEAVE SLIDE RULES HERE. Otherwise, he knew, someone would reach for his slide rule during the meeting, leap up and say, "Boss, you can't do it."

Creativity is like any other muscle. When we are taught not to use it, taught not to exercise it, the muscle grows pale and atrophies from disuse. Too many teachers and executives push their employees and students away from building that muscle, blinding them to its potential. And the potential of humanity is dealt a fatal blow.

"We've always done it this way," people say, and nothing gets done, except by men like Dick Fosbury, men who have the ability to see through the barriers. Fosbury was an Olympic high jumper. For years, every high jumper used the same technique, clearing the bar with their stomachs facing down, until Fosbury flipped over in mid-air, so his back faced the bar, and kicked his legs to clear. It was called the Fosbury Flop, and it's now the accepted way to teach high jumpers their craft.

"You can't use up creativity. The more you use, the more you have. Sadly, too often, creativity is smothered rather than nurtured. There has to be a climate in which new ways of thinking, perceiving and questioning are encouraged."

**Maya Angelou,
author and poet**

This is a story about elephants and creativity. If it sounds incongruous, bear with me. In Africa, they train elephants by chaining them to huge trees with deep roots and massive trunks. The elephant will pull at the tree, jerk at the tree, until its leg is bloody and sore. But he won't even wiggle the tree or budge the steel chain. He'll keep pulling for as long as three weeks, injuring nothing but himself, until finally he'll give in and stand still, never again attempting to pull at the tree. By then, you could tie the elephant's chain to a tent stake, and he'll never pull it out. He lives in fear of the tree, lives in fear of hurting himself again instead of fighting to be free.

Veeck refused to be straitjacketed. Even if he felt a conversation was lagging, or he wanted to delve deeper into a subject or expand a point, he would manufacture an argument just to show a differing opinion. The result was that you thought more deeply, that you were forced into making choices, forced into justifying your decisions, forced to exercise that creative muscle.

Thomas Edison accomplished this by fishing. He would sit on the end of a dock in Fort Myers, Florida, holding his fishing pole, the line stretched into the bay. He had no bait on the hook. So the fishermen on the dock asked him why he did it. What was the point?

"I fish with no bait because no one bothers me," he said. "Neither fish nor man."

"Every genius is a revolutionary who produces a great deal of commotion in the world. After he has abolished the old rules, he writes his own, new ones, which no one even half understands. Not always does the next generation comprehend and appreciate him properly. Sometimes, it may even take a whole century."

Fredric Chopin, composer

Not every idea works. There was Disco Demolition night, which became the one glaring failure of his career. It was actually Mike Veeck's idea, to invite fans to bring disco records to the park and destroy them between games of a doubleheader, but for years afterward, Bill Veeck's staunchest critics pointed to it as proof that he had taken the insanity of his imagination too far. And they used it to force him away from the game for good.

Fifty thousand people attempted to get into Chicago's Comiskey Park that night in 1979, well over capacity. After the first game of a twi-night doubleheader with Detroit, about

Mike Veeck. (Courtesy of the Tampa Bay Devil Rays)

7,000 fans jumped onto the field, shouting obscenities, tearing apart the batting cages, and setting fire to disco records in the outfield. The White Sox were forced to forfeit the game. It was a disaster. Even Veeck had to admit that. It was, he would later say, the one idea that worked too well.

It was easy for his critics to dwell on that day, to ignore the thousands of promotions that had worked and to point to the one that didn't. But that would be as unjust as suppressing creativity in the first place; as ignorant as rejecting 1,500 ideas simply because one didn't work. And so many of those ideas did. It got to the point where people came to the ballpark just to see what would happen next, to see how Veeck could shock them this time. "Once you have established a reputation for being original and imaginative," Veeck wrote in *The Hustler's Handbook*, "you will find that anything you do—no matter how unoriginal or unimaginative—becomes fun just because it is you who is doing it."

"The idea is there, locked inside; all you have to do is remove the excess stone."

Michaelangelo, artist

What Bill Veeck taught me was how to cultivate an idea, to transform the wispiest of thoughts into the most grandiose of events. In the summer of 1990, four years after Veeck died, our NBA team, the Orlando Magic, purchased the Double-A baseball team in Orlando. At the time, we were hoping to win a major-league franchise expansion and were in the midst of intense competitions with both Miami and St. Petersburg. St. Petersburg looked like the front-runner (though, in the end, Miami wound up with the franchise: the Marlins).

In the meantime, there were gentle barbs flying back and forth between Orlando and St. Petersburg. So at one of our minor-league games, we decided to hold a "St. Pete Night," honoring the good (though rather aged) people of St. Petersburg.

We brainstormed, created, tossed out ideas. We decided we would send St. Peter himself to meet people at the gates of the stadium. We served them Cream of Wheat as they came into the ballpark, with tenderizer. We played dusty big-band favorites from artists like Tommy Dorsey and Glenn Miller. We had pregame wheelchair races and cane-throwing contests. The grand-prize winner that night earned a year's supply of right-turn signal bulbs.

We generated a few laughs. Joe Henderson, a reporter from the *Tampa Tribune,* came to cover it, and, needless to say, the St. Petersburg Chamber of Commerce was not exactly overwhelmed with our activities. I guess you could say they gave me the key to the city. And then they had the locks changed.

But I had this feeling that night. The feeling that somewhere behind St. Peter's gates, Bill Veeck was humming along with us.

"This is an illusionary business. The fan goes away from the ballpark with nothing more to show for it than what's in his mind. When you sell a chair, or a house, or a car, you can develop a contented customer based on the quality of your product. Three years from now, he can look at it with a feeling of satisfaction— 'Best buy I ever made.' But in baseball, all he ever walks away with is an illusion; an ephemeral feeling of having been entertained. You've got to develop and preserve that illusion. You have to give him more vivid pictures to carry away in his head. Let me say it again. The only thing about a baseball game that matters is the ephemeral notion that you had a good time."

Chapter 4

That Sounds Like Great Fun

"Bill had a spirit, a sense of joy for life, like no one else. He had an instinct not just for fun but for joy as well. It was infectious, inspiring and had an effect on every life he touched. He left some of that with all of us. It just sticks with you."

Tom Weinberg, financial investor in the White Sox with Bill Veeck

o perhaps you're wondering, where's the midget? We haven't really touched on the midget yet, and you'd think that since this chapter is supposed to discuss Bill Veeck and his expansive sense of humor and his unquenchable zest for fun that the transcendent story of Veeck sending the midget to the plate in St. Louis, the singular moment that trailed Veeck to his grave,

would fit here. "My epitaph is inescapable," he once said. "It will read: 'He sent a midget to the plate.'"

Tom Weinberg. (Courtesy of Tom Weinberg)

Because of that, I thought I'd hold off on the midget for a while. After all, it would be a shame to delve into trodden ground when there is such fertile territory all around. There are so many other stories. There are tales of Veeck dancing and singing and playing practical jokes and dressing in costume and experimenting with the absurd in an attempt to find a punch line.

Start with the tale of the ice pick. Dick Schaap, the longtime sportswriter, tells this one about the time he met Veeck in a cab at LaGuardia airport to write a profile of him for *Sport* magazine. Veeck got into the cab. He pulled out an ice pick. He stabbed himself in the leg.

(The wooden leg, that is.)

He used to perform this trick for children as well. Then he'd ask, "Can your daddy do that?" He built the ashtray in that leg because so much of his notion of what was funny was built on shocking people; on the basic incongruities that diffuse the tension and make us realize how ridiculous our worries are in the first place.

It is hard to imagine today's owners stabbing themselves with an ice pick. Or squirting champagne at team parties. Or chasing children around a creek, swimming the butterfly, shouting, "I'm a giant sea monster!" He made fun of himself for being crippled, made fun of others if they called their infirmities upon themselves and, in the process, made everything so much blessed fun.

"His mind was 71," wrote Jim Murray of the *Los Angeles Times*, "but his heart was 12 years old."

"The human race has one really effective weapon, and that is laughter."

Mark Twain, author

Veeck knew how to laugh, and I would venture to say that he laughed more readily and more frequently than anyone in baseball history. At every one of those instructional sessions at his house, every time I visited him, every time we discussed my plans and his plans and the ways of this earth, the same word continued to surface.

And that word, of course, was fun.

He used it to describe his philosophy of life and family and work and sales and promotion because he knew it was too risky to sell your product on the basis of wins and losses alone. If that were the case, at the end of each season, only one team would have had a successful year, and everyone else would be recouping their losses. So instead, you don't disillusion yourself by placing your well-being on the risky notion of success. You sell your games on the strength of that ephemeral notion. You sell the fun of it all.

Fun and Bill Veeck were synonymous. (Author's collection)

Bill believed that when a person left the ballpark, they left with one thing: A memory. You hope they leave with a hat and a T-shirt and perhaps one of those giant foam fingers, as well, but for the most part, it will be the memory that stays with them. And what will they remember?

Bill once told me, "Anything that happens in a ball park, from the moment a fan arrives, to the moment he leaves, can ruin the impression of fun that you're trying to build. They will never forget what a good time they had. That requires an attention to detail."

We drew 114,000 fans to Spartanburg my first season as general manager—an amazing number for that level of the minor leagues. And yet the team was terrible. So when the season was over, I felt awful about it, as if I hadn't fulfilled some sort of promise. So I called Veeck.

"Pat," he said. "Just how many people did you draw to the park this season?"

I repeated the number.

"How many of those people had a good time?" he asked.

I said I hoped all of them did.

"Tell me one other thing you could have done this summer that would have provided that enjoyment to that many people."

I told him I didn't think there was anything.

"Let me tell you something," he said. "You never *ever* have to apologize for showing people a good time."

And this is how life should go, isn't it? The results are secondary. It is the process that matters, and in the process, one could find a wicked time if one surrounds himself with the right

Larry MacPhail (right) honored Pat Williams for being chosen as the winner of the MacPhail Promotional Trophy in 1966. (Author's collection)

people and the right places and is willing to approach absolutely nothing with a cold seriousness.

There was a way to tell whether you had truly captured Veeck with an idea. He would say, "That sounds like great fun." It was the word "great" that separated these ideas from the rest, for when Veeck burst forth with that phrase, you knew you'd struck on something. I still use that phrase today.

Bill used to challenge me to guarantee it; that if any fan didn't have fun I should refund their money on the spot. Of course, it was easy for him to say. He was an owner. I wasn't. I've never had the courage to do that myself.

So now you want to have fun. I've piqued your curiosity. You understand that it's not immoral or illegal or illicit to have fun, that actually, it's quite the opposite, that if there's not an element of riotousness in everything you do, you're missing something.

So I challenge you, just like Veeck always did. Come with me. Let's spend the night skipping from place to place and not fear the consequences. What are you going to do? Put the book down? You can't stop reading here. You'll never know what you might miss.

"The number-one premise of business is that it need not be boring or dull. It ought to be fun. If it's not fun, you're wasting your life."

Tom Peters, business guru

One basic premise: Never let work get in the way of a good time.

The coach of our Orlando WNBA team, Carolyn Peck, once said that she'd discovered what went wrong when her team started to slump a little as it headed toward the playoffs. She told people, "I thought we had to get more focused. It cost us our funness for a while there."

Funness? Is that a word?

Guess it is now. We're on a roll.

There should be parties at work. This does not mean work has to be a perpetual bash with your boss always wearing a lampshade on his head. But every so often, perhaps more often than not, absurdity should reign. And it starts at the top. The founder of Wal-Mart, Sam Walton, once danced on Wall Street in a hula skirt as part of a vow he had made. Another time, he flew his airplane to Texas, had it parked, and told the copilot to pick him up 100 miles down the road. Once there, he flagged down a Wal-Mart truck driver and rode the rest of the way, just because "it seemed like so much fun."

If I am asked that ever-present question about my ultimate dinner party, I would have to include two men with similar inclinations, Walt Disney and Bill Veeck. Now, let me explain my biases here. When I moved to Orlando to run the Magic in 1986, I became instantaneously Disney-ized. This is an insidious form of brainwashing that leaves you perpetually waiting in line for Space Mountain and mumbling the names of your oldest children, which you are quite convinced are Donald and Pluto. Actually, it left me fascinated with every facet of Walt Disney, and I wrote much of this in a book called *Go For the Magic,* which I encourage you to buy, because I have a lot of kids to put through college, and by doing so, you'll help add a measure of frivolity to my life.

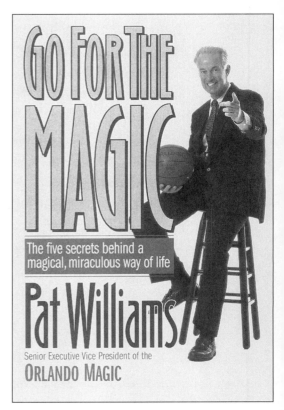

*The dustjacket cover of **Go For the Magic**. (Author's collection)*

But the point is, I learned that Walt Disney had formulated five secrets that will allow your dreams to come true. And number five was simple: Have fun.

"One cannot have too large a party."

Jane Austen, author

Veeck never missed many parties. This was his forte. He drove to Detroit once, when he owned the Indians, and arrived early on a Saturday morning. That night after the game he threw a large bash, and he and his friends and those who knew his friends and whoever happened to straggle along attended several night clubs and didn't get back in until eight on Sunday morning. Then Veeck went to the noon baseball game.

There are dozens of frivolous tales like this, of Veeck inhaling every spare moment. There was the morning that he and his friend Dizzy Trout, the former pitcher, came into the office after being out all night, and Veeck took off his open-collared short-sleeve white shirt, the same kind of shirt he wore every day. He opened a file cabinet, which is where he kept his clean shirts, took one out, put it on and started his day.

And on they went.

One night, at a banquet, after the night had moved from late to early, Veeck requested the table in front of him be moved. He eyed a low-hanging chandelier, about 18 inches above the table, called the room to order, adjusted himself in his chair and flipped up his artificial leg so that it nicked the bottom edge of the chandelier.

Then, with a straight face, he challenged everyone else to do it, and over the ensuing few minutes, as Veeck broke into laughter, he sat back and enjoyed another bizarre ritual he had just perpetrated on a handful of poor and innocent souls.

John Kuenster, editor of *Baseball Digest*, and his wife went out with Veeck and Mary Frances late one night, after Veeck had stayed late at a speaking engagement. They were going dancing, but it was past midnight, and Kuenster muttered, "Dancing? Everybody'll be gone by the time we get there."

Everybody was gone by the time they got to the Martinique Restaurant. But earlier that day, Veeck had called the owner and told the orchestra to stay around after they'd finished their gig. So at one in the morning, in an empty restaurant, two couples danced to their own private orchestra. "And I must say," Kuenster says, "Bill was a pretty good dancer."

"You can tell right away when you visit a company where no one is having fun…people look like they are running around with tight underwear on. They are longing to lighten up, but they have no permission."

**Ken Blanchard,
author and speaker**

I hear these stories, and it reminds me of one of the great mysteries of life, which is, why do people have so much trouble having fun? I think it pertains particularly to men. As men, so many of us have some sort of problem. We tend to adjust our faces in some permanent frown, like we are cheerleaders at a funeral, like we are professional lemon-tasters. Our day is a grind.

I don't know how this began. Perhaps it was the pilgrims. They did, after all, get off the boat at Plymouth Rock in quite a lousy mood. I have also heard a theory from one of our most respected contemporary philsophers, better known as Roseanne Barr. She thinks the reason people have so much trouble laughing is that the Puritans all came to this country, and the really fun people stayed behind.

This is what Veeck had to fight against in baseball, those who were offended by such a simple notion as laughter at a ballpark. They shunned his ridiculousness, his absurdities, the incongruities that endeared him to the common man. And that only made him laugh more.

"He was such fun to be around," said Mary Frances at Veeck's posthumous Hall of Fame induction. "He was a real Pied Piper."

The promotions, like the midget, like the circuses in the outfield, like the flagpole sitters, like the fireworks—we'll get to that …

For now, here is the tale of the man who danced with his wife in the kitchen, who played charades with his friends, whose idea of a good time was to startle someone with a notion so ridiculous they couldn't help but giggle.

Here is the tale of the clown.

One night, when the Yankees were at Comiskey Park, the Yankees' Gene Michael was sitting in the stands and relaying information to the dugout through a walkie-talkie. The next day, when Michael got to his seat, there was a clown in the seat next to him. And the clown stayed there for the whole game.

Gene Michael. (Courtesy of the New York Yankees)

"Laughter is an anesthetic. I could get shot five times, and if people think it's funny, I won't even feel it."
Conan O'Brien, talk show host

That brings us to the tale of the severed artery, which doesn't sound very funny, and really isn't, but tells a lot about how this man could turn just about anything into a punch line.

This was when he lived on a ranch in New Mexico, and he was painting a shed but decided the spray gun with the one-quart tank wasn't fast enough for his taste. So he hooked the spray gun to a gallon jar, and when he did, the pressure kept rising, until it exploded, severing an artery. His friend, Beth Smith Aycock, rushed him to the hospital, and Veeck, who was bleeding profusely, kept muttering that he wasn't going to make it, and Aycock rushed around 20-mph curves going 90.

When it was over, Veeck told Aycock he'd survived for one reason. He'd survived, he said, "Because I wanted to see how this came out."

Ba-dump-bump! How's that? A rimshot for a near-death story.

Once, when he was living in Maryland and thought he might have a brain tumor, he was reading a story to his children and suddenly slumped over with a "whooo…" and feigned unconsciousness. The kids freaked out, and Veeck popped up a few seconds later and said, "I was playing a joke on you."

Problem was, it didn't work on his own family. One of the kids looked at him and said, "What do we look like? Stupid? If it was a joke, it wasn't that funny."

"And by the way," someone else said, "get on with reading the story. You skipped a line."

When he was dying, this time for real, his daughter Lisa visited him in the hospital. Veeck was wearing an oxygen mask. His dinner was in front of him. "Are you going to eat your peas?" Lisa asked.

"No," Veeck said. "Are you?"

So perhaps he was a little morbid. But is there any better way to cope with life's most grievous ills than to look them squarely in the eyes and throw your head back and laugh?

"I challenge you to find a sad Bill Veeck story," Mike Veeck says. "Not a poignant one or a moving one, but a sad one. You won't find it."

The doctor who is treating Mike Veeck's daughter, a young girl named Rebecca who is in danger of losing her sight, once told him, "You guys are always laughing. You're always making silly jokes. Is nothing sacred?"

"Well," Mike Veeck says. "I learned that somewhere."

Which leads us right into the tale of the toupee.

One of Veeck's fellow owners, Charlie Finley, had watched with Veeck as Minnie Minoso became the oldest player to get a hit in a big-league game. And Finley began ragging on Veeck, telling him that he should step up to the plate and try to get a hit. "But no artificial devices," Finley said. "You've got to hit one-legged."

"Charlie," Veeck said, "I'll challenge you to that. No leg for me. No toupee for you."

With that, Finley walked away.

Charlie Finley. (Courtesy of the Oakland Athletics)

"You can't stay mad at someone who makes you laugh."
Jay Leno, talk show host

"Did he laugh because he was afraid?" Mike Veeck asks of his father. "I don't know. I never asked him. But I can tell you why I laugh. It has stood me in pretty good stead. People have described it as nervous laughter; laughter to get attention. I don't care what they think. I don't care what they call it. I can tell you now—looking down the barrel of my daughter's blindness—that laughter helps me defuse the hurt that I feel."

This comes from a man who, when he first owned the St. Paul Saints of the Northern League, hung up signs that read: "Fun is Good."

Joe Vitale, the motivational author, tells a story of a friend whose father survived during the Great Depression by getting people to spend a nickel on something they didn't need. He bought a small, fold-up merry-go-round, took it to parks and charged people a nickel to ride it. And people preferred to spend their last nickel just to squeeze out a single ounce of fun.

"Humor is the shock absorber of life. It helps us take the blows."

Peggy Noonan, former presidential speechwriter

As if you needed more convincing, there are mountains of scientific proof that laughter is beneficial to your health. A Stanford professor discovered that laughing heartily 100 times a day has the same beneficial effects as 10 minutes on a rowing machine. Laughter also unleashes chemical neurotransmitters and hormones throughout your body, contributing to an overall sense of well-being. It minimizes the intensities of both fear and anger, providing increased frequency and depth of respiration, expulsion and replacement of residual air in the lungs and coughing out of mucous accumulations.

Not only that, it feels pretty good too.

So I hope you've discovered the answer here. Having fun ain't exactly dependent on your knowledge of neurotransmitters. In every situation, in every bleak moment and dull moment and trying moment, no matter how inappropriate it might seem, you turn your cheek, and you laugh as loudly as you can.

And if, in a moment, everything is not fine, it will certainly seem a lot better than it was.

Veeck once sent away for a mail-order toy. When it arrived, he learned it had to be assembled. He spent the entire night before Christmas attempting to put that infernal toy together for one of his children. When he sent his check to the manufacturer, he tore it into tiny pieces, put them into an envelope and wrote: "I put your toy together. You put my check together."

No doubt he felt a burden lifted.

The manufacter had no choice but to accept the check.

"Sit in the moonlight and drink champagne or put beans up your nose and tell limericks. Do what needs to be done … Get together in a comfortable place with people you like a lot, dance, be romantic, be silly, and see if you can get each other laughing by making fun of your elders … Satire, kids, is your sacred duty as Americans. Be funny. Poke them cows and make them moo."

Garrison Keillor, author

Let's not stop poking them cows yet. Let's really venture into the absurd and the tale of the raw steaks. It comes from John Kuenster, who one night went to a speaking engagement with Veeck in a Chicago suburb. It was late, past midnight, by the time they finished, but Veeck said, "Let's stop at the ballpark."

"What for?" Kuenster asked.

"It won't take long," Veeck said. "I just need to pick something up."

They pulled up alongside Comiskey Park, on 35th Street, and they parked the car, and, after a security guard let them in, they climbed the stairs to the kitchen of the Bard's

*John Kuenster. (Courtesy of **Baseball Digest**)*

Room. Veeck walked to the refrigerators and pulled out six massive raw steaks. They dangled from his hands like catcher's mitts.

"Here," Veeck said. "You've got a big family. Take three of these."

But this is not where the story ends. Because after they got back in the car, Veeck began eating one of the raw steaks. And he ate almost the whole thing.

Wait a minute. Is that outrageous? Is it repulsive? Is it hilarious?

I suppose it's a little of everything. Which is why it's so amusing, so Veeckian, if there is a such a word, and I guess there is now because we're having too good a time to turn back.

Veeck was quick to admit that his sense of humor was patently lowbrow; that he could entertain himself and others quite easily. That was fine. "I have never objected," he once said, "to being called vulgar," and then he noted that the Latin of "vulgar" translates to "the common people." So as long as he was entertaining someone, he'd do whatever he had to do, from playing tricks with his leg to dancing until dawn to swimming and playing card games with his children to delivering live pigs for his players to take to their farms.

Make them smile. Make them laugh. Make them forget their car payments and their electric bill and their job at the factory. Allow your employees and your family to enjoy what they're doing without feeling guilty about it. Encourage them to make fools of themselves. Sing off-key. Dance in a hula skirt. Get shot five times and poke yourself in the leg with a sharp object.

Nothing should be off-limits in pursuit of lightening the moment. No toupee or slab of raw meat should escape your grasp.

"The only dirty word I can think of, offhand, is "conformity" because it is a word which tells a man he has no mind, no opinion, no name of his own."

Chapter 5

Who Do You Think You Are, Bill Veeck?

"When Bill gets dressed up, he looks like he forgot his pants."

Mary Frances Veeck

I've been dressed up before. And I'm not talking about a suit and tie, although I have done that because I have to, and because I think Bill Veeck was perhaps the only man in history who could get away without wearing a tie anywhere, including at his own wedding. But in this case, I'm talking about the type of suit with colorful fur and a head the size of a zeppelin.

I'm talking about a mascot's suit.

This was in the early 1980s when I was with the Philadelphia 76ers. We were trying to introduce a new mascot, and it wasn't going over very well. But the problem wasn't the mascot itself. The problem was the person inside the suit.

So one night, I relented. I said, "That's it. I'm going to wear it tonight."

We were playing Seattle, and I put on the suit and became a new person.

My inhibitions vanished beneath the comfort of anonymity. I did things in that suit that they would have arrested me for out on the street. The highlight of it was when I tried to sneak into Seattle's huddle during a time-out, and their coach, Lenny Wilkens,

Lenny Wilkens. (Courtesy of the Atlanta Hawks)

pushed me away and tried to kick me in my plush posterior.

Here's what I'm saying: Bill Veeck lived like that without any need for anonymity. The only fuzz on his costume was the kinky hair that sometimes took on a shimmering pink hue. He refused to wear a tie, to build a door for his office, to hire a secretary, to screen his phone calls, because that's who he was.

You really want to know how to have fun? Here it is. Perhaps the most important advice Veeck ever imparted to me or to anyone else.

Be yourself. Or as Mary Frances Veeck put it, "You cannot pretend. You must be."

That's all. Just be yourself. Let your inhibitions go. No matter how ridiculous or silly it might make you feel. Don't try to please anyone else. Don't try to mimic anyone else. Don't try to fit an image because as much as you strive for it, as meticulously as you attempt to contrive another you, it will all fall apart in the end.

"The reasonable man adapts himself to the world; the unreasonable one persists in trying to adapt the world to himself. Therefore, all progress depends on the unreasonable man."
George Bernard Shaw, playwright

We've talked about this already, about the way people tighten themselves up, pull inward, rein in their personality. It's especially prevalent in men, closing themselves off, building up walls.

Why?

I'll tell you why. Because we're afraid of rejection. We think if people see through our defenses, see through to ourselves, they might not like us. True, it's a gamble. I can assure you that there *will* be people who won't like you. Veeck alienated the bulk of baseball's establishment with his carefree attitude, with his gentle treatment of the common fan, with his refusal to acknowledge the walls that baseball's owners had erected between themselves and their constituents.

Mike Veeck observed, "My dad would walk into a room, look for the three biggest stuffed shirts, pull out a verbal pin and go after them."

No tie. The same style of white open-collared sport shirt every day, a shirt he began wearing because buttoned collars gave him a rash, and stayed with because it fit his image so readily. The hair curling in all directions. The shirtless old man in the stands at Wrigley Field. Call me anytime. Approach me anywhere.

Roland Hemond tells a wonderful story in *ESPN Magazine* that captures this perfectly: "Bill and I were to speak at a luncheon. That day, J.C. Martin, a retired player, was waiting to see Bill about a broadcasting job. I thought J.C. might make Bill late for our appointment. (I didn't know that J.C.'s meeting with Bill was scheduled for after the luncheon.) See, I wanted to protect Bill. So I went into Bill's office and closed the door behind me. Bill peered over his glasses and said, 'Don't ever shut my door. I *never* shut my door.' When I got back to the office, I broke out laughing. There's no door to his office. He'd had it removed. Now, I've heard of the open-door policy, but this was a little extreme. Next day, I go on a road trip with the ball club. When I return 10 days later, there are *no outer walls* to Bill's office. He'd had *them* knocked down too. Later I told him, 'Bill, this is remarkable. I used to have meetings behind closed doors and read everything that was said the next day in the newspaper. You don't have any walls and there are never any leaks.'"

As far as I could tell, Veeck had two enemies: formality and conformity. Because neither of them had anything to do with who he was. Bill frequently said, "When there is no room for individuals in ballparks, then there is no room for individuals in life."

"We are what we pretend to be, so we must be careful about what we pretend to be."
Kurt Vonnegut, author

We compare ourselves to each other, and we imitate each other, and we fall all over ourselves in our attempts to surpass each other's achievements. We measure our progress, our stumbles, our success, our failures, against what's already been done. Certainly, there's nothing wrong with emulating those we admire; with following the examples of those who have come before us. That's what this book is about.

But in the end, there is only one judge.

And here's a hint: It's not anybody else.

"Don't bother just to be better than your contemporaries or predecessors. Try to be better than yourself."
William Faulkner, author

This brings us to Charles Barkley.

There will never be another Charles Barkley, NBA power forward, outspoken individualist. Love him, hate him, there is no question that,

Charles Barkley. (Courtesy of the Philadelphia 76ers)

like Veeck, he forces you to acknowledge his existence as a human being. Title of his autobiography: *Somebody's Gotta Be Me.*

Having drafted him in 1984 while I was with the 76ers, I can vouch for the legitimacy of that title. When we brought Barkley in for an interview before the NBA draft, we asked him what his major was at Auburn. He said it was aeronautical engineering. We asked why. Barkley said, "If I don't make it in the NBA, I can always be a skycap."

"A great philosopher once said there's only three things in life," Barkley has pontificated. "There's what other people think you are, there's what you think you are, and there's what you really are."

Now I've heard that Charles wants to enter the gubernatorial race in Alabama. And when someone asked him why, he said, "I've always wanted to be the gubernor."

Somebody's gotta be you, Charles. I'm just glad it was you.

"Wearing underwear is as formal as I ever hope to get."
Ernest Hemingway, author

Veeck's wardrobe never changed, not even to conform to social norms. Once, his friend Andy McKenna called for dinner reservations at the Drake Hotel in Chicago. He told the maitre' d that one of his guests would not be wearing a tie.

The maitre d' told him it was required, so McKenna said, "This is Bill Veeck. He never wears a tie."

The maitre d' said, "You should have told me it was Bill Veeck. Of course he can come without a tie."

People didn't expect Veeck to wear a tie. They didn't want him to because he represented the general populace in a sport where they've always been bla-

A tie-less Bill Veeck. (Courtesy of Jim Dyck)

tantly ignored. He charged those around him with his air of openness and integrity, a resentment of all things formal and proper. A tie would have shattered that image (although Veeck's childhood friend, Marsh Samuel, insists Veeck wore a tie at his first wedding, something Veeck denied, most likely to heighten the dramatic effect).

And he felt the same about ties as he did about closed doors.

The first thing Veeck did when he bought the White Sox in 1975 was to take off the door to his office and order that the opening be expanded to three times its current size. He encouraged walk-in visits. In an article he wrote for *Sports Illustrated,* he gave out his phone number and emphasized that the phone calls would be forwarded directly to him, no questions asked. He answered all of his mail himself, writing in longhand in the margins of letters.

He once wrote me a letter with the typed heading of "Dear Mr. Williams." Next to it, he added in long hand, "Boy, are we formal today."

A baseball owner tearing out his office door, distributing his phone number in a national magazine and answering his mail by hand. It was Veeck at his finest. It was bizarre, and it was unique, and it was unprecedented. It was everything baseball had come to expect from its pre-eminent character, and yet he wasn't doing it because it was expected of him.

But others, like me, began to emulate his principles. For me, it was one of the first steps to discovering my own identity.

"When I heard Bill had his phone number listed in the book," says Chicago sportswriter Rick Telander, "I did the same thing. And I have ever since."

Of course, I can't recommend that everyone start wearing open-collared sport shirts and flicking ashes into an artificial leg and combing their hair in thick burrs. In fact,

Rick Telander (Courtesy of the **Chicago Sun-Times***)*

if anything, I'd recommend against it, because the chances are pretty strong that this is not who you are. It worked for Veeck because he was who he was. There will never be another. There never should be.

A man named Mike McCarney told me about the time his father went to a union meeting in downtown Chicago. He showed up in a shirt and a jacket. He wasn't wearing a tie. The doorman examined his outfit and told him he'd have to buy a tie before he could be admitted. Then he said, "Who do you think you are, Bill Veeck?"

"When I was a child, my mother said to me, 'If you become a soldier, you will be a general. If you become a monk, you will end up as the Pope.' Instead, I became a painter and wound up as Picasso."

Pablo Picasso, painter

Let's face it. Most of us aren't fortunate enough to be able to drift through our lives without having to slip a tie around our neck every so often (at least at our weddings). But that doesn't mean we have to choke away ourselves. And if we expect to accomplish anything truly original and important and satisfying, we can't lose sight of who we are. And we shouldn't let it happen to anyone else.

Bear Bryant, the late Alabama football coach, had this advice to those trying to mold young coaches or young executives or even young children, "Don't make them in your image. Don't even try. You don't strive for sameness. You strive for balance."

I give you the story of two composers, Irving Berlin and George Gershwin. When they first met, Berlin was already famous, and Gershwin was struggling, working for $35 a week. So Berlin offered Gershwin a job as his musical secretary, writing songs for three times the wage he was already making.

And then Berlin told him not to take the job.

"If you do," he said, "you may develop into a second-rate Berlin. If you insist on being yourself, someday, you will become a first-rate Gershwin."

Gershwin didn't take the job. Today, both men are recognized for their genius.

"Early on in my career, I started out pretending to be Barbara Walters. All the time, I was trying to hold my posture like Barbara and sit like Barbara and talk like Barbara. It didn't feel like myself. Life is about becoming who you are."
Oprah Winfrey, talk show host

When he worked at Suffolk Downs, a race track in Massachusetts, the first time he'd drifted away from baseball, Veeck noticed the place had fake flowers. So he took them and threw them out because he despised artificiality, because it was no substitute for the real thing.

He could sniff out phoniness. Had no tolerance for it. Problem was, many of those who ran baseball were hemmed in by the status quo, and they had no true desire, no inclination, to think on their own. They were boxed in by what had come before. They did nothing to differentiate themselves, to sell themselves, to make the game enjoyable. Instead, they dwelled on its sanctity and its tradition and its everlasting rules.

_____

"I am still puzzled as to how far the individual counts; a lot, I fancy, if he pushed the right way."

T. E. Lawrence, author

_____

When I began soliciting people for stories and anecdotes about Veeck, Mark Kram was one of the first I talked to. He'd been there at that first meeting I'd had with Veeck, and he'd spent time with Veeck again and again through the years.

It was Mark Kram who gave me that T.E. Lawrence quote. And it strikes me because it evokes Veeck's utter disdain for those who, instead of bursting forth with their own thoughts, cowered behind the sanctity of their so-called "rules."

"I try not to break the rules," Veeck once said. "Merely test their elasticity."

So he deliberately poked and prodded at the traditionalists. He questioned their values and their attitude about baseball as a "way

Besides his family, no one was more important to Bill Veeck than his players and the fans. (Courtesy of Bob Broeg)

of life"; as a religion. He questioned the rules. Nothing had to be that way, did it?

"The rules tell you what you can't do," Veeck said in a speech one night, "which means you can do anything that's not in the rules."

"Nancy Reagan adores her husband; I adore mine. She fights drugs; I fight illiteracy. She wears a size three; so's my leg."

Barbara Bush, former First Lady

He never really fit in. They were millionaires in suits, and they'd made their fortunes in business, and they'd never set their pricey posteriors on a bleacher seat in their lives. He'd inherited the family business from his father. The family business was baseball. He loved the game, and he loved people, and all he cared about was how more people could be drawn to this game, and how he could keep them there.

He didn't fit their image. He didn't satisfy their profile.

This is the price of being yourself. Not everyone will understand. Not everyone will accept it. Veeck and his first wife, Eleanor, separated in part because she couldn't understand his moods. She was somewhat introverted. He was … well, he was not.

And so many of his fellow owners also had personality clashes with Veeck. One described him as a "capital-gains gypsy." They found him brash and unapologetic and irritating. He had a long-running feud with the New York Yankees—long his chief rival for power and influence in the American League—and general manager George Weiss, and later, owner George Steinbrenner.

Veeck also testified in the trial of Curt Flood, which would open the doors for free agency in baseball. He arrived at the federal courthouse that day in his open-collared shirt. No jacket. He lit up a cigarette, and the bailiff announced that the judge was preparing to enter the chambers, and a lawyer whispered to Veeck, "You aren't allowed to smoke in a federal courthouse."

Veeck said, "I didn't know that." Then he hiked up the leg of his trousers and put out the cigarette in the ashtray in his wooden leg.

"As a baseball owner," says former Baseball Players Union head Marvin Miller, "Bill was a fish out of water."

Not that it bothered him. There was a part of Veeck that reveled in his own rebellion. Sometimes, he even flaunted it. But in the end, this was what drove him from the game, that his welcome had worn thin, and those who opposed him finally wore him down. "My time has passed," he said late in his career. "I'm an individualist. Baseball has become a syndicate business."

But they could not dull his impact. It's what happens sometimes when you muster the courage to think for yourself. You produce ideas and thoughts and policies that are years ahead of your time. And you are criticized. And you are considered a radical.

But remember this, even in defeat, Veeck's ideas remained revolutionary. They still exist today. They serve as the foundation for modern-day baseball promotion. And don't you think that was worth the price?

"If a man does not keep pace with his companions, perhaps it is because he hears a different drummer. Let him step to the music which he hears, however measured or far away."
Henry David Thoreau, philosopher and writer

That Thoreau phrase, those words, appeared on the program at Veeck's memorial service. There couldn't have been more a fitting epitaph.

Remember how we talked about fun in the last chapter? Well, you want to know why Veeck had so much fun? This is why. He was stepping to his own music. He was dancing to his own beat.

I've tried to remember that, even in the darkest moments. When I was the general manager of the Chicago Bulls, in Dick Motta's second year as head coach, he was thrown out of a game. I walked into the locker room along with Bennie the Bull, our mascot.

I had an idea. I told Dick he should put on the Bennie the Bull suit, go back onto the floor, stand next to the bench and coach the rest of the game.

Dick thought about it. He chose not to do it.

But years later, he said, "I wish to this day that I had gone back and coached the rest of the game in the suit."

Don't let yourself get caught up in regrets or in the shadow of those around you. Don't measure yourself against your family, or your friends or your colleagues. Don't spend your life trying to please people. That's how comedian Chris Farley lived, always acting, always playing the clown to please others. He wound up dead from drugs and alcohol.

"If you need love from everybody," says his friend and Saturday Night Live cast member Rob Schneider, "it feels good, but eventually the nightclub audiences go home. Eventually, the TV shows are over, and the movies end, and you've got to live with yourself."

So shed your tie, open your collar, roll up your pants, if that's who you are. Step to your own music, even if, like Bill Veeck, you have only one foot to step on. Not only will you liberate yourself. You'll also have so much fun you might never want to wear that tie again.

"As a major part of our promotion, I moved around and met people. If the attendant in the men's room wanted to talk baseball for half an hour, we talked baseball for half an hour ... No subject I know is as interesting as a human animal."

Chapter 6

Keep the Change and Buy a House

"I learned from the greatest team builder I ever knew. He would've laughed and said, 'Life is about people.'"

Mike Veeck

There was a man in Chicago with four children and no job. The gas in his apartment had been shut off, and he had no hot water, so none of them could bathe. The man was approaching desperation. His wife had left him. Every day for eight months, he'd been looking for work. But this was during the recession of the 1980s, and there were no jobs to be found in the city.

So the man made a desperate confession to a newspaper columnist, Bob Greene. He said he would start committing crimes to feed his family. He had never committed an illegal act in his life, but there were no other options, no jobs, no place else to turn.

The day that column ran, Greene's phone rang incessantly. With every call, another voice offered to help or offered money. But the man did not want money. The money would run out eventually, and then he would be back where he started. What he needed was a job.

Greene asked each one of his callers if there were any jobs. They had no answer. They had no job to offer. Greene grew discouraged. All this sympathy, all this emotion, and no one willing to help.

And then, around noon, the phone rang one more time.

"This is Bill Veeck," the caller said.

Bob Greene had not met Bill Veeck, who was then the owner of the Chicago White Sox. Veeck asked Greene, quite pointedly, "Is this fellow willing to work?"

Greene said he was. "Well, I've got a big old ballpark out here," Veeck said. "I could probably use an- other hand to help keep things up."

*Bob Greene. (Courtesy of the **Chicago Tribune**)*

So here, in the midst of this drought, a strange man was offering a job. And Greene had to ask why Veeck was doing it. "Oh, I went through the Depression. I've seen this before," Veeck replied with nonchalance. "Sometimes, when a fellow is in trouble, you want to go out on a limb for him."

"The sign of a great man is that the closer you get, the greater he seems."

Chofetz Chaim, philosopher

This is the story of Bill Veeck's life. Climbing out onto limbs. For all the outwardness and flamboyance, all the over-the-top promotions, all the pennant-winning teams, all the independent thought he produced and sleepless nights he endured and books he pored over, he was, in the center of those complexities, a person who couldn't resist people.

Bill adulated them. He listened to them. He engaged them. He hugged them. He shook their hands. He pulled them aside and offered them advice. He treated them as equals. He valued their company. He surrounded himself with them. He felt their anger, their pain. His every act was a service to them.

Sometimes, in listening to the stories of the people who knew Veeck, or who worked for him, or who just brushed past him on a summer afternoon, you find it all a little hard to believe. And it's true, that while this book lauds virtually every quality Bill Veeck personified, he was not a saint. That's not what I'm out to prove.

But Veeck loved people unabashedly. And when you consider the swarm of good will that still pours forth almost 15 years after his death, it drives you to wonder how any man could have touched so many lives.

"The most generous man who ever lived," an old friend once said of Veeck.

That's not exactly an easy thing to measure. But sometimes, I wonder what would happen if you could.

"The most useful person in the world is the man or woman who knows how to get along with other people. Human relations is the most important science in the broad curriculum of living."

Stanley C. Allyn, president, National Cash Register Co.

I am merely one of a legion of people whose life's path was altered by Veeck's kindness, by his seemingly boundless capacity to engage. There are legendary sportswriters and Hall-of-Fame players and longtime baseball executives and fans and secretaries and janitors on that list. Sometimes, all it took was a moment. Sometimes, as with me, it was a steady diet, over the course of years, from someone who was willing to care about you as much as he cared about himself. And, many days, probably more.

He was the definitive people person, which is a skill in itself, one that can be built even if it isn't inherent in your personality.

How do you become a people person?

Understand, first, that nothing happens without getting involved in people's lives. You have to take an interest in a person, even if you have to force yourself to do it. In Veeck's case, he became absorbed in you. He asked you questions; tried to gauge your interest in certain subjects. And he exuded a sense of caring.

When people approached him with questions (and they always had some), he would turn it around and start asking them about their lives. This wasn't some corporate strategy to sell tickets, although it certainly helped. This was genuine curiosity.

There was that time I went to see him at his house in Maryland, and one of his daughters was working on her school project. I sat there for an hour without Veeck speaking to me, or even acknowledging my presence, and when he was done, he turned to me. And there might as well have been no one else in the room but the two of us.

Bill Veeck tried to answer every letter he received. (AP/Wide World Photos)

"The biggest strain of being a manager is that you must think constantly about others, and you have to be in a good mood … or at least you have to pretend. It is performance art, and the show must go on."
Michael Knisley, magazine editor

And the second truth of becoming a people person:

You must be visible. And you must be available. Veeck carved out the time, regardless of how many other duties he had to complete that day. When he worked for the White Sox, people would walk in and stand by the switchboard and ask to speak to Veeck. And he would lumber down the steps to spend time with them. Besides his thousands of speeches and his near-daily ambles around the bleachers and his rounds in the press box (or the Bard's Room, the press lounge in Chicago), there were private moments, shared moments, from a man who was determined to know everyone.

When he worked in Cleveland, he rode the streetcars, gauging people's thoughts. He stood on a street corner, after news arose that he might trade star shortstop Lou Boudreau, and let the people berate him from their cars. Whatever they wanted to say, however they might say it, he was there; he was available. The only time he didn't answer his phone was if he was preoccupied with someone else. Otherwise, he'd lift the receiver and bay a "Hallloooo…"

There are drawbacks to such accessibility, to a phone number that can be so readily dialed at any time of day. Or night. "I get a lot of calls from saloons at two in the morning to settle arguments," Veeck once confessed. "When a guy gets on and asks me if so-and-so played for the White Sox 30 years ago, I say, 'Of course he did.' When he puts on his friend for verification, I tell him I never heard of him. Then I go to sleep contented, thinking of them belting each other on a barroom floor."

The rest of the time, of course, Veeck was in those barrooms, those saloons, chatting away.

"When I was in the Army, I used to tell the junior officers that the day enlisted men stop coming to you with their problems is the day you cease to lead them."
General Colin Powell

It is the same with generals and presidents and baseball managers and coaches and principals and teachers and CEOs. If you are not there for them, if you are not co-mingling, if you are not available and accessible and willing to listen, your authority will diminish. That's why Colin Powell used to make a point of taking the same walk around a base at the same time every day. Soon enough, a soldier knew that if he had a complaint, or a problem, or just needed to talk, all he had to do was find Powell while he was on that walk.

And so it is in sports. Without visibility, respect diminishes. In the summer of 1997, I was in New York on business and took in a Yankees game. While standing in line at the will call window, I bumped into David McMakin, a former player for Bear Bryant at Alabama.

"What's your most vivid memory of the Bear?" I asked.

David thought for a moment and replied, "It was probably at the training table. The assistant coaches would always jump line, get their food and then sit together at a corner table. Not Coach Bryant. He'd wait in line with everyone else and then end up sitting at a table with a different group of guys every meal." Then David laughed and said, "Of course, we were always praying it wouldn't be our table."

Paul "Bear" Bryant. (Courtesy of the **Chicago Tribune**)

Vince Lombardi understood that when he observed, "There are other coaches who know more about Xs and Os. I've got an edge. I know more about football players than they do."

Jack Stallings, my baseball coach at Wake Forest, once told me, "When I was a graduate assistant at North Carolina, Coach Walter Rabb said, 'Jack, never forget, you are not coaching baseball, you're coaching baseball players.' "

If you stop treating people as real individuals, you lose them. When they start thinking you don't care.

(Left to right) Wake Forest coach Jack Stallings, Don Roth, Pat Williams and Bob Muller. (Courtesy of Don Roth)

When they start thinking you've got better things to do than preoccupy yourself with their problems. When you start delineating the luxury-box holders from the bleacher seat regulars. When you thrust your nose in the air and start to sniff after your own sense of self-importance.

Veeck never sat in the back seat of a cab or limousine. Always in front, with the driver. He co-mingled with players' wives, with young reporters and broadcasters, with clubhouse attendants and janitors. He tore up $10 bills (or $50 bills) when people dropped them on tables in an attempt to pay restaurant tabs. He carried his mailbag on road trips, sometimes responding to letters on the letter he'd received, never giving dictation because it took up too much valuable time. "He even seemed to like the people he disliked," said his old Maryland neighbor, Douglas Wallop, the author of the musical "Damn Yankees."

"It's often a good idea to let the other fellow believe he's running things, whether he is or not."

William Feather, writer

In Dale Carnegie's book, *How to Win Friends and Influence People,* he offers six principles that are essential to eliciting friendship. I give you the principles, and I give you the Veeck stories that personify each one. Perhaps it is the simplest way to examine the breadth of his ability to endear himself to people. And perhaps it will show you how easily it can be done, if you simply take the time to do it.

Principle One: Become genuinely interested in other people

A car jumped the curb in California and struck Marvin Miller's son as he walked down a sidewalk. His leg was broken, and the break was severe, and the former head of baseball's players union didn't know where to turn. So Veeck turned to him.

"I read about your son's accident," he said during a telephone conversation. "I also see you are at a labor relations seminar in Washington soon. I'll be in Washington too. I'd like to see you."

They met at a local restaurant, and Veeck shared all he knew about leg injuries, about surgery, about amputations. It was a simple gesture. It was enough to persist as a memory for Miller for almost 30 years. "I'll never forget how much that meant to me," he said.

Principle Two: Smile.

Two brief interludes here, both from fans who were around when Veeck owned the Milwaukee Brewers in the early 1940s, both that leave you with a snapshot of Veeck's infectious grin.

Ron Meredith was 10 years old in 1943 when Veeck began holding morning games to benefit the third shift of workers, handing out milk and cereal at the gate. Then he'd walk through the stands to sit with various groups of fans.

One day, Veeck approached Meredith, pondered his boyish face, dotted with freckles, and said, "You know, I'm going to have a Freckles Day."

Says Meredith, more than 55 years later, "I've never forgotten that."

Carlos Roffa was 12 in 1942 when he delivered the

Freckle-faced Ron Meredith. (Courtesy of Ron Meredith)

Milwaukee Journal. Papers were three cents. Every day, Veeck bought one, gave him a nickel, and said, "Keep the change and buy a house."

Once this had happened numerous times, and Veeck had delivered the same line, Roffa told him, "By now, I should be able to own a mansion."

It was those spontaneous and joyous exchanges, those brief conversations, that persevere in people's minds, even after a generation of wear, that made Veeck's toothy grin his most powerful weapon to win people over. Says Russ White, the ex-baseball writer for the *Washington Star*, "Bill made every day like a day at the amusement park."

Principle Three: Remember that a person's name is, to that person, the sweetest and most important sound in any language.

Richard Smith served in the army from 1955-57, then was in the reserves. When Veeck held a "Smith Night" in honor of White Sox left fielder Al Smith, Richard Smith had reserve duty and couldn't make it. But when he went to the park two weeks later, he walked down the left-field line, caught Veeck's attention and told him what had happened.

Two weeks later, Richard Smith got a hand-written note from Veeck, congratulating him for serving his country. Along with it were four box seats to a future home game.

White Sox left fielder Al Smith inspired Bill Veeck to hold a "Smith Night" promotion. (Brace Photo)

Principle Four: Be a good listener. Encourage others to talk about themselves.

He had this way of furrowing his brow when he was intent, and his words would come out as a mere whisper, which was unusual for someone who struggled with his hearing for most of his life. Broadcaster Bob Wolff once worked a major-league game of the week on television with Veeck as his partner. He anticipated an overbearing flamboyance. Instead, Veeck came across as shy, almost reserved. "Maybe," a friend of his once said, "it's because he's such a good listener."

In all those meetings we had, in all those phone conversations we had, Veeck would take extra time to focus on my problems. He did it with so many people, with writers like Mark Kram, who through Veeck gained the confidence to expand his writing into essays and novels. It's something called empowerment, and we'll discuss it more fully in the next chapter.

All this through silence and an encouragingly furrowed brow.

Principle Five: Talk in terms of other people's interests.

Veeck had a way of bringing people together. He was so attuned to everyone's interests that he conjured ways to build new friendships. It was through Veeck that I met Larry Ritter, author of the classic oral history of baseball, *The Glory of Their Times.* Bill arranged for us to meet at half-time of a 76ers vs. Knicks game back when I was working for Philadelphia. And it's also how I met Jerry Krause, now general manager of the Bulls. Veeck brought us together when we were young baseball executives in 1965.

It was also how I became the Chicago Bulls' general manager in 1969 at age 29. One of the Bulls' owners, Phil Frye, was a former investor in Veeck's baseball ventures. Bill talked me up to Frye, who called me in Philadelphia to arrange an interview in Chicago. A few weeks later, I was working for the Bulls.

If you know people well enough, these connections appear naturally. You want to pull your friends together because creating new friendships between others becomes as important as solidifying the ones you already have.

Principle Six: Make the other person feel important ... and do it sincerely.

Al Widmar hadn't seen Bill Veeck for 23 years when he attended baseball's winter meetings in Miami. He'd pitched for Veeck in St. Louis, with the Browns, and he was at breakfast that morning when he saw Veeck. Next thing he knew, a pair of grizzled hands were waving in his direction. Widmar looked around.

It was Veeck, waving to him.

"How did you remember me?" he asked.

And Veeck replied: "You were part of the family."

Didn't take long to enter that family. Milwaukee sportswriter Ken Bunch only met Veeck once, before a flight to Chicago's O'Hare Airport, through a mutual friend. Next thing he knew, Veeck was dragging Bunch's luggage to the gate. Then Veeck ducked into the restroom, stopping before a shoeshine man, asking him how his wife was doing in her recovery from surgery.

As they continued toward Bunch's flight, Veeck stopped for two more shoeshine men. He knew them both, of course. "An old friend," he kept saying.

Weren't they all?

"During the six years of the American Revolution, George Washington literally spent every waking and sleeping moment in the field with his troops … It is simply the process of stepping out and interacting with people; of establishing personal human contact."

Donald T. Phillips, author

The phone rang at eight one morning in 1948. "I want you and your wife in my office in 30 minutes," Veeck told catcher Ray Murray. It had been a tumultous season for Murray, who'd been called up to the Cleveland Indians the night before and had spent much of the year bouncing between the minors and the majors.

Ray Murray. (Brace Photo)

He'd arrived in Cleveland at three the previous morning. He and his wife were staying at a downtown hotel, a sizeable walk from the stadium, and Murray said, "Bill, we can't walk that far. We've been traveling. I'll come down later."

"Take a cab," Veeck said. "I'll pay for it."

So Murray and his wife rousted themselves from their bed, left their hotel room, hopped into a cab and took it to the Stadium. Murray told the cabbie to wait. Only be a minute, he said.

He walked into Veeck's office. Veeck said, "I appreciate the way you've cooperated with me. I want to do something for you."

He held up a key.

"This is for a new Pontiac car," he said. "If you can find it, it's yours."

He wouldn't tell Murray where it was. Wouldn't even tell him where to look. He was laughing, but Murray stared at him, and he knew this wasn't a joke. So Murray started thinking. He remembered Veeck was conducting business with a car dealer on the west side of Cleveland. He and his wife ran back to the waiting cab and ordered the driver to take them there.

There, in the showroom of the dealership, was a new Pontiac. Murray walked over, the key in his hand. He opened the door and inserted the key in the ignition. And it started.

The car was his.

Veeck had that kind of relationship with his players; one that's almost unfathomable in today's button-up business world of baseball. "The only owner I ever knew who gave a damn about his players was Bill Veeck," said his close friend, Hank Greenberg. "Bill genuinely cared about them, and he always worried about them individually. It was almost like hero worship for Bill. The ballplayers were first in his book, and he would do anything to help their families or ease the way if they got into trouble."

He endeared himself to their wives, as he did with so many women, his capacity for courtliness always on display. He bought the players suits for game-winning hits, for game-winning saves or simply for playing on his team. Once, he dropped a $25 gift certificate for a local men's store in every player's locker. He gave away stacks of his patented white sport shirts. He had replica uniforms made for each player's children in St. Louis. "My son is 45," said one of those St. Louis players, Jim Dyck, "and still has his little Brownies uniform."

He played cards with them in the locker room before games. He shagged balls during batting practice and once knocked down a screaming line drive with his wooden leg. And so people wanted to play for him. They wanted to come back. He was a man they could trust, and he wasn't in it simply for the profit margin and the gate receipts.

He treated everyone in the media with the same overwhelming decency. Large paper. Small paper. Weekly paper. Television. Radio. It didn't matter. He introduced himself, endeared himself, and, in turn, they treated him with the same reverent respect. It's hard to find many reporters willing to rip Veeck. Honestly, it's hard to find a single one.

And through all of that, he built an immensely loyal following.

"The people are what it's all about. If I'm trying to get away from them, how can I sing to them?"

**Garth Brooks,
country singer**

How many companies have trumpeted customer service as their slogan, have promised *People First*, have blanketed us with their seeming concern for our welfare—and then left us on hold on their customer service hotline for an hour-and-a-half?

That *People First* commitment is perpetuated so often because it is the only philosophy in this sensitive and competitive business world that truly works. Yet so often, it gets trampled by the bottom line, by profit margins, by arrogance and obliviousness and arcane ideas.

For our best leaders, the presidents and generals and civil-rights leaders, it's what fostered their immense popularity. The people can't like you if they don't know you. They can't be loyal to something that lacks a face. It's been called MBWA, Managing By Wandering Around, or "the technology of the obvious." No one did it with more passion than Veeck.

After a while, after hearing all these fans and colleagues and players and even one-time acquaintances of Bill Veeck's spill their stories, I discovered a trend. People remembered. And it was almost as if they were surprised by how much they remembered or what sort of mementoes they kept. It was as if they hadn't realized how much those small encounters had affected them.

Carmella Hartigan called me one day as I was gathering research for this book. She was born in 1902, and she sat behind Veeck in the bleachers at Wrigley Field. His back touched her knees. As she recited pieces of her experience back to me that day, her voice reflecting the radiance of Veeck's presence, she told me, "I still look for Bill whenever I go to Wrigley Field."

His legacy remains so encompassing because people continue to stand behind who he was; behind what he represented. His life was about the people, and he showed it with such unassuming and generous gestures that anyone who brushed alongside him can't let go. Not even if they tried.

Through the people, Veeck has been rewarded with the ultimate compliment; the one we're all striving to achieve. Through the people, Bill Veeck lives.

"My daddy taught me a lot of things ... Early in life, after I had done something deserving of punishment, he told me: 'When you do something stupid, I'm going to embarrass you. Then it will be up to you whether you want to keep on being stupid or change.'"

Chapter 7

A Ph.D. in Veeck

ı

"Bill would motivate you in subtle ways. We'd be sitting around a table after a game with a bunch of people, and Bill would quietly say to me: "You don't know how good you are. Just look at yourself in the mirror and see all that potential."

**George Koch,
ex-White Sox employee**

ill Veeck would hate this chapter. He'd be disgusted with me, and he'd be embarrassed, and yet I don't care. I'm going to do this anyhow. I'm going to discuss his influence and his ability to construct self-worth. I'm going to glorify the things he would never have admitted he possessed.

I can envision his protestations. He'd shudder at the assumption that his words could redirect people's lives. Only an arrogant fool, like certain members of Congress and sports owners (cities and teams will go unnamed here), would shelter their egos with a thought like that. Utterly ridiculous, he'd snort. Preposterous.

I'm sorry, Bill. I can't ignore it. You were an influence to me, to those who worked for you, to those who worked around you, to those who merely spoke to you, even to some you've never met. That's what you are, even now, with dog-eared copies of *Veeck—As in Wreck,* your magnum opus, perched on bookshelves of sports promoters and sportswriters and general managers. And I'm sorry if that makes you blush, wherever you are, but it's the truth.

How many times have I asked myself: What would you do? How many times have I thought to myself: What would you say?

*My tattered dust jacket cover of **Veeck—As in Wreck.** (Author's collection)*

I still use your phraseology, the words you might have uttered at this juncture, to accept a compliment, which is never an easy thing to do gracefully. I do it by saying, "You're very kind."

Those were your words. That was your influence. I would not be where I am today without you. Neither would an entire industry.

"Every man is a hero and an oracle to somebody, and whatever he says has an enhanced value to that person."
Ralph Waldo Emerson,
philosopher and writer

I can't keep pace with the language of the business world. I don't even try anymore. My children like to tell me I'm a 1940s kind of guy, which means I'm trailing the rest of the Wall Street suits by about 50 years, and so any mention of matrices and triangulations and paradigms leaves me grasping my forehead and turning helplessly toward my colleagues. By the time I discover what a paradigm is, it's already undergone a paradigm shift.

But I am going to insert a buzzword here, if only because it fits.

Don't be afraid if you're as clueless as I am about business gibberish. I'll define it first.

Empowerment: 1. To give power or authority to; 2. To enable or permit.

What I'm talking about is actually a hybrid of both definitions. What I'm talking about is a sense of enabling, of uplifting and exhorting and edifying, of believing in someone so they believe in themselves. Because it's so much easier to pull yourself along if someone's pushing behind you.

That's what Bill did. He pushed. Gently, subtly, so that you might not even notice it. But every time you left him, or hung up the phone, there was this glow, as if you'd just undergone a full-on caffeine transfusion, as if the world were pliable and manageable and waiting for your orders. As he grew older and his involvement in baseball lessened, this became his most obvious pleasure: the steady stream of disciples who flooded his Maryland house, pining for direction.

When I was in Spartanburg, in minor league baseball, I'd hang up the phone on a Sunday night after talking with Veeck, all the papers on my desk blanketed with furiously scribbled notes, my heart jabbing at my chest, my pulse on fast-forward. I had thoughts. I was inundated.

People used to ask Charlie Evranian, one of Veeck's old employees, where he went to school. "Got my B.A. in Detroit," he'd say. "Got my Masters in Atlanta. And got my Ph.D. in Chicago with Bill Veeck."

Ed Farmer pitched for Veeck's White Sox in 1979, although his first three starts could barely be considered pitching. His earned run average was around 13.00, which means he had about as much chance of getting people out throwing grapefruits while blindfolded.

After that third start, Veeck met Farmer outside the ballpark. "Young man," he said, "we need to go upstairs and talk."

So up they went, into the Bard's Room, empty and quiet except for the two of them. And Veeck said, "You know, you and I and Paul Richards are the only ones in the world who think you can pitch."

And on he went. He said, "I've been around baseball a long time. And I'm not wrong very often." And finally, Veeck said, "Now you go downstairs. And you do what you have to do to make us look good."

Ed Farmer. (Brace Photo)

So Farmer went downstairs. He went back to pitching. That summer, after moving to the bullpen, he saved 14 games. The next year, he made the American League All-Star team.

"Veeck always gave you the full course," says longtime baseball executive Ned Colletti. "Never skimped."

Empowerment: To enable someone to reach a new level of ability. That's what it means.

"If I've been able to see this far, it's because I've stood on the shoulders of giants."

Albert Einstein, scientist

Veeck's primary influence was unquestionably his father. From William Veeck Sr., who started as a newspaperman and became president of the Chicago Cubs, Bill learned that cursing was an unnecessary evil. He learned that there was no prudishness in avoiding profanity; that you could express yourself in more lucid terms without relying on four-letter qualifiers. More than that, he learned about baseball, about promotion, about treating people with dignity and respect. He learned to care. He learned to listen.

He didn't become everything his father was, didn't want people to address him as "Mr. Veeck," didn't inherit the same quiet dignity. But he absorbed his father's persona, what his lessons purported, and he molded himself based on those traits. And then he passed on what he'd learned.

He wielded the power of influence. People wanted to be friendly around him. They wanted to soak in his image, his knowledge, his unabashed enthusiasm and gregariousness. They wanted to be near him because everything he did was so real.

"Soldiers watch what their leaders do. You can give them classes and lecture them forever, but it is your personal example that they will follow."

General Colin Powell

People are not stupid. They know when they are poised before brilliance. And they stop. They examine it. They breathe deeply. Take

Michael Jordan. When he shaved his head, it was an aberration. There were six other players in the NBA with the same look. At last count, there were 76, and even in the aftermath of his retirement, the number continues to multiply at an exponential rate.

My wife, Ruth, and then-12-year-old son, Alan, were watching the Bulls in a playoff game in 1998. And Alan turned to Ruth and said, "Michael Jordan doesn't have any tattoos, does he?"

Jordan didn't follow. Jordan established trends, stepped to the music of his own persona. Hence, the influence.

Michael Jordan. (Courtesy of the Chicago Bulls)

People know when you're pretending to be someone you're not. They're not going to follow a liar. They can sense when genuine feeling is lacking, when a singer mouths the words to his or her songs, when a CEO becomes a mercenary, when a player swings or throws or shoots for the guaranteed contract. And they won't care what you do. And your opportunity to affect change will be lost. You have no hope. And you have no hope of building hope.

"Just the other day, I said to myself, 'Herb, as the chairman, are you satisfied with the results of Southwest Airlines?' And the response I gave myself was, 'Well, Herb, as president, I think you ought to be complimented for the outstanding job you've done.' And then, in my third capacity, I said, 'As CEO, Herb, I want you to know that both the president and chairman are proud of what you've accomplished.'"

Herb Kelleher, CEO, chairman and president, Southwest Airlines

Veeck built my belief. From him, gradually, I became confident enough to realize that I could do this job. The smaller lessons piled on each other. Swearing was a crutch. You answered your own phone calls. You wore a tie only at the most formal of occasions. You listened. You asked pertinent questions.

Because of him, I became a different person. I became a better person. I became confident. I became a man. Bill always told me, "A big-league pitcher's utter confidence is almost as important as his stuff."

Understand that I did not *become* Bill Veeck. First, that would be impossible. And second, that's not being true to me. Veeck drank beer incessantly. I don't. He trailed a steady stream of cigarette smoke. I don't. But everything I admired about him, I emulated. And in emulating Veeck, I discovered myself. I stumbled across my own self-worth.

Norb Wojtanowski was 13 in 1961, when the *Chicago Daily News* sponsored a contest to select the batboys for the White Sox and the visiting team. Wojtanowski was picked as a finalist. He went to a luncheon in the Bard's Room, was interviewed by a panel of local dignitaries, and sat next to Veeck. They talked for 45 minutes. As Wojtanowski was leaving with his parents, Veeck ambled over and told him, "I hope my son Mike turns out to be as pleasurable and well-mannered as you."

That brief conversation, that lone compliment, sunk indelibly into one man's psyche. "I can honestly say that aside from my father," Wojtanowski says, "Bill Veeck has had the greatest influence on my life."

I also spoke to a man named Roy Rivas, who talked succinctly and powerfully about Veeck's influence, how he was like a son to Veeck, how Veeck came to his home and played with his children. "I am what I am," he told me, "because of Bill."

Thing is, Roy Rivas never played for the White Sox. Never worked in their front office. He wasn't a reporter. He wasn't in the business of baseball, or the business of sports.

It's true, Roy Rivas did work for the White Sox. He was the chef.

"How often do we come in contact with men and women in whose presence we may dwell only for a short time, but we can never look upon their countenances or be in any way associated with them without being made better or lifted up?"

Booker T. Washington, educator

In 1983, Veeck had lunch with a Chicago police sergeant named Jim O'Brien. It was a typical Veeck lunch, lasting four or five hours, friends joining together and floating away, conversation flowing freely. When it was over, O'Brien turned to Veeck and told him that he'd noticed that as people came and went through the afternoon, some used profanity, but Veeck never did.

"Neither did you," Veeck said.

"That's because I was so impressed you were doing it," the sergeant said, "that I became aware of my words."

So we can all become influences, if we want to. I've even formulated an equation that captures the simplicity of this process. I promise, it will be the closest this book comes to calculus. It goes like this:

Influence develops from empowerment.

Empowerment develops from listening and building confidence.

Therefore, influence develops from listening and building confidence.

So the foundation of this chapter is based on two principles: Listening, and building confidence. The rest blossoms from there.

"I like to listen. I have learned a great deal from listening carefully. Most people never listen."

Ernest Hemingway, author

So many people turn themselves off when someone else is talking, then flip the switch back on when it's their turn. You wind up talking at each other, two subway trains passing through a hollow tunnel in opposite directions, and by the time you come through to the other side, nothing's changed. You're the same. The person you're talking to is the same. No one's learned anything, and no one's gained anything because no one was listening.

That's our nature. In one ear. Out the other. Back into our own muddled world we go, preoccupied by the seeming complexity of our own problems. And so all of our problems go prancing around, unchallenged, unanswered because the only help we have in solving them, the people we talk to, don't care enough to immerse themselves in what we have to say.

That's why a good listener is so rare. That's why a good listener is guaranteed to be surrounded by friends. And that's why Veeck became the man he did. Because when he talked to someone, suddenly, he shed who he was. And he became who they were. He wanted to know about them, what they did, where they lived, how many children they had, what they wanted to do with their life, how they were going to do it. He already knew his story. He wanted to hear yours.

Author Larry Ritter didn't know Veeck at all when he began research for his book on old-time baseball players, an oral history of their stories. But he called Veeck and told him his idea, and Veeck said, "Come on down. We'll talk about it."

Ritter was a professor of economics and finance at

Larry Ritter. (Courtesy of Larry Ritter)

New York University. He had no baseball background, but Veeck had invited him to his house, on a whim, without knowing him, and for hours, he listened to what Ritter was thinking, to the spore of an idea.

The spore blossomed into *The Glory of Their Times,* one of the most lauded and respected sports books of the 20th Century. And all it took was Veeck's time, his welcoming ear, to change Ritter's approach to people. "If Bill would do that for me," he says, "so should I for others."

Veeck had an ulterior motive for listening so keenly. Because that's how ideas blossomed. They can come from anywhere, from anyone. There is no premium on ideas, on original thinking. It does not come with a nameplate on your door or a six-figure salary. Sam Walton, founder of Wal-Mart, says his best ideas came from clerks and stockboys, and in the same vein, Veeck often admitted that some of his best ideas came from the fans. The best thoughts, it seems, stem from those immersed in the daily experience, those who rarely get the chance to voice their opinion.

But when someone becomes receptive, when someone listens, it is usually not forgotten.

Donnell Rawlings was a cab driver in the early 1980s in Chicago, and through the din of his rickety radio, he'd anticipate Veeck's name being called by the dispatcher. A couple of times, he'd picked Veeck up, and each time, the experience moved him.

Both times, Veeck sat up front. Both times, he asked questions. And then he sat back and let Rawlings tell his story. "He seemed to want to know all about me," Rawlings told writer Thomas Boswell in an *Inside Sports* magazine profile of Veeck. "I don't tell many people that I write poetry, but I told him. He sat there with a big smile on his face and made me recite everything I could remember."

"I know how to listen when clever men are talking. That is the secret of what you call my influence."
Hermann Sudermann, writer

So how do you listen?

It is not a question regarded with much academic gravity. There are no college classes in listening, and if there were, half the students would probably skip class in the first place. But the secret to becoming a better listener is not hard to figure:

First, let the speaker know you're interested. Don't let your eyes stray. Be responsive. Show signs of understanding by interjecting phrases such as, "You're right," or "That's true" or even just, "Uh-huh," or a nod of the head...anything to show that you're interested and not preoccupied with your Christmas bonus or tonight's lottery numbers.

Second, ask questions. That's probably the best path toward listening well. It doesn't matter your position or the situation. A few well-placed questions will carry you along like nothing else can. If you're having trouble drawing someone out, if they're shy or reticent, give them the simplest and most flattering of queries.

What do you think?

When Chuck Swirsky became a Chicago sports announcer in 1979, he walked up to the Bard's Room and introduced himself to Veeck. And Veeck said, "Kid, do me a favor. Look around this park. And in a couple of weeks, let me know what we can do to improve things."

Swirsky was stunned. But he did formulate some ideas, and he passed them along, and Veeck listened.

Chuck Swirsky. (Courtesy of WGN Radio)

Bill would constantly remind me, "Listen to what the fans say about the ballpark. Learn from everybody."

I've seen the trip to better listening described as a six-step process, the steps forming the word **LADDER**:

Look at the person speaking to you.
Ask questions.
Don't interrupt.
Don't change the subject.
Empathize.
Respond verbally and non-verbally.

And by climbing the ladder, you may elevate something else in the persona of the person you're responding to. You may find their confidence soaring.

"Listening, not imitation, may be the sincerest form of flattery."

Dr. Joyce Brothers, psychiatrist

Larry Doby needed someone to believe. And in the bleakest of circumstances, facing the heaviest of barriers, Veeck was there, standing behind him, holding him aloft as prejudice caved in around them.

Veeck had always campaigned for minority involvement in baseball. But it wasn't until 1947, weeks after Jackie Robinson signed with the Dodgers, that Veeck scouted and signed the first black baseball player in the American League. It was Doby, a second baseman for the Newark Eagles.

Veeck rode in the taxi to the ballpark with Doby that first day he'd

Larry Doby. (Brace Photo)

signed with the Indians. Remember that this was an era of blatant prejudice and racial polarization; an era when some whites were afraid to shake hands with blacks for fear that the color would rub off on their hands.

That day, in the cab, Veeck turned to Doby and said, "If you have any troubles, come and talk them over with me."

And he said, "Larry, we're in this together."

It was all Doby needed to survive, that one lifeline, that one boost, that infusion of empowerment in a brutal world. Doby was taunted. He was spit upon. He was isolated. But whenever life had reached its bleakest point, Veeck was on the phone, saying, "Let's go out. Let's get something to eat."

There weren't many places for a white man and a black man to go, together, in 1948. But when they were in New York, they would go to Harlem, and they would find a jazz club. They would go to see Dizzy Gillespie or Duke Ellington or Oscar Peterson, and when they walked in, Veeck would be the only white face. "But he didn't care," Doby says.

Today, Larry Doby is in the Hall of Fame. And all it took was a push to get him headed in that direction.

"Most of us, swimming against the tide of troubles the world knows nothing about, need only a bit of praise or encouragement to make the goal."

J.P. Fleishman, educator

Bill Jauss was a young reporter with the *Chicago Daily News* in 1959 when the White Sox played in the World Series. He wanted to write a sidebar, covering the final game from the bullpen, so his editor told him to talk to Veeck, to ask for approval.

Veeck glowered. He said, "Don't you know that the Baseball Writers Association has rules to protect against this very thing? There's no way they'd allow this."

So Jauss turned to walk away. But Veeck stopped him, and when Jauss turned around, he was facing the most mischievous grin. "Be resourceful," Veeck told him. "And good luck."

Ken Brett was traded to the White Sox in 1976. First thing Veeck did was invite him to his apartment and bombard him with questions about himself, about the team. He asked Brett what the team needed to improve itself, and Brett told him about a player named Bill Stein, from the Texas Rangers.

"Well," Veeck said, "let's try to get him right now."

So Veeck called the Rangers and left messages, as Brett sat in Veeck's apartment, astonished at the receptiveness to his thoughts from a man who could do whatever he wished with his team.

This is how Veeck fortified your self-image. He made you believe that you were supposed to believe. He built you up. It's why the best coaches, the best teammates, like John Wooden, like Larry Bird, don't waste their time preoccupied with incessant yelling. "I think yellers and screamers," Bird has said, "are the ones who don't know what they are doing."

If you motivate by stacking positive reinforcement, by empowering, you're concocting a more confident individual. And even if you do use that harder edge, you have to balance it with a softer, more encouraging side. Vince Lombardi, the legendary Green Bay Packers coach, once spent a large portion of a scrimmage berating lineman Jerry Kramer, who was leaping offsides and missing assignments. When it was over, Kramer sloughed off the field prepared to give up football.

So Lombardi approached him in the locker room. "Son," he said, "someday you're going to be one of the greatest guards in football."

That was all Kramer needed. He no longer yearned for motivation; just concentrated on Lombardi's singular vision. And the words of his coach soon became a self-fulfilling prophecy.

"Doubt is a thief that often makes us fear to tread where we might have won."

**William Shakespeare,
dramatist and poet**

It's natural to doubt yourself, and I say this with absolute certainty because I have seen some of the most outwardly confident men in the world struggle with their own self-worth.

You ask for proof? I present proof—I have seen Howard Cosell wrestle with insecurity.

I was on his television show once, when I was young myself. It was 1975, back when I was with the Philadelphia 76ers, and once the microphones had been turned off, the soundboard shut down, Cosell turned to me and asked, "Did I do a good job? Did I ask the right questions?"

So if Howard Cosell, one of the most dynamic and absorbing personalities in our nation's sports history, can struggle with angst, then it can happen to anyone. But we can help alleviate these feelings through empowerment. We can enhance confidence. We can produce the cocksure swagger of a Joe Namath, who persevered in the face of doubt, who, when asked about his chances of success at a press conference the day he signed an enormous contract with the Jets, said simply, "I'll make it."

You've probably heard that quote from Dizzy Dean, the old Cardinals pitcher, "It ain't bragging if you can do it."

Veeck leapt into the stands to break up fights; a one-legged baseball owner taking shots to the face from his own fans. He stood up to those who strangled his values and stood behind those who perpetuated them. He exuded confidence, and he cultivated confidence. And once—with the gentle push of influence—you've solidified that commitment to what you're doing, your sense of belief will guide you.

When, in 1975, former White Sox second baseman Nellie Fox was dying of cancer in a Baltimore hospital bed, Veeck would call to cheer him up; call to say how much the organization missed him.

"Honey," he'd tell his wife, Joanne, "I'm going to make it. Bill Veeck needs me in Chicago."

Veeck: "There's no dignity in my makeup. I'm Bill.

There is no 'Mister.' If there's a job to be done, I'll do it."

Reporter: "What do you do for a living?"

Veeck: "I'm a bum. I speak."

Chapter 8

Spoken Like a True Bum

"If I were writing a book about Bill Veeck, I would start out by saying: 'Bill Veeck had the horrible misfortune of being born on the right side of the tracks. As soon as he was able, he crawled to the other side to complete his education.'"

Mary Frances Veeck

I ride in a limousine more often than I'd like to admit because I'm frequently invited to speak at events, and those who extend the invitation feel the need to pamper me. So perhaps to counteract the pretentiousness of the situation, possibly as a tribute to Bill Veeck, or maybe as a product of my own insatiable curiosity, I delve into a certain ritual. I like to chat with the driver, up in the front seat, right beside him.

I enjoy learning their names; asking them about the people they've served. I extract stories about the most memorable celebrities they've driven; about the rides they've given that were unique and unforgettable. Sometimes, I do it with flight attendants and cab drivers, as well, in my attempt to form a workable mosaic of the human experience as seen through the eyes of the common man.

A driver named Robert told me how Tom Hanks wouldn't get in the stretch limo because it was too showy and insisted on riding in a regular sedan. A woman named Joan recalled how Arnold Palmer smiled and talked and signed every autograph on a flight, and then fell peacefully asleep. Louis talked of Denzel Washington's approachability. Barry said that John F. Kennedy Jr. refused to allow him to carry his bags. "Too heavy for you," he said.

You learn something by weaving these stories together. You learn that the most memorable people are not the ones adorned in diamond necklaces and Armani suits, not the ones who hold pretentious chats with studio executives or with Congressmen on their cell phones.

You learn that the most memorable people are the ones who are just like the rest of us.

"My life is a simple thing that would interest no one. It is a known fact that I was born, and that is all that is necessary."
Albert Einstein, scientist

Kenny was my limo driver at a convention in northern Idaho. He'd spent 12 years ferrying guests to the "Tonight Show" with Johnny Carson. Kenny's most memorable celebrity was Vincent Price, the horror movie actor. One night, Kenny drove Price to his home and parked the limo in his driveway. Price invited Kenny inside, then said, "Call the limo company. Tell them you have a flat tire."

"I don't have a flat tire," Kenny said.

"Yes you do," Price said. "And if you don't tell them, I won't get the two hours I need to cook dinner for you."

So Kenny called the limo company, and that night, he ate Chateaubriand and steamed mushrooms with Vincent Price.

The reason I pass along these stories is because they epitomize the spirit of Bill Veeck. He was the most humble man I've known, and I say that because he lived the definition.

Humility: The state or quality of showing a consciousness of one's defects or shortcomings.

All those conversations with cabdrivers and janitors, all the moments Veeck took to step into others' lives, they were facilitated by a recognition that he was no better than anyone else. That's the way I see humility: Carrying as much—or more—interest in others' lives as in your own. Veeck was a mere servant; a poor hustler struggling to provide a moment of happiness for those around him (and make enough money to keep himself afloat in the process). He was proud to be called a hustler, even titled his legendary promotional bible *The Hustler's Handbook,* because it afforded him an attunement with the common man.

He had no pretenses about who he was. Once, after a lively discussion with his traveling secretary Spud Goldstein in Cleveland, Veeck admitted that he could quite rightly be called a "sincere phony."

How many presidents and CEOs and executives have the impudence to admit that?

"The best definition of humility I've ever heard is this: 'Humility is not denying the power you have but admitting that the power comes through you and not from you.'"
Fred Smith, founder, Federal Express

We've just finished talking about building a layer of confidence. Now you've got to understand how to temper that layer with a coating of humility. Humility does not entail constant self-deprecation. It wasn't that Veeck was continually disparaging of his own abilities; if he had a glaring fault, it was that he could be unfailingly stubborn in defense of his ideas. But somehow he never projected self-importance. If anything, he leaned in the opposite direction. Which is strange because in watching him from afar, one could form an impression of a seemingly bombastic and self-centered promoter, wallowing in his own flamboyance.

First time I met him, driving up that driveway toward his country house, that was the impression imprinted in my head. And in a matter of seconds, it was displaced.

He had a way of dispelling that myth while maintaining a healthy self-image. An example: A reporter once asked Veeck where he came up with his ideas.

"Where do ideas come from?" Veeck replied.

The reporter who asked the question was veteran sportswriter Dave Kindred. When he heard the answer, first thing he thought was that this was Veeck's modest way of saying, "How do you account for genius?"

Veeck was too utterly grounded to make himself into anything more than he was: a common fan who'd lucked into the right circumstances. So much of his joy was fanned by his interaction with others, and he couldn't accomplish that with aloofness; with a false impression of his own intelligence. "What made him special," says baseball writer Tracy Ringolsby, "is that he wasn't special."

Dave Kindred. (Photo courtesy of Dave Kindred)

When he bought the team in Milwaukee, Veeck cleaned the stands when the work staff was short. He did the same thing when he owned the White Sox. He could have been sipping chardonnay in his private box, and no one would have said a word, but that just wasn't him. Sometimes, when the groundskeepers in Chicago were short a man, Veeck would grab a rake or one of the hoses and help out.

"If you get to feeling that you are too important; that you're indispensable, or that you can do the job without real effort and hard work; without the correct preparation ... that's arrogance. Arrogance is weakness."

John Wooden, Hall of Fame basketball coach

It grows ever rarer, in these days of exploding flashbulbs and overwhelming media attention, that a star is able to maintain such perspective, but it happens. I saw Julius Erving, in my days with the Philadelphia 76ers, appear at free clinics, continually slough off the privileges of his fame and extend a hand in thanks to the least recognized of club employees.

Even if you have no inclination toward country music, you can't avoid Garth Brooks. He's one of those megastars whose name resides in its own stratosphere, and

Julius Erving. (SPI archives)

I was fortunate enough to witness a side of him that belies the fame. It happened when he came to the Orlando Arena to put on a show and during the afternoon rehearsal, I slipped downstairs to watch. I was standing at the back of the building, turned, and there was Garth, standing next to me.

I introduced myself. I told him of my 19 children, of our 14 adoptions. I asked him to sign a message for the children, and he wrote, "To the Williams children. Always stick together as a team, and love each other."

The next week, the arena's public relations director called. He said Garth Brooks had called and told him he wanted to reach me.

"Ha-ha," I responded.

"I'm serious," he said. "Here's his phone number."

So I called, and to my surprise, Garth Brooks answered. He was in Nashville, and as we talked, he addressed me as "Mr. Williams," or as "Sir," and he told me his sister in Oklahoma was interested in adopting children, and would I mind calling her and helping. I called his sister, and we talked at great length, and even though I never learned of the outcome, it was one of those transcendent moments that helped me to realize how simple this life is, how everyone is linked by our humanity regardless of our station.

I met a limo driver named Bill. One of his most memorable trips was with Garth Brooks. He told me how Garth had let his 11-year-old daughter sit on stage during one of his concerts. "Garth loves to do significant things for people," Bill said. "Things that will impact their lives forever."

"Half the harm that is done in the world is due to people who want to feel important."

T.S. Eliot, author

I know what you might be thinking, that Veeck's job was to sell himself and his product, that perhaps he only hid his ego in order to sell tickets. And it's true, as I told you, that if Veeck had a singular weakness, it was that he could be stubborn and was often married to his own ideas.

But his humility was not part of the hustle. It was just him. He had no sense of his own fame; of his endless opportunities for wealth. He would use $20 and $50 bills as bookmarks. He gave away more cash than he ever spent. Despite his stubbornness, he was quick to apologize when something went wrong. He despised pretense. He apologized to fans when the team was struggling, told them to bring their ticket stubs, and he'd treat them to another game. "Bill never thought of himself as a person of influence," says his longtime coauthor, Ed Linn. "He was humbled by his fame."

Connie Mack with Bill Veeck. (Brace Photo)

He struggled with self-doubt, especially later in life, when he went on a hiatus from baseball, and it appeared the modern engines of the game had left him facing extinction. "I only have a leg-and-a-quarter, a lung-and-a-half, my hearing is shot, and my eyes are gone," he once told writer Mike Lupica. "I've given the world all the edge I'm going to give it."

It is the paradox of humility: That the best at what they do seldom realize what makes them the best. And this is part of what makes them the best.

There is a story of Bobby Jones, the great golfer, who was in the gallery once watching the U.S. Amateur, when someone hooked a recovery shot around a tree and landed it 10 feet from the cup. It was an extraordinary shot, and Jones muttered, "I don't think anyone else in the world could have hit that shot."

And a fan said, without recognition of who he was speaking to, "Bob Jones could hit that shot with his eyes closed."

And Bobby Jones told the fan and his friend, "You're wrong."

So they argued, two strangers unwittingly touting the merits of the man they were speaking to, as the man they spoke to decried his own legend.

"I think I may boast myself to be, with all possible vanity, the most unlearned and uniformed female who ever dared to be an authoress."

Jane Austen, author

Jimmy was my driver in Memphis. Said he once drove a former Miss America, Heather Whitestone. Picked her up at a bookstore, where she was doing a signing. She wouldn't leave until she'd signed everyone's book, which took two hours. Then Jimmy and Heather had lunch, and he drove her to Nashville. The whole time, they were talking, and she was leaning over the back seat.

Finally, she said, "I want to sit up front."

"Let me stop the car," Jimmy said.

"You don't have to do that," Heather said, and, tangling her elegant dress, she clambered over the back seat, into the front and sat down.

Greg was my driver in Palm Springs. His most memorable passenger was the richest man in America, but not because he was the richest man in America. Because he came across like any other man in America.

At least until Bill Gates gave Greg a $43 tip.

There is a story that Joe DiMaggio loved to tell of the time he got lost in upstate New York with a friend of his after visiting the baseball Hall of Fame in Cooperstown. They called to a farmer on a tractor and asked for directions. The farmer spoke directly to the driver, ignoring DiMaggio, giving his directions, then turned in mid-sentence, patted DiMaggio on the arm and said, "I see you, Joe."

And with that, he finished dispensing the directions.

"All this attention that I'm getting now is very nice. But it's perfume. I smell it. I don't eat it. So I'm enjoying it, but I'm not buying it."

Jerry Seinfeld, comedian

Joe DiMaggio. (Brace Photo)

What irked Veeck was when life became a game of rankings; when someone would call to lodge a complaint, and they'd be asked, "Who's calling?" To him, that didn't make a difference. "I won't be one of those mechanics who tries to make people manageable in large numbers," he said.

That would have been self-serving, would have been self-important. And Veeck was afraid of that more than anything; of being perceived as something more revered than the rest.

There is nothing owed to you.

It was one of Veeck's pet phrases. It appeared just like it does here, highlighted in italics, in *Veeck—As in Wreck.*

When he wrote columns for various newspapers during the World Series, he would sit with the writers, clacking away at his portable typewriter in the frigid auxiliary press bleachers, draped in an ancient frayed overcoat. He was a working stiff, no bigger than his friends, his colleagues, his ushers. And certainly no bigger than the game itself.

Baseball belonged to the fans; to the players. Veeck was their servant. He subsisted in their shadow. "Bill never lost his hero worship for the people who played this game," said Mary Frances Veeck.

He was one of us. Which is why people were disgusted when they roped off a special section for the press at his funeral. It was the kind of act that would have disgusted Veeck. So no one sat there.

That day, as the service began, the Church of St. Thomas the Apostle was shrouded in silence. A lone trumpet shattered the stillness, warbling an Aaron Copland song.

The title was: "Fanfare for the Common Man."

"That's the reason I'm so lucky – my kids are pretty rare. From youngest to the oldest, they're people in their own right. They bel. in Mary Frances and me ... If I seem to wax lyrical about Mary Frances, then I do. She's quite a girl."

Chapter 9

A Little Pizza Smell in a Crowded Car

"There's something marvelous about going off and getting pizzas. You are in the station wagon. Every seat is being used, and there are these steaming pizzas. And it's raining, and you're going down these little Maryland roads. Children don't want Disneyland. They want a little pizza smell in a crowded car where everybody's happy, and all is right with the world."

Gregory Veeck,

son of Bill and Mary Frances

hat I remember is not how they loved each other, because to love each other is merely a brushstroke in the entire sprawling portrait of a marriage. What I remember about the relationship of Bill and Mary Frances Veeck is their absolute interdependence, their constant intertwinement, the way they sculpted the direction of their lives through the liquid of each other's aura.

I didn't know what I was seeing then; how powerful a substance this was. I was young, and I hadn't been through the langorous progression of a marriage, through the barren space of divorce, hadn't recognized the trepidation and skill required to sustain a long-term relationship.

Now that I have—now that I've been through a wrenching divorce like Veeck and have remarried to the woman of my every yearning like Veeck—I can recognize the sanctity of the relationship of Bill and Mary Frances, how it served as a model of partnership. Without Mary Frances, Bill was lost. Without her to encourage him and temper him and embrace him and stand alongside him, his impact would have been dulled. He needed her to become what he did. Theirs was a symbiosis that strengthened them both.

"The trait I admired most growing up was my mother's unwavering loyalty to my father. To the world, they presented a consolidated whole: respectful of each other, always each other's first priority."

Janice Burns, author

It begins with examples, and for Veeck, growing up, the example was his "Daddy," the man he called, to whoever would listen, the kindest and gentlest person he'd come across. He was shielded by love, from William Sr., from his sister, Peggy, from his mother, Grace. That was the model he was presented in childhood, one of tight family relations, of bonding and sharing, of absolute joy. It was how he attempted to forge his own relationship with his first wife, Eleanor. She was a childhood friend of Veeck's, a horseback rider in the Ringling Brothers circus. They were married at 21, had three children, and, in typically effusive spirit, Veeck gave them all odd nicknames: *Pinkeye Pete* for Peter, *Sissiebritches* for Ellen, *The Ape Man* for William. But Eleanor didn't share Veeck's propensity for theatrics. And just as Veeck's career was ascending in Cleveland, as the Indians were gliding to the pennant, to the World

Series, their marriage had already frayed, succumbing to the friction of their differences.

Eleanor was not as overtly outgoing. She shied from the odd hours and the flamboyant behavior that's readily accepted in baseball. She disapproved of Veeck's nightly outings, the way he consistently waded into conversation. They began to lose their understanding of each other. They drifted in disparate directions. Veeck bought her a ranch in Arizona, tried to show interest in her love for horses to preserve their marriage, but it wasn't enough.

Bill and Eleanor Veeck and son Billy. (Brace Photo)

Navy nurse Verna Hanson with Pete and Cissy Veeck in 1944. (Courtesy of Jean M. Breithaupt)

Bill and Billy Veeck spend time together in 1944, fishing in Azusa, California. Bill had just been discharged from the Marines. (Courtesy of Jean M. Breithaupt)

They were separated in 1946. They divorced three years later. It became the loneliest period of Veeck's life. And I know, because it was the same way when it happened to me.

Perhaps one reason I was so drawn to Veeck is that there were such parallels to our lives. We wanted so many of the same things, and it seemed like so many of the same things happened to us. In fact, when you consider our family situations, our divorces, our hasty remarriages, our inclination toward children (although I've got him more than doubled on that count), the similarities are almost eerie.

The loneliest period of my life? It was when I separated from my first wife, Jill, after 22 years of marriage. We had tried so hard to keep it together. But in the end, the ingredients that formed our relationship fell short of what we needed. We were different, too much so to share our lives together. The elements weren't there, and because they weren't, it didn't matter how hard we tried. It was destined for failure.

"If you marry, you will regret it. If you do not marry, you will also regret it."

Soren Kierkegaard, philosopher

So how do you quantify a successful marriage?

I don't know if my answer is more complete than anyone else's. But I can tell you this, I am convinced my second marriage will not fail. As soon as I began dating Ruth, as soon as we laid out our interests, our influences, our Christian beliefs, I knew. This was right. This was the one.

One day, Ruth and I sat down and created our formula. It is a primer to what charged our marriage and what did the same for Bill and Mary Frances' marriage. Perhaps it is not the ultimate guide, approved by pastors, psychologists, counselors and divorce lawyers, but we'd like to think it makes a pretty solid grounding for those embroiled in couplehood or those on the verge of plunging toward choppy waters.

Each one of these 10 principles is something I discovered first by watching Bill and Mary Frances interact, so as I take you through this list, I will lead you through the aspects that lent such solidity to their marriage.

1. Love each other

As I've said, this is not everything. It is, however, the starting point, the foundation for everything that comes after. Bill met Mary Frances Ackerman in the fall of 1949 while she was a New York publicity agent for the Ice Capades. The press had already billed her as "The World's Most Beautiful Press Agent," but Veeck was skeptical.

They met. They were repelled.

At least, at first.

But after that initial dinner together, after both came off with spoiled impressions, as the night was nearing its end, they mined a common ground, they talked politics. And from there, the conversation took off. And a week later, they were in love, and Bill proposed, and in another week, they'd quietly become engaged.

It was hasty. But there was an electric chemistry. That was love. For the next 37 years, it never waned. Bill called her "Mairfrances," blending his words together, almost as if he were awkward about the depth of his feeling. He wasn't. They danced and hugged and kissed in front of their children, in front of their friends, in front of strangers, undaunted and unabashed by the strength of their feelings. "They sailed together," Gregory Veeck says, "in the good times and bad."

2. Like each other

I've never understood this, what exactly is the point of spending your life with someone you can't stand? What struck you about Bill and Mary Frances was the strength of their bond, the amount of time they spent together. This was because they agreed on so much, and when they disagreed, they abided by a mutual sense of respect. They were always together because they always wanted to be together, because they couldn't think of anyone else they'd rather spend their time with. "It was always Bill and Mary Frances," says Bill DeWitt Jr., now one of the owners of the St. Louis Cardinals. "They were a team."

3. Enjoy each other

A few years ago, after Bill had died, Mary Frances held a benefit for him in the Drake Hotel in Chicago. She did it there because when they'd first met, one of the places Bill had wanted to take her was to the lobby of the Drake Hotel to share with her the majesty of it and his passion for the intricacies of old hotels.

Mary Frances, however, had already been there. But it was that urge to share that resided with her as the years passed. It was uncanny; the com-

Bill Veeck and his "Mairfrances." (Courtesy of David Dombrowski)

monality of their interests. They danced. They listened to jazz. They read voraciously. On that first night they met, during that first dinner, one of the things that brought them together was when Bill mentioned he had read *American Freedom and Catholic Power,* a controversial best-seller back then. Mary Frances hadn't read it, although it happened that Veeck had a copy in the pocket of his jacket to loan to her.

They moved on to various subjects, disagreeing on virtually everything until they struck on politics. It was then that Mary Frances brought up a theory: The country should set up graduate schools to train diplomats and bureaucrats, instead of throwing them into their jobs without training.

That was the first of the eerie sensations Veeck had, as if someone had mined his thoughts and was expressing his own idea. They went from there, bandying each other's ideas, Veeck finding, for the first time, someone "as it were, to dance with."

4. Trust, respect, loyalty

There was a phone call. Every day there was a phone call, be it from the ballpark, from the hospital, from the hotel. Every day he called her, and every day they talked because they were on each other's minds, because they wanted to share, because they had established an immense trust and loyalty for one another. The call was the manifestation of that bond. The call was their moment, the reaffirmation of their vows, even when they were separated by hundreds of miles: Bill in Chicago, Mary Frances in Maryland. "The emphasis," Mary Frances said, "is on who you're with, not where you are."

5. Become each other's biggest fans

Mary Frances on Bill: "This is a brilliant man. His mind is always going, always curious, looking for new challenges."

Bill's dedication of *Veeck—As In Wreck*: "To Mary Frances—Not because I think I should, but *because I want to*."

6. Don't attempt to change each other

Mary Frances had no false conceptions of what she was diving into. She understood the hectic cadence of Veeck's life, his late-night excursions, his frenetic pace, and she accepted it. More than that, she was eager to become part of it, and because of her public relations background, she fit naturally into the scheme. In St. Louis, Veeck was already desperate for help, for innovation, so Mary Frances came up with the idea of sending a Browns contract to every newborn boy (presentable in 16 years), along with two tickets for the parents; and two tickets, plus a poem Mary Frances composed, to every girl.

She interacted with the sportswriters, something she'd already done with the Ice Capades, and she and Bill hosted radio

Bill and Mary Frances in 1959 on the TV set of "Bill Veeck Reports." (**The Sporting News**)

and TV shows together in both St. Louis and Chicago. She wanted this life as much as he did, and so there was a constant synergy, as if their thoughts were both swirling along the same path. "We have a great respect for each other's minds and opinions," she once said. "I think that's true of any good marriage."

Of course, Bill was ecstatic merely to find someone else who could comprehend the grinding gears of his mind.

7. Share the same values and grow at the same rate

This was back when they were searching for an apartment in St. Louis, after buying the Browns. They knew they needed a place close to the ballpark, and Bill began thinking, and Mary Frances began thinking, and it turned out they had the same thought: Move into the ballpark. So that's what they did, because that's what they both wanted, this place with an authentic jukebox and pole in the middle of the kitchen that supported the left-field stands, an apartment that hosted parties and son Mike's earliest years. It became, as Mary Frances has said, "the swingingest place in St. Louis," Mike sleeping in his highchair as the crowd's rumble sifted through the walls.

They grew together like that; always had their minds drifting in the same direction. When Bill was ready to move, so was Mary Frances, and with each decision, each shared moment, they became more deeply devoted to each other.

"Women look at their men, who are thinking silently, and assume they are ruminating about an important issue, but what the men are really wondering is if there's any pizza left in the refrigerator."

Karen Llewelyn, author and speaker

---

8. Communicate easily

After a time, Bill and Mary Frances' synergy became so tight that they could detect each other's intentions, so that when Bill met someone and drew a blank on their name, he could give Mary Frances the sign, and she'd walk over and introduce herself. And when Bill came back, she'd be talking to the person. "You know Jim Brown, don't you Bill?" she'd ask.

"Of course I know Jim," Bill would say. "We're old friends."

9. Serve each other

In their brief period of courtship, one of the things Mary Frances mentioned was that she liked to swim. So Veeck had a pool built at his Lazy V Ranch in Tucson. It was Olympic-sized. It cost $35,000, and that was in 1950. "That was the first time I learned that if I liked something, I'd have it the next day," Mary Frances says. "Maybe 17 of it."

Those first months were also a test for Veeck, because his divorce meant that he and Mary Frances had to appeal to be married in the Catholic church, and while the Church court reviewed the case for six months, they were forbidden from seeing each other; from even being in the same town.

Of course, Veeck did all he could to dance around the rules. He offered sizeable contributions as bribes; even went to New York and spoke to a Cardi-nal. He asked his friend Buzzie Bavasi to call the Pope on his behalf ("To

Bill Veeck enjoys the water in this Olympic-sized pool in Corona, California, circa 1944. He devised a way of wrapping his cast with rubber bandages so that he could jump in the pool. (Courtesy of Jean M. Breithaupt)

this day," Bavasi says, "I think Bill thought it could be done"). No luck. So in the end, he persevered six months without Mary Frances, his penance, until they were married in a cathedral in Santa Fe, on April 29, 1950.

Over time, their acceptance of each other's unique quirks was as crucial as their shared philosophies. Mary Frances happily purchased all of Bill's personal effects: toothbrushes and razor blades and slacks and shirts. And after a loss, when Veeck would tend to brood, Mary Frances knew to stay away, to drop a tray of food in front of him, to tolerate his moodiness and his dour expressions and keep him at a distance from other breathing creatures.

"I didn't want to marry someone I could devour," Mary Frances says, "or someone who would try to dominate me."

"I think the trouble with a lot of people is that they work too hard at staying married. They make a business out of it. When you work too hard at a business, you get tired. And when you get tired, you get grouchy. And when you get grouchy, you start fighting. And when you start fighting, you're out of business."

**George Burns,
actor and comedian**

There is one more principle to my "successful marriage" ladder, and this will lead us to an area in which I would like to think I have some expertise, since there have been more little feet pitter-pattering through my house at times than in a block's worth of day-care centers.

10. Have the same philosophy on children

There was a commonality among Bill and Mary Frances' six children. They had the same upright manners, the same ease in the presence of adults, and yet they mined their own natures. Mike following his father into baseball, Marya into painting, Gregory as a geography professor, Lisa an editor of a trade publication, Julie a clinical psychologist, and Christopher in the concession business before passing away about five years ago. "They were very much their own individuals, rolling around their rooms doing their hobbies and being themselves," says Douglas Wallop, Veeck's old neighbor in Easton, Maryland. "Then they'd come into the room and be perfect."

"We have not completely fulfilled our responsibility as parents until we bequeath to our children a love of books, a thirst for knowledge, a hunger for righteousness, an aware-ness of beauty, a memory of kind-ness, an understanding of loyalty, a vision of greatness and a good name."

William Arthur Ward, poet

Former Tampa Bay Devil Rays vice president of marketing Mike Veeck poses with a team logo. (AP/Wide World Photos)

I have a friend, Josh McDowell, a well-known speaker and author, who works extensively with youth. And since we're on a trend toward lists, I thought I'd share his six principles, or six "As," that lead a parent to becoming a "hero," to his or her child—along with examples that I've gleaned from the Veecks and their children. Once again, I emphasize that this list cannot cure all ills. Trust me, with 19 children, I know what a conun-drum parenting can be. I hope this helps.

1. Acceptance

This is the path to bolstering security and self-worth; to inducing a child to comprehend his own vulnerability and open a more powerful sense of trust. The Veecks always encouraged their children to clear their own path, and they did. Each found summer jobs—as waitresses, at nurseries, painting lines on a bridge. And each discovered a career path. There were no taboos, nothing off-limits. Especially considering the rather rambunctious nature of Bill's own childhood. "One thing I tell our sons," Mary Frances once said, "is that there is nothing they need to keep from their father. There isn't any kind of trouble they can get into that he hasn't seen."

Yet it was more than just turning a wisened cheek. It was an exercise in character development. Every major decision—college, a career—was to be made by the child. Sometimes that path led to a rather confounding end. "Mom and dad taught us how to get up on the wire," Marya says. "Dad didn't always teach us what we do when we splatter." But it was the Veecks' way of encouraging without coercing, of leading their children to the understanding that whatever they did, whatever they chose, as long as they felt it was the right path, so did their parents.

2. Appreciation

I cannot tell you how many times I have caught my children doing something wrong. But the moments that are most rewarding are when I discover them doing something right, because this is how they develop a feeling of significance and leap beyond the wall of criticism.

During his first temporary retirement in Easton, Veeck reveled in driving his daughters to horse-jumping shows. He was ignorant of the final results. He didn't really care. Instead, in the car on the way home, he'd turn to them and ask, "Did you enjoy it?" That was all he wanted—for his children to appreciate what they were engrossed in as deeply as he appreciated each enriched moment of his own life. And to have a good time while they were at it.

Mike Veeck remembered, "Dad loved to laugh. He understood that laugher is the great equalizer. The creation of laughter was always very hallowed in my house. I grew up in a large family with lots of laughter and lots of noise."

"I think the dilemma of being a 13-year-old girl is best summed up by a book I've heard about, titled something like, **I Hate You and I Wish You Would Die, but First Can You Drive Me and Cheryl to the Mall?**"
Tony Kornheiser,
newspaper columnist

---

3. Affection

There is an awesome power to a singular family moment; to Gregory Veeck's notion of the pizzas in the car on the country road in the rain. These are the images children carry forth into adulthood. This is why those who lack the presence of affection so often wander astray in our society. This is why, when Veeck retired to Easton, he dove into rhythm with his family, sitting at the end of a long table, quizzing his children on multiplication tables, geography, state capitals, history, a load of trivia and admittedly useless facts. The Veecks would cut out doilies on Valentine's Day and make masks on Halloween and plant a tree on Arbor Day. There were times when Veeck spent the entire day at home, digging through his sprawling collection of books when one of the children had a report due, sticking matchbook covers between the pages so they knew where to look.

4. Availability

This is one of my prevailing concerns, as a father of a small army, especially since I am deeply in love with my work; consumed by it at times. I fret as to whether I do it well enough, but all I can do is my best. And I figure if Veeck could find the time amid everything he did, all his activities and ideas and interaction, why can't I?

Because without time, in great sprawling quantities, there are no memories. A child grows around you instead of through you. It is why Veeck (William) and Veeck (Bill) and Veeck (Mike), three overlapping generations, gravitated toward baseball. To know each other. To share each other.

"Baseball's unique possession, the real source of our strength, is the fan's memory of the times his daddy took him to the game to see the great players of his youth," Bill Veeck once said. "Whether he remembers it or not, the

The Veeck family and their Chicago White Sox limousine. (**The Sporting News**)

excitement of those hours, the step they represented in their own growth and the part those afternoons—even one afternoon—played in his relationship with his father are bound up in his feeling toward the local ballclub and toward the game. When he takes his own son to the game, as his father once took him, there is a spanning of the generations that is warm and rich and—if I may use the word—lovely."

It holds true for so much that we do. If we open our calendars to our children, they will carve out the time for us.

"Unattended children will be sold as zoo animals."
Sign at a gift shop in Red Lodge, Montana

---

5. Accountability

Limits are necessary. Limits develop self-discipline and decisiveness. But there is no room for hypocrisy because without a parent's account-ability, children are rendered helpless. This means an air of humility and a constant display of patience. It's why even though Disco Demolition Night in Chicago, the one Veeck promotion that went horribly awry, was actually Mike's idea, Bill shouldered the criticism among the media and the fans. ("Dad loved me so much," Mike says, "that he took the blame for me.")

Yet Bill was not above accepting blame, however begrudging. On one of those nights in Easton, Bill was lecturing his children about authors, dispensing the merits of Frank L. Baum, until finally Mike Veeck chimed forth and said, "It's L. Frank Baum." They went on debating, until Bill finally was cornered, and admitted he was wrong, and it became a small victory that Mike cherished; the reason, he joked, why his father was cremated. Because otherwise Mike would have written on his tomb-stone, "Frank L. Baum was the wrong answer."

Yet Veeck never failed to turn his humbler side to his children, refusing to use his clout to pull strings for them. He took Mike to Wash-ington, D.C. to view President Kennedy's coffin, and as they walked through the capitol Rotunda, along the snaking line, people greeted his father with a "Hey, Bill," or "Good to see you, Bill," or "Do you want to get in line?" Veeck kept walking, to the end of the line, accepting no favors. "And I loved him for that desperately," Mike says, "until the 11th hour, when I was so cold I thought that my arms and legs were going to fall off."

6. Authority

This is never easy, but it must exist. Children must have the will-power to submit to someone else, or they'll never be able to submit to themselves. They'll wind up lost. It wasn't like Veeck ever tortured his children, ever spat through long fits of temper. Usually, it was merely the tone of his voice, the furor of his expression, the mere weight of his footfalls that told them they'd overstepped their bounds: this wasn't the day to ask a favor. The line was subtle. But the line had been spread before them. They knew where their space for comfort ended, and this was all they needed to hear about it.

"I got a fortune cookie that said, 'To remember is to under-stand.' I have never forgotten it. A good judge remembers what it was like to be a lawyer. A good editor remembers being a writer. A good parent remembers what it was like to be a child."

Anna Quindlen, writer

Bill Veeck was always a bit of a child, existing among a child's game, viewing the world with a child's glee. It's what made him the father that he was, so wonderfully encouraging, so decidedly unbiased. Pool him with Mary Frances, and you were observing the wondrousness of family at its most vivid and sparkling best. "A love story," Mary Frances called it, one that endures. As proof, Mike Veeck, the baseball executive, while general manager of a minor-league team in South Florida, walked to center field after games and talked to his father. The connection was so strong that to this day, Bill's ashes reside in the Folgers coffee can on Mike's desk: a sign of their unique relationship.

THE HUSTLER'S HANDBOOK

Bill Veeck

WITH ED LINN
Co-authors of
Veeck -as in wreck

"You can be anything with a book. You can be in any part of the world. You can be with Marco Polo in China. The next day in the South Sea Islands with Herman Melville. Or you can be Tom Sawyer or Huck Finn on a raft. No other way can you find that ability to be so many different people in so many different places."

Chapter 10

That First Fine Careless Rapture

"I loved being in Bill's presence, but he intellectually embarrassed me. It was not on purpose. He just had such a wide-range of interests because he read so much."

Frank Deford, writer

He was sleeping in his hospital bed with the lights gleaming from above when Bing Devine walked in to visit him. This was 1983, and Devine, once a baseball executive, was in football now, passing through Chicago with the NFL's Cardinals franchise. Under the heavy glow, Bill Veeck dozed, and Devine tiptoed quietly around the room, peering at the stacks on chairs and desks, crammed into open spaces, all these heavy hardcover books piled up. Must have been 50 of them.

And every one had a bookmark.

Veeck read dozens of books at once, six pages at a time from each. He read almost entirely hardcover first editions, because to Bill those were books in the purest sense. He once read the entire Encyclopedia Brittanica. He entered used bookstores with great heaps under each arm—biographies, novels, poetry, historical accounts—and exited with new and equally massive piles. He brought stacks to lunch with his friends. He read while soaking the stump of his missing leg in the bathtub, read before bed, read in the brief interludes between the hubbub. He read when the dysfunctions of his body forced him into long hospital stays, skipping from book to book, marking each one: sometimes with scraps of paper; sometimes with $50 bills.

He read as a child, his father wrapping up the complete works of two or three authors and giving them to him at Christmas—sometimes as many as 50 books. Bill read them all in three months. His father read to him and his sister after dinner every night. One afternoon, when he was sick, his friends went to see a show, and when they went back to his house to check on him, he'd read an entire historical novel. By the time he was 14, Bill had read most of the classics.

That's where it starts, in youth, buoyed by the prodding of teachers and parents. For me, it was my mother. She was the reason that at seven years old, I was bent over on my hands and knees, poring over the sports section of the *New York Times.*

William Veeck Sr. (Brace Photo)

The rest of my education in self-improvement came from watching Veeck. He read on planes. He read on trains. He read anything that was laid in front of him. First time I saw him, when I was a kid wandering up his Maryland driveway, he was reading that book of Civil War poetry on his porch. Every time I spoke to him, he mentioned a book. Every time I saw him, he was either holding a book or in the process of acquiring one. "I have the literary digestion of a garbage-disposal unit," he once said. "I can go from Gibbon to the best-seller list to a trade journal and find something to interest me in all of them."

Bill Veeck reminded me of writer William Faulkner who told English students at the University of Mississippi, "Read, read, read. Read everything—trash, classics, good and bad, and see how they do it. Just like a carpenter who works with an apprentice and studies the master. Read! You'll absorb it. Then write. If it is good, you'll find out. If it's not, throw it out the window."

"Books are the carriers of civilization. Without books, history is silent, literature dumb, science crippled, thought and speculation at a standstill. Without books, the development of civilization would have been impossible. They are engines of change, windows on the world, 'lighthouses' (as a poet said) 'erected in the sea of time.' They are companions, teachers, magicians, bankers of the treasures of the mind. Books are humanity in print."

Barbara Tuchman, educator

I will crawl onto a limb here. I will assume since you are reading this book, you enjoy reading, to some degree. I'm going to guess that you will finish this book within a month, which if you do, and if you continue to read just one book each month, puts you among the top one percent of intellectuals in this country.

Historian David McCullough once stated at a commencement address, "Reportedly, the average American watches 28 hours of television every week, or approximately four hours a day. The average person, I'm told, reads at a rate of 250 words per minute.

"So, based on these statistics, were the average American to spend those four hours a day with a book instead of watching television, the average American could, in a week, read:

•the complete poems of T.S. Eliot

•two plays by Thornton Wilder, including *Our Town*

•the complete poems of Maya Angelou

•*The Great Gatsby*, and

•the book of Psalms

That's all in one week!"

We all know reading has dwindled in social importance. Children's test scores dip. Illiteracy rates skyrocket. Our best guess as to why this is happening is because reading is not like watching television. Television is the instant warped gratificiation of tabloid talk. Reading is intrinsically more challenging, more time-consuming, a burden. People don't read for the same reasons they don't exercise: no time, no compulsion, no self-discipline. Reading is sifting through the minutiae of James Joyce. Television is zoning out while watching *Three's Company.*

Bill Veeck, then president of the St. Louis Browns, wheels and deals on the telephone in his cluttered office. A picture of Baseball Commissioner Landis hangs on the wall. (AP/Wide World Photos)

But those of us who do read, the apparent minority of "intellectuals" in a remote-controlled society, can comprehend the wondrous buzz of knowledge that we acquire by burying our nose in the pages. The mind is a muscle, the book its Nautilus machine, and once fed, it screams for more, to be filled, to be challenged, to be educated.

Why read? Because it is the only way to expand our education. Because without reading, we are stagnant, unflinching, our brain matter congealing into slush on the side of the road, our upward mobility flattening. One-half of those who graduate from college never read another book, which means they've thrown away their parents' fortune (or their own) for no good reason.

In fact, let me challenge you to do more. Author Brian Tracy writes, "You should read one hour a day in your field, which equates to one book a week, 52 books a year and 520 books in ten years." Imagine the impact this could have in your life and career!

Bill Veeck's own formal education was a joke. He never finished high school. His father squeezed him into a spot at Kenyon College, and Veeck dropped out after a year. So how did he become one of the most widely educated men of his day, with knowledge in tax law, in gardening, in Indian lore, in the Civil War? How did he acquire so much about so much? How did he become the ultimate *Jeopardy!* contestant?

The answer is obvious. The answer is in his library. Because a deep immersion in reading can overcome the most serious faults in education. And Veeck is not the only evidence of that.

William Faulkner never finished high school and dropped out of the University of Mississippi. He became postmaster general, reading every book and magazine that came through the office, slipping into the library next door, reading *Moby Dick* and *Madame Bovary* and *The Brothers Karamozov* until he began to write himself and became one of the most honored authors of his generation with barely a breath of formality to his education.

"Outside of a dog, a book is a man's best friend. Inside a dog, it's too dark to read."

Groucho Marx, comedian

It wasn't just the way Veeck read. There's got to be more to it than that. You've got to use what you read, expose it, share it. Leonard Koppett, a sportswriter, was carrying a book on the Roman Empire under his arm one day before the Yankees played at Comiskey Park, and Veeck stopped him and told him he'd read the book, and off went the discussion.

Veeck was the most prolific talk-show guest of his time because of this; because he could expound on any subject the interviewer wished to discuss. Irv Kupcinet of the *Chicago Sun-Times* hosted a talk show for a while, and whenever he invited Veeck to appear, Veeck would ask who else was on and what books they had written, and by the time he appeared on the show, he'd read everyone else's book. He could have hosted the show himself.

He wrote a column about his favorite books each year, and once, he put a Jimmy Breslin novel first on his list, and for Breslin, a noted author and journalist, it became one of the thrills of his life; to know that this man—so literate, so erudite—could choose his book above the hundreds of others he'd perused that year.

How many of today's sports executives could elicit such a response?

"The two great laws in life are growth and decay. When things stop growing, they begin to die. This is true of men, businesses or nations."

Charles Gow, philosopher

Mike Lupica is a sports columnist in New York who saw Veeck at the 1983 World Series, when Veeck had been hired to write a guest column for the *Chicago Tribune.* It was after the final game, and they were in the pressroom, and Veeck asked Lupica about the theme of his column. Lupica told him he was writing about the Phillies—Pete Rose, Joe Morgan, Tony Perez—who also played with the dynastic Reds teams of the 1970s, the Big Red Machine, and how this was their last flourish of glory. Veeck muttered, "That reminds me of a poem I learned as a kid," and on the back of a sheet of statistics, he penned the lines to a William Blake poem:

> *A wise bird is the thrush*
> *He sings each song twice over*
> *Lest you should think*

He could never recapture
That first fine careless rapture.

Lupica still has the stat sheet with the lines of poetry scribbled on the back. He once looked them up in *Bartlett's Quotations*. Through 60 years, Veeck had recalled virtually every word. He was blessed with that sort of mind: to wade through a sea of information, catalogue facts and sort through them; to pull them like cards from a Rolodex when he needed.

Yet the last thing Veeck wanted to be thought of was an intellectual. He was the anti-intellectual: a self-admitted vulgar hustler, not above kitsch and silliness. When his friend, Hank Greenberg (who constantly bought Veeck books to add to his collection), would chide him for his brilliance, Veeck would demur quietly. "Hank," he'd joke, "here's another beer."

"When I have a little money, I buy books. If I have any left, I buy food and clothes."

Erasmus, educator

Chuck Daly. (Courtesy of the Orlando Magic)

A couple of years ago, my wife and I went to the NBA's All-Star weekend. We flew in the team plane, rode on the team bus, stayed in a hotel in New York City and flew home on Sunday night. The next week, at a team luncheon, Chuck Daly, the ex-Magic coach, pulled me aside. He asked me, "Do you remember what you did last weekend in New York?"

I told him I didn't.

"You read," he said. "On the flight. On the bus. During the game.

You read the whole time. I don't remember you even talking to your wife."

I told this to Ruth. She stared at me for a moment. She said, "Praise the Lord for Chuck Daly."

The message is this, read with passion. Read with hunger. Read widely, and read intelligently and read in great bursts. Let it slip into the pattern of your life. But don't read so much that it interrupts the flow of your life. Otherwise, it's doing you no good. The best thing about Veeck's reading is that it fit into the otherwise uneventful periods of his existence: those interminable hospital stays; the langorous soaks in the bathtub—therapy for his leg and his mind. Then he'd get out, walk around, sit with people—and pollinate his path with knowledge. Every one of his conversations stemmed from something he read. As he learned, he taught. He imparted as fast as he could absorb. "He could take you anywhere in the world," says Chicago sportswriter Bob Logan, "just by telling his stories."

And this is why he was such a success as a writer.

"All good books are alike in that they are truer than if they had really happened, and after you are finished reading one, you will feel that all that happened to you. Afterwards, it all belongs to you: The good and the bad; the ecstasy, the remorse and sorrow; the people and the places; and how the weather was. If you can get so that you can give that to people, then you are a writer."

Ernest Hemingway, author

I have already mentioned, numerous times, what *Veeck—As In Wreck* did for me in for my burgeoning career. It became an indispensable guide for a generation of writers and executives—for Mike Lupica, who kept the dog-eared copy he'd read as a teenager and had Veeck sign an index card inside the front cover; for Terry Cannon, executive director of the *Baseball Reliquary*, who still has the copy he read when he was nine—

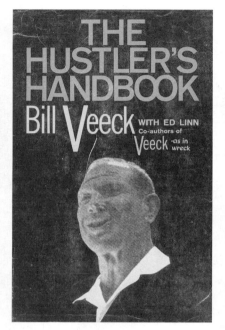

*The Hustler's Handbook is considered a
virtual bible of sports promotion.
(Author's collection)*

who still considers it the most powerful baseball book ever written; for
Larry Ritter, who after reading Veeck's
book wrote *The Glory of Their Times*,
another of baseball's more well-known
books; for baseball executive Ned
Colletti, who marvels at how the
book seems to read like it was just
written yesterday, even now, almost
40 years after its publication; and for
author Roger Kahn, who was encouraged by Veeck to write *The Boys of
Summer*, widely considered one of the
top baseball books ever published.

Another of Veeck's books, *The
Hustler's Handbook*, is considered a
virtual bible of sports promotion. But
it's not just the content. It's the way these books are written, the way he
and his co-author, Ed Linn, capture the essence of Veeck's voice and

spirit. Read aloud, these books are the
quintessence of Veeck—of all his
wonderful quirks—dozens of yarns
spun in a voice only he could possess.
"Bill was a really good writer," says
Linn, whose job was to edit down the
hundreds of thousands of words
Veeck dictated into a tape recorder.
"He loved words and took a great
delight in turning a colorful phrase.
He'd look for the perfect way of
saying something."

He did the same thing as a
guest newspaper columnist for the
Chicago Tribune and *USA Today*,
among others. He had a compulsion
to write. "I leap at any opportunity to

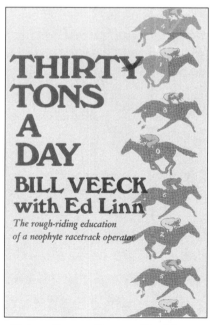

Thirty Tons a Day *was Veeck's
third and final book. (Author's
collection)*

write a sports column or book review," he wrote in *Thirty Tons a Day*, his account of his days running Boston's Suffolk Downs racetrack. He once admitted he'd written a 50,000-word novel that was never published.

The reason he wrote so prolifically and so well was because he had so much to say. Just to listen to the words pour forth from the page was an engrossing journey into the complexities of his mind. It's why he made such a great interview subject for sports-writers as well. Sometimes his presence was so deeply felt that people lost themselves in his words.

Jerry Colangelo. (Courtesy of the Phoenix Suns)

Arizona Diamondbacks and Phoenix Suns chairman Jerry Colangelo was once so involved in an article about Veeck from *Sports Illustrated* that he lost his bearings and left behind the fact that he was in a hospital waiting room. When the nurse asked for Mr. Colangelo, he absent-mindedly raised his hand, and when she said, "You have a new son," he said, "Thank you very much."

And for a moment, until he awoke from the dream, he went on reading.

"We are not even trying to say things right in our society. We give our thoughts the way we might give somebody arithmetic … add them up; see what they mean. Most people don't even care how they say something. If we are wrong about our words, we are wrong about a lot of things."

J. F. Powers, novelist

I can sense your curiousity here. You're wondering how this applies to you, if you don't write, if you're not interested in writing, if you have no overbearing desire to write the Great American Novel.

Why write?

Because you have to. You have no choice. In virtually every professional position, communication is always championed as one of those elusive buzzwords that lead to success. "People don't communicate properly," the experts say, and why don't people communicate? Because they don't read, which means they don't know how to write, which means they don't know how to form their thoughts in a proper and organized manner, which means no one can figure out what the other person is talking about.

So here we are, a nation of functionally illiterate Jerry Springer-watchers, our library cards tucked in a desk, our eyes fixed to a television screen, bemoaning the fact that our children can't write a simple essay. And we wonder why.

"I only went through 10th grade, but you'll see all kinds of textbooks around me. The more popular I become, the more I miss education. Whether you play blues or whatever, don't let people keep you like you were."

B.B. King, blues musician

I have heard of a phrase called "intelligent ignorance." What it means is that one is able to dance around the negativity of everyday life, to "intelligently ignore" the doubt and the imperfection and the inconsistencies of humanity. It means that one's vision is able to soar past the mistakes and the errors, and to comprehend only the possibilities; to understand that what we are doing is merely a fraction of what we could be doing, that the potential for invention and innovation and improvement has no ceiling, and that there is always more.

No one craves ignorance, but to experience intelligent ignorance is to gain a sense of wisdom about what our energies are capable of producing. And wisdom is what we acquire through years of reading and writing and experiencing, and of listening to those who read and write and experience what we haven't. Wisdom is learning. It is the culmination of a lifetime of self-education, the sum of every page we turn, every class we take, every sentence we scrawl. It is the reason Veeck spent his life buried in self-improvement. But wisdom is also what makes a teacher. And it's why Veeck was so able to impact the improvement of others, to pass along that knowledge, to impart all that he'd spent his life inhaling.

Mary Frances once told me, "At heart, Bill was a teacher. One of his greatest pleasures was passing along his knowledge and experience to other people. "

"We do not receive wisdom; we must discover it for ourselves after a journey through the wilderness, which no one else can make for us—which no one can spare us—for our wisdom is the point of view from which we come, at last, to regard the world."

Marcel Proust, novelist

In 1941, James Thurber wrote a story for the *Saturday Evening Post* called, "You Could Look It Up," centering around a 2' 9", 34-year-old French Hungarian named Pearl du Monville who bats for a major-league team. The manager of the team gets the idea after seeing the midget in a bar and brings him to St. Louis for a series, and when Monville bats, writes Thurber, "They was eight or nine rule books brung out and everybody was thumbin' through 'm … 'cause this was somethin' never'd come up in the history of the game before."

Ten years later, in St. Louis, in a moment of inspiration that became his epitaph, Bill Veeck sent Eddie Gaedel, a 3' 7" inch midget, to the plate.

There is some debate as to where the inspiration for the midget came from, and Veeck himself has said the notion that he stole the idea from Thurber was "pure libel." (He actually stole it from New York Giants manager John McGraw.) But it still seems like a fitting twist. A literary precedent for a literate man. If nothing else, I'm sure Veeck appreciated the allusions that he could formulate such an homage.

THIRTY TONS A DAY

"I spoke from church pulpits, and I spoke standing on a bar, and I once went down into a coal mine. On a year-round basis, I averaged better than a speech a night. There were days when I made as many as 15 separate appearances. It's hard work, traveling around like that. But look at the opportunity that is being handed to you."

BILL VEECK
with Ed Linn

*The rough-riding education
of a neophyte racetrack operator*

Chapter 11

Speaking in a Coal Mine

"I owned a chain of radio stations and asked Bill the best way to promote. He said: 'The best promotion is touching people. Go meet people. Speak everywhere you can and tell your stories. Get people talking, and then they become your ambassadors and spread the word for you.'"

Curt Gowdy, sportscaster

I don't even remember what my first speech was supposed to be about. Doesn't matter. It never really got that far. All I can tell you is that I was in the ninth grade at Tower Hill School in Wilmington, Delaware, and our English teacher was Mrs. Barbara Ford, and we were allowed one index card on which to keep all of our notes. So I did what any sensible teenager would have done in the face of such unspeakable trauma—I copied my entire speech onto the notecard, filling each space on the front and back with print so small that I would have needed a team of scientists and an electron microscope to actually read it.

Still, somehow I got off to a wonderful start that day, commanding the room in a dynamic display of whatever I was supposed to be talking about. And then after one paragraph, my eyes blurred, and my head went blank, and the room began to spin. My synapses collapsed, and I folded, tripping over my tongue until I gave up altogether.

I think we all have horrific stories about public speaking. Like my childhood friend Reeves Montague, who once gave a speech at our weekly high school assembly. Had a killer first line too, "Are you a cool cat?"

But that was all Reeves had in him. He stood there for what seemed like an hour, the room shrouded in silence, his knees knocking together.

Those surveys about public speaking—the ones that sink it below cancer and killer bees and standing in the left lane of a Los Angeles freeway on people's lists of their greatest fears? There's a reason for that. I speak more than 100 times a year—sometimes for money; sometimes for charity—and I talk about virtually any subject, and I still find it one of the hardest things I've ever done. And the feeling never changes.

"You can lump almost all nonprofessional speakers into either of two categories:
1.   Boring (the lectern-gripping, monotone reader)
2.   Nervous wrecks (scanning, fidgeting, sweating, talking too fast presenters)"
Paul LeRoux, author

Perhaps because I have such a fathomable apprecation for its difficulty, I also have an abiding fascination with the spoken word. And I believe I owe that to sports. And to my youth. I listened to Byrum Saam broadcast Philadelphia A's games, listened to Gene Kelly doing the Phillies and Bill Campbell doing the Eagles, to the voices of Harry Caray and Bob Elson and Vin Scully and Ernie Harwell warbling over the 50,000-watt stations. It is so rare to discover a voice like that, a speaker with such a gift for storytelling, for captivating an audience.

Our high school used to bring in outside speakers, and I can remember my father giving a stirring speech at an assembly. I remember the silver tongue of my football coach, Bob DeGroat, who preached to us, "Just because one person puts chewing gum under a movie theatre seat, doesn't mean you do it." (Which also tells you something about the dire disciplinary problems of youth growing up in the 1950s.)

I majored in physical education at Wake Forest, because I was young and a baseball player and beyond that I had no idea where I was going. If I could do it again, I'd do what Gerald

Pat Williams as a prep baseball player. (Author's collection)

Ford once proposed and concentrate on two things: Learning to write and learning to speak publicly. Two of the most crucial classes I took at Wake Forest were Introduction to Speech and Oral Interpretation of Literature because they forced me to talk, to express myself, to communicate, to stand before a classroom and force myself not to congeal or scream or run away and take the next bus out of town.

We had weekly assemblies at Wake Forest. I heard Eleanor Roosevelt and Billy Graham. I heard our basketball coach, Bones McKinney, who talked about the time he told a referee, "You're so stupid, you don't even know what the score is," and the referee said, "I sure do— we've got you by seven," and I began to realize that perhaps the best way to captivate an audience is not with reverence and unflinching solemnity.

Sometimes, you just have to tell a good story.

"My research indicates that only three people have died while making a speech. Since 12 billion people have lived and only three of them died making a speech, I'd say it's a fairly safe thing to do."

Zig Ziglar, motivational speaker

My first year in a baseball front office was in Miami in 1964 under Bill Durney, who was a Veeck disciple. At the time, most professional sports owners shied away from public speaking. Today, most of them still do. Some are hopelessly reclusive. Others are merely more interested in counting their money than in connecting with their fans. But Veeck was different. Sure, he was just as interested in making money. But he cared, and he yearned for his fans to feel wanted. And he taught his disciples the same thing (he wrote heavily of it in *Veeck—As In Wreck*). When I worked for Durney, one of the first things he did was push me forcefully out into the public to speak, to promote, and to sell.

That's the thing that people fail to realize. By speaking, you sell. When I became general manager in Spartanburg, and there was a

Bill Durney was Pat Williams' first boss in baseball. (Author's collection)

church supper or a Kiwanis meeting, I made an appearance. Those people couldn't have gotten rid of me if they tried. My livelihood depended on it.

This was me imitating Veeck.

Here was a man who spoke to anyone who would have him. To Rotary Clubs. To banquets. To assemblies. Bill spoke to charity groups and fund-raisers. At every stop in every city during his career, first thing he did was get out and meet people. He'd get there early. He'd stay late. He once drove 170 miles to speak to 25 boys in a high-school key club when he owned the Browns. He spoke to an all-black high school in the midst of the civil-rights movement. He appeared at sportswriters' dinners, apologizing profusely for the haplessness of his team. Three days after he moved to Boston to run Suffolk Downs racetrack, Veeck was in front of the Arlington Touchdown Club. Over the next two years, he delivered 400 speeches all over New England—typical of his frenetic attempt to lure every man, woman and child within a reasonable distance of his team or business to become a customer.

"Speeches are weapons in the marketing arsenal."
Ann Winblad,
business advisor

When Veeck was in St. Louis, his front office ran a check system, scheduling talks in one county and skipping the next. What they found was that six times as many fans attended the games in the counties in which they spoke. The more they spoke, the more offers came in to speak at other places. In Cleveland, 85 percent of the groups he spoke to showed up at the ballpark, even though Veeck never overtly asked for their patronage during his talks.

The point was this: How could you expect people to come see you if you didn't go to see them? They were as far away from the ballpark as you were from their house.

Veeck had two conditions for accepting a speaking engagement. Well, actually three. The first was that he never charged a fee. Second was that he never wore a tie, but everyone already expected that. Once, he appeared at a formal dinner—1,500 men decked out in tuxedoes, and Veeck in a brown sport jacket and an open-collared shirt. "First time I ever saw 1,500 waiters for one customer," Veeck cracked.

The third criterion of a Veeck speaking engagement was that his audience be replete with potential customers. George Mitrovich, a civic leader in San Diego, once invited Veeck to speak out there while he was with the White Sox. Veeck was friendly enough, but he asked, "How many White Sox season-ticket holders are there in San Diego?"

"I don't think there are any," Mitrovich said.

And Veeck said, "Then I'm not coming."

He had to turn down dozens of local engagements, only because, for all his virtues, he couldn't appear in three rooms at once. Yet when he'd committed to an engagement, he was there. This was a firm guarantee. He figured he owed people that courtesy. The day before he checked into the Mayo Clinic with health problems, fighting blackouts and weakness, he spoke at a golf club in Chicago. He walked a mile-and-a-half through the worst blizzard in St. Louis history to make it to a luncheon at the Chase Hotel, only to find that he was the only one there because who else would have been crazy enough to venture into a blizzard for lunch?

"He who approaches the lecture platform in the frame of mind other than that he is a humble petitioner…which does not at all signify that he can't, at the same time, be witty, mischievous, funny, acerbic and passionately convinced of the truth and right of what he is saying … is wasting his time … and that of the audience."

Reid Buckley, speech coach

"The only person who could turn a phrase like Bill Veeck," says Chicago sportswriter Bob Logan, "was Winston Churchill."

The thing is, Veeck was a terrible speaker. At least in the traditional oratory sense. He studied great speakers. He was just nothing like them.

A professor of speech once stood in the back of the room and graded Veeck. He flunked. His voice was weak, his delivery lacking, his organization senseless. He twisted his finger through his hair while he spoke. He scratched his wrist. "The only thing I can say for you," said the professor, "is that you seem to be completely effective."

By the time his legend had been solidified in the late 1970s in Chicago, people were flocking to see him. Lester Munson, a former lawyer now with *Sports Illustrated*, once invited Veeck to speak to the DuPage County Bar Association, usually a group of 30 men in suits with dour faces. But when Veeck was scheduled to appear, 400 people showed—so many that they had to move out of the banquet area and onto the adjoining bowling lanes. They filled 10 lanes with lawyers, with people sitting on the floor, bowling balls crashing along the empty lanes at the far end. And among the din, Veeck gave a mesmerizing performance. "I've heard Billy Graham, Jesse Jackson, Oprah Winfrey, John F. Kennedy and Bobby Kennedy." Munson says, "but nobody could deliver a speech like Bill Veeck. Bill was the most effective public speaker I've ever heard."

But how? With all his flaws, all his unorthodoxy, what was it about Veeck that could captivate a crowd of riveters and a crowd of lawyers and a crowd of small children?

One thing. It is the most important aspect of public speaking: Storytelling.

We've already discussed Veeck's ability to unravel a yarn, the way people would sit and listen to him speak in bars and restaurants and the Bard's Room at Comiskey Park until light turned

*Lester Munson. (Courtesy of **Sports Illustrated**)*

into dark and dark became light again. But he could translate that onto a podium, so that he could hold an entire room spellbound and anxious. I've only seen a few others who could do it so well: Tommy Lasorda, the former Los Angeles Dodgers manager; Frank Layden, the ex-coach of the Utah Jazz; Terry Bradshaw, the great Pittsburgh Steelers quarterback.

But no one was like Veeck. In gathering information for this book, a college professor sent me an audiotape of Veeck speaking to his sports theory course. He is endearing, he is charismatic, and, more than anything, he tells a good story, even if it might be the same one he told hundreds of times. He often used a standard opening line: "I used to own the St. Louis Browns, and I'm not used to seeing so many people gathered together like this."

He'd tell the same story of a man knocking on the box office window in St. Louis, arousing him from his slumber, and asking for tickets for that day's game.

"What time does it start?" the man asked.

"What time can you get here?" Veeck said.

He used that story thousands of times, and many others like it, and yet they never grew stale because each audience was different, and because the delivery was so charming, so rich with Veeck's character, that it sounded like he was telling it for the first time.

"When you listen to effective speakers, make a point of concentrating not on what they say but how they say it. You will notice how a dynamic speaker can breathe life into the most ordinary topic ... Remember that the two close companions of the spoken word are timing and delivery."

**Robert L. Genua,
speech coach**

In her book *Paths to Power*, syndicated columnist Natasha Josefowitz emphasized the power of the spoken word. "Speaking is the most visible of the four uncommon skills," she wrote. "You may not be well read, you may not know how to count, you may write poorly, but as soon as you open your mouth, people get an impression of you based on the content of your message and on the way you deliver it."

I am going to tell you something you might not want to hear: You are going to have to speak.

If you haven't done it already, you will, whether it's on the radio or in a classroom or at a board meeting or at a Rotary Club function. No one can avoid it forever. The problem is that it takes you by surprise, crawls up and accosts you, and you're not prepared. You wind up like me in the ninth grade, or like poor Reeves Montague, speechless and seeing double, nerves popping.

The first thing I can tell you is that there's nothing you can do about that feeling. One of Veeck's ex-employees told me that even after thousands of appearances, Veeck was still anxious before every speech he gave, and that most of the time he felt like running into the bathroom and lightening himself of the contents of his nervous stomach.

So it never goes away. But don't jump out that 30th-floor window yet, because there are ways to step around the anxiety. And the first step is in preparing your speech and catering to what people want to hear. Once, when I spoke at a convention, the organizers gave me an analysis of what the audiences had liked and disliked among previous speakers. The results are probably what you'd expect. They didn't like *preachy presentations*, or a *negative tone*, or *yelling* or a *failure to personalize the presentations to the specific industry.* They liked tales of personal experience, practical tips (as opposed to theories), humor and a *personalization to the specific industry.*

Veeck had four keys of his own, which mesh quite well with what we've just said: No off-color jokes, no profanity, talk about baseball (and the big stars especially) and be organized.

In other words, prepare, and tell stories, and make them funny, and make them apply and come off as a likeable person. Doesn't sound so hard. But there's the small matter of actually delivering the speech you've written. And this is where the lump begins to form in your throat.

> "*A speech is part theater and part political declaration. It is a personal communication between a leader and his people. A speech is poetry: cadence, rhythm, imagery, sweep! A speech reminds us that words, like children, have the power to make dance the dullest beanbag of a heart.*"
> ### Peggy Noonan,
> ### former presidential speech writer

With all I've read and studied, I could give you thousands of tips on public speaking, and you'd probably be so confused that you'd wind up right back where we started. So I'll keep it relatively simple. Four basic principles:

1. *Be Prepared*

Know what you're talking about. Know who's listening. Have a strong start (Veeck usually had that same joke or a variation thereof) and an emotional finish. Don't subsist off notecards (I learned my lesson early here). Veeck, in fact, often spoke without notes. "If you write out your remarks," he once said, "it's an insult to an audience. It shows that your first priority is to protect yourself from them. They sense it. If you just have a few notes on a scrap of paper, you'll walk away with more friends. They'll think: 'Hey, he's honest.' "

Veeck knew the stories so well, had such encyclopedic intelligence and such broad certainty of what he would say and where he was going, that he could arrange everything in his head. But he impressed his audience as offish and casual, and that only heightened his endearance. The fewer notes you can get away with the better.

Get there early. Know the room, the layout, the placement of microphones and seating and lighting. Find friendly faces. Don't leave hurriedly. Visit with people afterward. They've invited you; make them feel like you want to be there. "The fans make a big thing of your appearance," Veeck once said, "but they don't want you to duck out as though you had done them a favor and were glad to get it over with."

This was a regularity of a Veeck speaking engagement: staying late. Sometimes too late. Usually he could outlast his guests, hanging around at the banquet or at a local tavern until six in the morning. And in a sense, he was stealing something from them besides their time and their sleep.

He was listening to them and he was pilfering their ideas.

2. Stage Presence

First, dress well. I realize that Veeck was in direct violation of this rule, but here is where his unorthodoxy worked for him: He simply had the charm to get away with it. Ninety-nine percent of us don't. Also, move crisply, be aggressive with your eyes, speak slowly, be instinctive with your gestures, and don't slouch. Get as close to the people as possible. Remove all the barriers. I realize that it's intimidating to emerge from behind the podium, but it removes so much of the inhibition, the barrier between speaker and audience that we face.

I was at an Orlando Magic fund-raising gala once, and General Norman Schwarzkopf was there. I found him standing alone. So before he could sneak away, I cornered him, and the conversation turned to public speaking because Schwarzkopf is one of the best I've heard. "The most important thing," he told me, "is removing that barrier between you and the audience. It's scary to come out from behind there. But it works."

That's the crux of effective public speaking. Beating back our fears. In moments of extreme terror, I calm myself by reciting the starting lineup of the 1950 Phillies. Veeck overcame his nerves by picking out a single face

A. Rosen. (SPI archives)

and concentrating on it. In the process, he was shattering the same barrier. He became one with his listeners. "He made people feel he was speaking directly to them," says Al Rosen, who played for Veeck when he owned the Indians. "He could make personal contact, even in a large setting."

Ronald Reagan, the great communicator, had a fundamental speaking rule: Always talk to your audience. "Audiences are made up of individuals," said Reagan, "and I try to speak as if I am talking to a group of friends. I lock in and focus on one person while delivering a key line."

3. *Be An Entertainer*

Even if it's just a board meeting or a speech class, in some sense, this is show business, right? So be enthusiastic. Speak clearly. Don't have a fear of pregnant pauses, another device Veeck used to extreme advantage, especially when unveiling irreverent humor, which was certainly the overwhelming theme of his speech. Most of all tell stories. Write down the best ones when you hear them or when you experience them. One rule I like is that you should inject some sort of creative angle every six minutes. At least.

Best-selling author Ken Blanchard once wrote, "The best way to learn is through stories. I know that because of the way people respond to my stories in my lectures. Stories permit the audience and readers to identify and get into the characters and learn right along with the characters themselves. It makes learning effortless and enjoyable."

Blanchard continued, "I look at everything in life as a potential story So, to me, life is very exciting, because human beings are very, very interesting creatures. I learn every day from examining life and the lives around me."

4. *Believe It and Live It*

There must be conviction behind your words. They must reflect your own reality in order to endear yourself to your audience. If you don't believe what you're saying, why should they? When Veeck spoke, the words rang true. Judy Shoemaker, one of Veeck's White Sox employees, heard him speak once at Goshen College in Indiana, and he said one thing that has resonated for almost 20 years, "The rules tell you what you can't do. Which means you can do anything that's not in the rules."

That was the essence of Veeck. It was rebellious and playful and bold, and Judy Shoemaker insists it's affected her entire life. "Every time someone says I can't do that, or that it's never been done before, I stop and wonder why," she says.

"The voice is the sounding board of the soul. If your soul is filled with truth, your voice will vibrate with love, echo with sympathy and fill your hearers with the desire to do; to be and to become."

E. Hubbard, orator

This is the immense pull of a wondrous speech. This is the reward for executing one of life's most vigorous and demanding acts. The first time I felt the extent of it was in the summer of 1986, when I came to Orlando to drum up interest in an expansion NBA team that didn't even exist. The NBA had no definite plans to expand to Orlando, and the city had no history of professional sports, no guarantee of an arena. I was literally selling air. I stood at podiums across central Florida and emerged from behind them, selling a city on a product that had not yet been born.

It is still one of the hardest things I do: standing before that audience appearing poised and dignified while somewhere in the recesses of my mind those images of ninth grade, of Reeves Montague, taunt me. But here to temper my fear are those images of Veeck, scratching his wrist, twisting his hair, doing everything wrong and still doing everything right; speaking with such conviction, such sparkling attraction, that the whole room wanted to buy a ticket to a game just so they could see him again.

"I have a legitimate product. It's the best entertainment buy, dollar for dollar, in the world. So I want to sell it hard. If I'm the president of U.S. Steel, I wouldn't mind selling steel to my customers, so why shouldn't I sell baseball tickets?"

Chapter 12

A Pest,
A Salesman

"Selling was the story of Bill Veeck's life. In fact, he was the greatest salesman I've ever seen. He didn't wait for people to come to the games."

Sid Hartman, sportswriter

I n a way, I owe my livelihood to Mr. Mugge.
Success begins with that first sale, which eventually bursts forth into another, which leads to another, until the trail blossoms. And my first one came in 1964, in Miami, when I was working in a minor-league front office hawking ad space for our game programs. I'd spent days slamming my head into a wall of rejection, bursting through the doors of local businesses who had already been besieged by every ladies auxiliary club president and high-school yearbook publisher within 50 miles. I sidled out with nothing, my head and my confidence scraping up sparks along the sidewalk.

And here was Mr. Mugge to save me.

Mr. Mugge was the first to accept. He bought a $75 ad for his restaurant in the program. I'm guessing my boss, Bill Durney, had called ahead and set it up. But it didn't matter. I'd made a sale—and I was a salesman now. I could do this! I lifted my head and nearly skipped along the street.

At some crux in our lives we are all salesmen. We sell our no-load mutual funds, our scientific research, our paintings, our luxury sports cars, our stories. We sell our skills. We sell in order to survive. If we are motivated, and if we have any aspirations toward success, we sell something that we hold dear, something that arouses the tendrils of our spirit.

Bill Veeck sold baseball. He was branded a *promoter,* but what is promotion except a way of selling? He once said, "Anything you do to enhance sales is promotion." And he was indisputably the best salesman the game has ever seen. Through every speech he gave, every late-night belly-up session at the local tavern, every liaison with fans in the left-field bleachers, every newspaper interview and every radio show, Veeck was selling. Each meticulous promotion was built on the premise of inflating sales. Selling came first. Selling was his main priority. The game was his Fuller Brush, and the box office his briefcase of samples.

Before Veeck, no one bothered to sell the game. They figured the people would come to them, and in the past, in the early part of this century when Veeck's father was running the Chicago Cubs, they had. Baseball was the sole product. There was no competition. There was a built-in market. There were seven people in the entire front office, and all they did was heat the popcorn and open the gates and wait for the fans to stream forth.

By the time Veeck owned the White Sox, he had 40 people in the front office. And there was no built-in market. Any salesman can tell you there is no such thing as a built-in market anymore. There are so many choices. The world is a furious and unwavering bazaar, malls and web sites and television commercials, and the entertainment dollar is a stack of microscopic splinters. The success of your business is tied in to the success of your marketing plan.

And what's a marketing plan?

It's another of those '90s corporate buzzwords for what Veeck was doing before anyone else.

It's an embroidered euphemism for a sales philosophy.

"Before we had marketing guys," says Veeck's ex-employee, Judy Shoemaker, "we had sales guys."

"I guess if I had to narrow it down to one piece of advice to succeed, I'd say, Learn to sell. And realize that every interaction, whether it's baldly commercial or intimately personal, is in essence a selling situation."

Mark McCormack, sports executive

That first day, before my first sale, Bill Durney pulled me aside.

"There are hundreds of scouts in this game," he said. "Hundreds of personnel people and instructors and coaches. But do you want to know what's rare?"

"What?" I asked.

"People who can sell."

Then he said: "Participation."

"Huh?" I replied.

"Don't just sell. Invite them to participate with us," he said. "Don't ask them to support us. We are a business, not a charity. There is nothing owed to you. Give them a choice of location, whether they want their ad on the top of the page or the bottom of the page."

I hustled out of the office that day on my way to invite companies to participate. It was merely a phrase, a way of framing what I was doing. But it was my first sales advice. Give people a choice, and they are led to a decision.

I would venture to say that since that afternoon with Mr. Mugge, I have accumulated one of the world's most cluttered collections of books on selling. I have studied from Ted Turner and Ben Franklin. I can recite a hundred separate approaches to the art of the sale. I can also tell you

Pat Williams, the young salesman. (Author's collection)

without hesitation that Veeck was as effective as anyone I've ever known or studied. He understood how to motivate, how to persuade, how to convince. In St. Louis, he set up teams of front office people to sell ads and season tickets, and he rewarded the winners with television sets and free dinners. It's more commonplace now, but it wasn't then. It was another instance of Veeck stepping ahead of his contemporaries merely by utilizing his instincts.

Years before TicketMaster computerized ticket sales, Veeck implemented his own remote sales system. He made an agreement with a chain of department stores in the Chicago area so that fans could buy tickets at more convenient locations than the box office. He cultivated relationships with local businessmen, with the media, with those who could help boost his sales figures. And more than anything, like any successful salesman, he was present, stationing himself at ticket gates, on the field, in the bleachers. "Bill Veeck," says Mark Mulvoy, former managing editor of *Sports Illustrated,* "understood marketing and selling when no one in baseball had a clue."

"If you scratch a good salesman, you'll find a philanthropist, because selling is in fact giving. You give a little bit more than you ask in return, and invariably, you receive a little more than you expected."

Maxwell I. Schultz, business author

Sell: To give up, deliver or exchange for money or its equivalent.

So selling, at its essence, is giving. People want something. We deliver it. That's why Veeck did this so masterfully. He didn't *sell* anything. When he spoke to groups, when he spoke to the media, he didn't blatantly shill for his product like a seedy carnival barker; didn't invoke pressure or untoward tactics. But he was always convincing, always touting the merits of his club, of the baseball experience. And people wanted to come, either to see what sort of unfathomable promotion he'd conjure next, or to brush against his charisma again or just to see the game.

There are universities (and now, even high schools) that offer classes in the Veeckian branch of sports marketing, and virtually every successful business has mimicked his approach of customer care, of customer satisfaction, of customer priority. It is the best way to sell, and those who can sell are still among the rarest of commodities.

I will admit this. Remember how I just said public speaking was my most prevalent fear, even though I do it constantly?

Selling isn't far behind.

So here's my advice, culled from various sources, sprinkled with Veeck's wisdom. As with the rest of this book, my list is not the only undeniable truth. But for those of you who are as confused as I once was, who have yet to encounter Mr. Mugge's kindness, it's a start.

1. Personality

Be kind to your customers and their families. Be generous. Be humble. That should be obvious. Your livelihood is based heavily on first impressions. Have a sense of humor. Exude charm. Avoid deceitfulness. A study by the Professional Training Institute revealed buyers' five least-admired traits in a salesman: *Flattery, overstaying your welcome, too much talking, not keeping promises and arguing.*

The most admired: **Product knowledge (see the following section on *Preparation*), a presentable appearance, courtesy, honesty and sincerity.**

The best salesmen, wrote Mark McCormack, the sports executive, "may not be liked by everyone, but they have an instinct for getting some people (usually customers) to like them."

Old Sales Joke: There was once a salesman with such chutzpah that he addressed Henry VIII as Hank. (A distant Veeck relative perhaps.)

As you know by now, there weren't many people (besides fellow owners) who had problems with Veeck's persona. That made his base for sales, well, virtually everyone in the city. He could address every employee by name at the grocery store where he shopped. His timeless quote: "Those who depend on the dyed-in-the-wool, dedicated fans will be out of business by Mother's Day."

Reasons salespeople fail No. 1: Not presenting what the customer wants

Those who attended the games, Bill called "his customers," and his goal was their utmost satisfaction. The money was important (he was prideful that every team he owned made a profit), but each crowd, with its unique demeanor, was where Veeck drew his deepest satisfaction. That's why he once gave away tickets when people were waiting in a long line, why he was always asking himself, "What can I do for them?" That's why he wrote everyone back, why he spoke to everyone who called, why he treated people as if they belonged. They remembered that, and when it came time for them to attend a baseball game they turned to him. He didn't even have to persuade.

"Sell value. Sell service. Sell benefits. Don't sell price. Sell yourself. You will eradicate the competition."
Paul Karasik, sales trainer

---

2. Preparation

Know what you're selling. Pay attention to the details of your product. Know enough that you don't need to refer customers to someone else, even if their questions are rather complex. This takes work, but a dedication to work, to researching and pitching until the sale is closed, is

The encyclopedic Bill Veeck. (Courtesy of Russell Schneider)

the only way to succeed consistently. This is why Veeck drove three hours to speak to a group of 15, and why he'd answer his home phone at four in the morning.

Reasons salespeople fail No. 2: Not prospecting enough

Know the needs of the person to whom you're selling. In fact, know as much as possible about the person: names of family members, of pets, sprigs of detail that endear you more readily. People remember that you remembered. Veeck once spoke at T.F. South High School near Chicago, and a year later, some students were out at a White Sox game and asked if he remembered their teacher, Jim Kijewski.

"T.F. South," Veeck said without hesitation.

Reasons salespeople fail No. 3: Not planning and preparing

It didn't hurt that Veeck's memory was encyclopedic, that he could recognize one-time acquaintances after 20-year separations. But no one is telling you to memorize the dictionary. All it really entails is echoing a detail or two—enough to make your customers feel that they're more than just customers, that they're not just an expendable asset. All it takes is a keen ear.

"All the world is a store, and all the people in it are sales-people. That is to say, every one of us human beings is trying to transfer an idea from his own head into some other brain. That is the essence of salesmanship."

Arthur Brisbane, journalist

3. Listening and understanding

There is simply no way of comprehending what someone wants, of comprehending their needs, without hearing what they're saying. Veeck set attendance records in Milwaukee and Chicago and Cleveland and St. Louis not because he concocted an atmosphere that he assumed the fans would thrive upon. He broke attendance records because he listened to the fans, because he took their needs into account, because he was not arrogant enough to believe that he could assume what they wanted. His job, wrote Gordon Cobbledick in *Sport* magazine, was to give "the people … the feeling that (the team) was theirs." He owed them the value of their opinion. So, as much as he spoke, he listened.

Reasons salespeople fail No. 4: Not probing enough

"You ask yourself," Veeck once wrote, "if there's any other business in which the customers virtually command the salesman to come to them and extol the merits of the product … You can't hire representatives to go out and deliver your spiel for you. The prospective buyers want the head of the firm."

*"One of the staples of my life is the moment I get off a plane
… I spend my spare minutes at a pay telephone. The phones
are generally in a line, close together, and you are able to
hear what your neighbors are saying … What I hear, time
after time, is one of the melancholy stories of our modern age:
the sales people checking in with their home office, to confess
they have not been able to make the sale they were sent out
to consummate. I see them everywhere, and I have come to
understand that they are among the bravest of us all."*

Bob Greene
newspaper columnist

4. Persistence

There is a daunting statistic in the sales world known as the
10:3:1 ratio. What it means is that for every 10 calls a salesperson makes,
he will be allowed to give a presentation to three. And if his success rate is
relatively *high*, he'll make exactly one sale.

Reasons salespeople fail No. 5: Not handling objections well

More statistics: 80 percent of new sales are made after the *fifth* call
to the same prospect. Nearly half of all salespeople give up after the first
call.

Reasons salespeople fail No. 6: Not following up enough

So don't let go. Keep trying. Use every tactic short of anything
that induces annoyance. Remember that you're trying to convince this
person of something you believe in. You're trying to provide. And be
prepared for the answer you don't want to hear, to lift yourself above the
rejection, to absorb a flurry of blows to your ego. "I'm not sure you can
teach thick skin," writes Mark McCormack. "You have to be born with
it."

Here is why people fear selling almost as much as they fear public speaking: At least in public speaking, even if you're terrible, people feign politeness.

There is no room for shyness in sales. It is an arena that rewards persistence. "I have been told by some of my best friends that persistence is one of my finer qualities," Veeck once said. "In other words, I can be an awful pest."

And a wonderful salesman.

"Take my factories and my money, but leave me my salesmen, and I'll be back where I am today in two years."
Andre Carnegie
industrialist

To quell any alarm and to soothe your ego, you should know that there are no flawless salesmen. Even Veeck had a glaring weakness, one that's almost laughable, in that it's the most facile part of the sale. Yet it is also the one aspect of a sales call that stands above the others.

Reasons salespeople fail No. 7: Not closing often enough
Veeck could charm a businessman for hours, could pitch his product, could listen and inform, could persist and wait until the sale was pending. But when it came time for the deal to be closed, he couldn't do it. He had to take someone with him to close the order. He was so steeped in giving, in providing, that when it came time to take something, he faltered. "The best salesman in history," said my old boss, Bill Durney, "who couldn't ask for a check."

"My philosophy as a baseball operator could not be more simple. It is to create the greatest enjoyment for the greatest number of people. Not by detracting from the ballgame but by adding a few moments of fairly simple pleasure. My intention was always to draw people to the park and make baseball fans out of them."

Chapter 13

Fifty Thousand Bolts and a Bunch of Nuts

"My father's ballparks were monuments to the foibles of mankind; to the idiosyncrasies. He loved characters. He loved incongruities. He was a visionary."

Mike Veeck

That day, August 19, 1951, as a 3' 7", 65-pound midget leapt from a paper-mache cake, as he stood in the on-deck circle swinging three souvenir bats, as he ambled toward the plate and a Detroit pitcher named Bob Cain dropped his hands to his side and stared, as a St. Louis doubleheader crowd of more than 18,000 whooped and hollered, as Detroit manager Red Rolfe protested and home-plate umpire Ed Hurley's neck reddened, as a newspaper photographer skulked onto the field a few feet from the batter's box and snapped a picture that will carry into posterity, the entire infrastructure of professional sports quaked.

There would have been a Bill Veeck legacy with or without Eddie Gaedel, the midget who walked on four pitches that day, and encapsulated the great promoter's

grandest and most daring stunt of all. I'm convinced of that. But this was the one that expedited his theory to the masses, that generated unprecedented waves of controversy, that gestated in every impressionable mind. This was his epitome, and it would be a virtual sacrilege to begin a chapter on Veeck and promotion without mentioning it.

Three-foot-seven-inch Eddie Gaedel was part of Bill Veeck's most memorable stunt. (AP/Wide World Photos)

Let's face it. No one will ever top the midget. I have wrestled bears in Chicago and hosted a trained pig act twice (more on that later) and

hired skydivers who have fallen into the bushes and given away every variant of product known to mankind. But I was only emulating him, only attempting to approach the unparalleled imagination of that day in St. Louis.

But Veeck was not some one-hit wonder. He was the best promoter of his time, the best promoter in the history of sport. In 1952, he bought 5,000 bats from a bankrupt factory in Arkansas and gave them away in St. Louis. Now every team in baseball has a Bat Day, a Ball Day, a Cap Day. It is all the progeny of Veeck.

And yet even as every major-league team appropriates

Every major-league team has a "bat day" promotion nowadays, but Bill Veeck was the first to do so in 1952. Pat Williams' first boss, Bill Durney, towers over Rudie Schaffer (foreground) and Bob Fishel. (Courtesy of Jim Dyck) those ideas, the essence of his work has been buried. He was so far ahead of his time that his craft was vastly underappreciated by his peers; so far ahead that even today, his ideas are greeted with a certain skepticism by baseball's rusty establishment, by men who still violate his basic principles. He was so far ahead that 40 years later his ideas are worth clarifying and classifying for the next generation—one that hasn't read *Veeck—As In Wreck*, that hasn't torn through *The Hustler's Handbook.* It is a society that could use a splash of water (perhaps the considerable splash of a Frenchman leaping 40 feet into an 18-inch wading pool, one of my Veeck-inspired promotions when I was general manager in Spartanburg) to liven up what's become a rather pedantic three-hour game.

John Quinn, the Phillies general manager in the 1960s and early '70s and definitely from the old school on promotions, once scolded my associate Dick Smith, "You take your nylons and flowers and give me nine good ballplayers, and I'll fill my ballpark every night."

Bill's cohort for 40 years, Rudie Schaffer, said, "Back before Bill stirred up the pot, the biggest promotion in the major leagues was to open the gates and say, 'We're playing at three.' "

So here in this chapter, we present the promotional genius of Veeck speckled with his voice and caveats in their most encapsulated, abbreviated form. If we spent time on these pages detailing every Veeck promotion, every Veeck idea on promotion, we would be on page 512 and still discussing Squirrel Night in Milwaukee and the notion of Marilyn Monroe riding a pink elephant (trust me, it all makes sense).

This is, after all, a man who gave away *a dozen lobsters and a 200-pound cake of ice and a thousand hot dogs and a thousand Cokes and six ladders and six squab (they're pigeons, in case you're wondering) and 50,000 nuts and bolts and 3,000 cupcakes and ...*

Well, you get the idea.

Veeck's Immutable Laws of Promotion #1:

The Power of Illusion
Bill Veeck: "Although you are dependent on repeat business, you have NO PRODUCT to sell. The customer comes out to the park with nothing except the illusion that he is going to have a good time. He leaves

with nothing except a memory. If the memory brings on either yawns or head pains, you have lost him until next year."

"You have to give Veeck credit. He was great at diverting attention. And that's what a good promoter does."
Eddie Einhorn,
Chicago White Sox executive

In 1960, nine years after Eddie Gaedel stunned baseball, I was a junior at Wake Forest, and the head of our Monogram Club. Jerry Steele, a mountainous 6' 8" basketball player, approached me, poked a long finger in my chest and, in a rolling Southern drawl, said, "I want you to run our freshman/varsity basketball game this week."

And with that sharp jab, I became a promoter. I could shape the event, could dictate the atmosphere, could hire dancing girls and marching bands and set up a halftime show. Of course, I had exactly no money, and I had six days, so the dance team and the marching band came from the local high school. And I don't really remember anything about the halftime show, but I know I planned that event with every anticipatory instinct I could muster, until I couldn't stand the tension anymore. But the game turned out to be competitive, and the crowd was happy, and these were the only things that mattered.

I went to Miami then, where I learned from Bill Durney, who had learned from Veeck, who taught me the value of illusion in enticing crowds. It was about nuance, about polishing your product until it began to gather a shine of its own.

For instance—food.

In Miami, our nights were themed. So was our food. On Hawaiian Night, we served Hawaiian Chicken and Cole Slaw of the Islands. And on New England Cookout Night, we served Cape Cod Chicken and Cole Slaw of the Colonies.

Are you sensing the overriding commonality here? You dress something up, and it always looks better. Example: In Miami, we made a deal with the South Florida Dairy Council to hold three "Dairy Nights." On the first, all someone had to do was say, "Drink more milk," at the gate, and they were in.

Terrible turnout.

On the second, all someone had to do was bring in the top of a milk bottle, and they were admitted free.

Terrible turnout.

On the third, everyone, along with their morning milk, was given a ticket that quite fancifully declared, "On behalf of the South Florida Dairy Council, we cordially invite you to attend a Miami Marlins game, free of charge."

We drew the largest crowd in the history of the franchise—nearly 8,000 people squeezing into our compact stadium.

Illusion. This is what you're selling. Once you've lured them, presented the product with such charm and radiance that they can't turn away, then you can have your way with them. Then you give away your lobsters and your pigeons and set off your fireworks. Then you surprise them with such a torrent that they don't know what to expect. And soon enough, you've become the illusion, and people are coming to the ballpark because they've been doused in such fun that they want to be there to see what's next.

Veeck's Immutable Laws of Promotion,#2:

The Incongruity Property

Bill Veeck: "You give away a radio or TV—so what? What does that do for the imagination? Nothing. So he's got a TV set. If I give him 50,000 nuts or bolts, that gives everybody something to talk about. A guy goes into a bar and he says, 'Hey, did you see that guy got 50,000 nuts. What's he going to do with them?' They have something to talk about."

"The best ideas for promotions were things that intrigued ourselves. We acted as if we were our own customers. If we thought up a promotion that didn't make him laugh or me laugh, then we wouldn't try it. All you hope to do is draw people to your park and make baseball fans out of them; maybe have some wonder to themselves, 'What's that wacko Veeck gonna pull next?'"

Mike Veeck

July 26, 1959. Giveaway Night at Comiskey Park. Veeck bequeaths to fans the following items: 4,000 pickles (kosher), 1,000 cans of chow-mein noodles, 1,000 cans of beer, 1,000 ice cream bars, 10,000 tickets to a Class D baseball game, and a free rental of 500 tuxedoes.

In Milwaukee, Veeck gave up pigs, horses, pigeons, ducks, a cake of ice, white mice, live eels and codfish, among others. None of it made any sense. That was the beauty of it, the spontaneity of watching someone attempt to deal with the sheer volume of 10,000 cupcakes. It was Veeck's dalliance in human psychology. What will they do? Will they collapse under the pressure?

With few exceptions, no one knew what was to be given away, what would happen next, until they walked into the park. This was a crucial element of the experiment. So when one person was given 1,000 hot dogs, and a second 1,000 buns, and the third 1,000 sodas, or 500 cans of fried grasshoppers, or when White Sox first baseman Lamar Johnson was chosen to sing the National Anthem, or when Veeck announced that food stamps were hidden under the seats and thousands of chairs galumphed all at once, that was when the true oddity of human nature ensued. That was when Veeck reached the height of his joy. The more situations veered into the absurd, the more attention they contracted, and the more interest you generated.

So Veeck had his odd giveaways, his 500 jars of iguana meat, his rigging of a drawing to be sure that a rather dignified man was handed six live pigeons and was forced to hold onto them for nine innings. What happens to people like that, proper business folks, in situations like this is an unprecedented liberation from the rather cold restrictions of their daily life. And they find themselves yearning to come back, to recapture that feeling.

Bill Veeck and his fife were part of the 1976 Opening Day festivities. (author's collection)

It wasn't only the fans. Veeck and his staff and his friends were a part of this as well. He couldn't stand merely to watch. On Opening Day 1976, the year of the American Bicentennial, he and his manager, Paul Richards, and his business manager, Rudie Schaffer, marched onto the field, one with a flag, one with a drum and Veeck with a fife, hobbling as he played. One night, he heard broadcaster Harry Caray singing "Take Me Out to the Ballgame" in the broadcast booth, and without a word to Caray (or so legend has it), flipped the switch that amplified his voice throughout the stadium. Caray's cacophonous song became a Chicago tradition.

Incongruity. The less sense it makes, the more sense it makes.

Harry Caray's seventh-inning crooning of "Take Me Out to the Ball Game" became a Chicago tradition. (Brace Photo)

Veeck's Immutable Laws of Promotion #3:

Clean Bathroom = Happy Fan

Bill Veeck: "Most of all, we showed the fans that we weren't just out for their money, that we cared about them and wanted them to have a good time. I can remember looking out the window after a game had been rained out (in Cleveland) and seeing a couple hundred out-of-towners waiting disconsolately for the train at the Pennsylvania Railroad depot. I called down to the locker room and asked (Lou) Boudreau and (Bob) Feller to dash over and barber with them until the train came."

"When you behave decently with the fans, when they sense your sincerity, they pay you back to the nines. So the first thing we must do is become method actors. You know, the method philosophy. You cannot pretend, you must be. "
Mike Veeck

Bill spent $500 extra each month to put cloth towels in the restrooms and used 15 different chemical sprays to kill the smell of rancid butter around the popcorn stands. He established contact with a radar screen around Chicago so he could be given advance notice of rainstorms, so he could hand out plastic rain capes to those fans who were about to get wet. He raged when one of his employees turned the lights out while fans were still leaving the park in order to skim a few dollars. "The people are still in the park," he shouted.

Veeck remodeled the women's restrooms everywhere he went, perking them up, installing individual vanity tables and fluorescent lighting and full-length mirrors, even manipulating the lights at the concession stand so they were more flattering. He offered a standing money-back guarantee after games. If someone hadn't liked what they'd seen, their cash would be waiting for them. If the performance was truly awful, sometimes he stood at the gates himself offering refunds.

One thing about a promoter: His job is steeped in the lives of people. Which means he must know them, understand them, be able to interpret their tastes. But more than that, it means he must care about them. He must be willing to sit with them, to apologize to them, to endow them with humanity instead of treating them as clicks on a turnstile, as empty commodities.

Mike Veeck said, "I think people look at it as quaint—Dad sitting in the stands. It was just his way of doing market research."

The love of people stems from Veeck's epic personality, one we've dissected, and will continue to unravel in these pages. He was a soft and giving man, and he cared deeply, and people were imbued by his flattery. To bring them back, Veeck reasoned, you had to treat them well. But this ascended beyond mere philosophy, beyond the principle of business and selling.

It was the kind of man he was. A giver. He would hold a night honoring virtually any player on his team, would hand out gifts until only the lint in his pockets remained. His first national publicity came when he began holding those morning games for the night-shift workers laboring in factories in Milwaukee during World War II. He held giveaway nights for "A" students and their teachers, for Boy Scouts and youth groups, for bartenders and cabdrivers and transit workers. He held a "Music Night," on which anyone who could play "Take Me Out to the Ballgame" was admitted free. Two pianos arrived, hauled in on the back of pickup trucks, along with hundreds of other instruments, and the rest of the fans were given kazoos, and a veritable symphony was formed. In the seventh inning, guided by the baton of an assistant conductor from the Chicago symphony dressed in a white tie and tails, thousands of amateur musicians produced a rendition of the song that would have sent music critics scampering off tall buildings. "But the next morning," Veeck said, "I got 20 calls from people who told me they'd never had more fun at a ballpark."

His populist principles soared to unfounded heights in 1948, in Cleveland, after a night watchman at the local Chevy plant, Joe Earley, wrote a letter to the *Cleveland Press* asking why the Indians held nights for players or dignitaries but never for an average fan like him. So Veeck had a night for the average fan built around Joe Earley. He gave away 20,000 Hawaiian orchids flown in on a temperature-controlled plane. He presented Joe Earley with a run-down car, an outhouse, and various livestock.

And then Joe Earley was given a refrigerator, a washing machine, luggage, a wristwatch and a new Ford convertible. And perhaps for the first time, the establishment of baseball was confronted with the unprecedented thought that the people who watch their games merely wanted to be treated with the same dignity as those who play it.

Veeck's Immutable Laws of Promotion # 4:

Winning is an End, But Not a Means

Bill Veeck: "Entertainment, beyond its more obvious purpose, softens the blow of losing. It gives the fan something else to think and talk about as he is leaving the park. Instead of the pain of another loss, he can think, with pleasure, of the fireworks or the circus acts or the band or the Harlem Globetrotters. But we are dealing here only with remedial action. All I ever said is that you can draw more people with a losing team plus bread and circuses than with a losing team and a long, still silence."

"Veeck was certainly a genius of merchandising. He believed in the fun at the old ballpark theme, too. But never forget one thing about Veeck: There was no substitute for winning."
Jack Brickhouse
broadcaster

Jack Brickhouse. (Brace Photo)

You start at the bottom. Unless you are blessed with the gift of an inheritance or the cool fortune of luck, you begin with virtually nothing, and you pull yourself up, rung by rung. And here is where the gaping fault of modern athletic promotion lies. It's that these owners, these executives, tumble their fortunes in with the wins and losses, and when they lose, they are downcast and aloof, and the newspapers swing a cheek in the other direction, and soon they've become the Los Angeles Clippers.

And they don't think that there are other ways to entice the interest of a community besides winning. That sometimes, just by being genuine and by being cordial and principally by being interesting, that one can accomplish what Veeck did with the dismal St. Louis Browns, literally eliciting support on the street, drawing 300,000 people away from the more successful St. Louis Cardinals in one year by staging outrageous stunts like the controversial Grandstand Managers Night, in which a group of about 4,000 fans voted on each major managerial decision during the game ("Never has a game been called better," Veeck wrote).

There were those, rivals mostly, who thought Veeck had no interest in producing a winning team but merely directed his efforts toward the ballpark circus, the gags and the giveaways, the marching bands and belly dancers, the "cheapening" of baseball, as Cubs owner Phil Wrigley called it.

This was an attempt to simplify Veeck's philosophy. And as we know by now, the complexities of this man, the tentacles of his persona, were such that any oversimplification of him can be easily disproven.

Veeck has written that he allowed himself three years to produce a pennant contender. If he hadn't done it by then, he considered his efforts a failure, regardless of the overflow of gate receipts, regardless of the adulation among the community. He accepted losing grudgingly. And he was openly competitive with rival franchises not merely because it made for a more interesting show, as was his perpetual explanation. In 1948, Veeck explained, "If you are going to have a fight with a visiting club, be sure to insult them the day they come to town and not the last day of the series. It pays off better." He was openly competitive because he was ferociously competitive. Winning mattered. Even if losing could be fun.

Veeck's Immutable Laws of Promotion, #5:

Spend Money (Preferably Someone Else's) to Make it
Bill Veeck: "Promotions are not without their drawbacks. For one thing, they cost money. That's deplorable. One of the secrets of being a promoter is never to doubt for a moment that if you spend your money right, the fans are somehow going to come. But sometimes the best

promotions come the cheapest. A hustler should always be scrupulous about having somebody else on hand to pick up the check."

"Bill always positioned us so that we were the little guys going up against the big guys who had all the money. Bill's mantra was, 'You can do anything you want, as long as it doesn't cost money.'"

Chuck Shriver, former White Sox publicist

So what you're wondering now is where the money came from: How did Veeck pay for all these giveaways, all these special nights, all these specially ordered flowers, all these pigeons, all these millions of pickles. Because ticket sales only cover so much unbridled extravagance. And there is always a price tag.

The answer comes on the back of those rain jackets that Veeck gave away in Chicago, the ones with the Pepsi-Cola logo on the back. Or on the bats with the Coca-Cola logo that were distrib-

Chuck Shriver. (Courtesy of Chuck Shriver)

uted on Bat Day. Or in the essence of one of Veeck's most potent ideas that never reached fruition: A tarp with the Morton Salt slogan, "When It Rains, It Pours," splayed across the infield in gargantuan type.

There is no shame in sponsorship. Promotion, in the Veeck school, is a shameless business anyway. The midgets in spacemen costumes that

Veeck once unleashed at second base in Chicago (Eddie Gaedel among them) were provided by Continental Airlines. Certainly, you are aiming to please, to excite, to exhilarate, but there is the underlying impetus of profit guiding your thoughts. And so for every idea, there is a financier. On Joe Earley night, the generous gifts, the washing machine, the luggage, the refrigerator, the clothes, were all provided through the generosity of local merchants in exchange for a place among the torrent of publicity. His $350,000 exploding scoreboard in Chicago cost him precisely nothing after a local executive advanced him the money and was paid back with the cost of billboard advertising. Everybody won.

Here we come to another misconception about Veeck, voiced by ex-Twins owner Calvin Griffith, who said Veeck would "spend two dollars and one cent to get two dollars in the till."

The truth? Veeck had the money. He made it everywhere he went. He just never needed it; never kept it. And sometimes he spent it rather openly, and sometimes he gave away tickets, even though he often said that a good promoter should give away everything but tickets. But his philosophy went like this: If you give something away, give it away. Don't dally in 10 percent discounts, in half-price days. Either give or don't give. It's the only way to achieve respectability, to earn a measure of honor among the community.

Calvin Griffith. (Courtesy of the Minnesota Twins)

So it's true. Veeck never had more than a few thousand dollars in his bank account. He invested money he'd earned in new enterprises, new teams, new ideas. And the money he had, he spent cleverly. He maximized his return. When he spent money, he made it clear to the public that he'd spent freely, at his own expense, to provide for them. Even if it wasn't always the case. Like with Nellie Fox Night.

This was in Chicago, and they'd had to widen a gate in right field to accommodate the concession trucks. It was purposeless money spent— this construction. It provided no profit. Unless …

And so Nellie Fox, on the way to becoming the American League's Most Valuable Player in 1959, was given his night, and since he lived in inland Pennsylvania, far from the water, Veeck invoked the incongruity principle and gave Fox a sailboat. And word was spread to the local papers that the White Sox had knocked down the walls and expanded the right-field gate just to fit Nellie Fox's sailboat into the ballpark. Twenty-four hours later, the sailboat had been returned to a company in Toledo, and Veeck had given Fox his true gift, a patch of farmland in Pennsylvania. The papers reported on the extravagance of Veeck's gesture and Bill quipped, "We would have given him the land, of

Nellie Fox. (Brace Photo)

course, but you can't tow a piece of land into a ballpark." No longer had needless money been spent. What Calvin Griffith misunderstood is that to every cent there was a purpose. Even if it only went toward the cause of endearment.

Veeck's Immutable Laws of Promotion #6:

The Promotion Never Ends

Bill Veeck: "When Bob Hope tells a joke, his audience enjoys it far more than if it were being told by a comedian of lesser stature; not simply because Hope tells a joke exceedingly well but because his audience *expects* him to be funny, *wants* him to be funny, and is rather flattered that he is being funny for *them*. Once you have absorbed that invaluable lesson, you become aware that you are entitled to steal from yourself by taking one basic identifiable idea and playing as many variations on it as you can find."

"When you don't promote, a terrible thing happens: Nothing."

From a Sign on my desk

There was a time the steelworkers went on strike and Veeck had special tickets printed and gave them out for free. There was a time the neighbors near the ballpark began to complain of the noise and Veeck held a "Good Neighbor Night." Promotion demands a sense of what's current, what's necessary, what issues are pressing outside the doors of your business. It demands a knowledge of what people are talking about. And more than that, it demands a constancy of thought and action.

What bothers me most is those who apply these principles once at one event. And it performs marginally well or perhaps very little. And they come back and tell me, "I tried it. It didn't work."

It can't be done sporadically. Effort must be continuous. Ideas can be clipped and shaped into hundreds of fragmented forms, just as Bat Day has become Cap Day and Poster Night. Or ideas can be formulated based on what's happened, by tapping imagination and taking the obvious chance of annoying a subject or two. Like what I did to Don Nelson.

This was in the early 1980s, and the Milwaukee Bucks and what was then my Philadelphia 76ers used to face each other in the playoffs virtually every year. Nelson was coaching the Bucks, and once, in a fit of anger, he took off his sportcoat and heaved it impetuously, and it fluttered and landed softly.

At center court.

In the middle of the game.

Don Nelson. (Courtesy of the Golden State Warriors)

There went Don, ejected from the arena. And there went that joy buzzer in my head, and the next time the Bucks came to Philadelphia, our halftime promotion had been solidified: A coat-throwing contest. Farthest toss wins. NBA coaches ineligible.

So you succeed and you fail, and you tweak here, and you jab there, and in the end, all that matters is that you keep trying. Everyone has their Disco Demolition Night, their crushing defeats, their Uncle Heavy and His Pork-Chop Revue.

Ahem. I believe an explanation is necessary here.

Uncle Heavy and His Pork-Chop Revue was a trained pig act. Well, in constant search for divergent halftime entertainment, I invited this group to perform while I was in the front office of the Atlanta Hawks. Here was a pig pushing a baby carriage, a group of pigs performing synchronous rolls. They were bright animals. I was rather impressed. But the president of the Omni in Atlanta, John Wilcox, was not.

He summoned me to his office the next morning. I believe his face was actually blue. "I watched that show with my friends," he said. "I've never been so embarrassed in my life."

Now, this wouldn't have been so bad if the story ended there. But I was so enthralled with the Pork-

Uncle Heavy and His Pork-Chop Revue was an ill-fated Pat Williams promotion. (Author's collection)

Chop Revue that I invited another trained pig act to perform in Philadelphia when I moved there. This time, it was the Ham'n'Egg Revue, and there was a trained chicken and a pig named Pepper, and Pepper could sing. Just not very well. And if you know the fans in Philadelphia, you know that they've booed Santa Claus, and most would probably boo their own mother if she sang as poorly as Pepper of the Ham'n'Egg Revue. So you can imagine how they treated a pig. I believe they expected Pepper to sing a dead-on rendition of Sinatra's "New York, New York." Instead, the handler poked Pepper in the spare ribs to get him to sing, and the pig squealed, as pigs tend to do when they're poked, and the fans jeered, and Pepper became so upset that he promptly relived himself at center court.

Headline in the next day's paper:

Pat Williams Has His Own Bay of Pigs Fiasco

You win. You lose. The promotion does not stop at the behest of one off-key pig.

Veeck's Immutable Laws of Promotion, #7:

None of these laws are immutable.

Bill Veeck: "No one has a monopoly on ideas. You can always think of something."

"Years ago, Bill Veeck asked if we could have foul lines that could light up, or have multicolored water coming through the irrigation system or if we could light up the base when a runner hits it. Back then, we didn't have the technology to do things like that. Today, we could."

Roger Bossard,
White Sox groundskeeper

I said that no one could ever top the midget, and I honestly wonder if anyone could. But I shouldn't say it's impossible. There's room for anything. It's just a matter of stretching, of dreaming, of thinking outside the realm of simplicity that reigns in today's world. It's Mike Veeck planning Vasectomy Night in a minor-league park in Charleston, S.C., and referring all the outraged calls to his mother (eventually, it was called off). Or Mike's "Lawyer Appreciation Night," where the lawyers pay double and then get billed by the third of an inning. It's an homage to lunacy, like the Missing Tooth Night we had for our minor-league hockey team in Orlando. Those lacking teeth were admitted free. Those with chipped teeth got in for half-price. Dentists were stationed outside the box office. We thought about creating the world's largest piece of dental floss until we realized that that was a thoroughly disgusting idea.

But at least we thought of it. And at least we had the courage to try it. The problem is that very few want to try anymore, and here so many of these ideas, the Veeckian philosophy of promotion, brilliant and understated, have been buried under sheets of dusty thought.

So here it is again. Doesn't matter your business. You can steal these ideas. You can tailor them. You can follow the rules. Or you fabricate your own. You can try any-thing really. There is no shame in promotion. And if it's funny, and if it makes some-one laugh, and there is plea-sure tied to your actions, then you've won. Even if you lose.

Tuffy Truesdale and Victor the Wrestling Bear were invited by Pat Williams perform at an Atlanta Hawks game in 1974. (Author's collection)

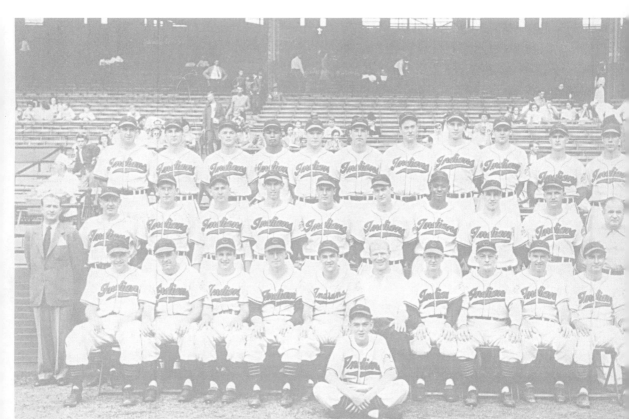

"I tell you, I have no patience with people who think everything i

coming to them. If a man wants to work, I'll work right alongsid

him. The only way I know how to run a ballclub is the hard way.

don't know any shortcuts and probably wouldn't take them if I

did. If you can't outsmart people, outwork them."

Chapter 14

One Will Do It

"He could work for 20 hours a day, sleep for four hours, and his generator would be recharged; his eyes would be bright. His eyes were never bloodshot. He was always ready to go."

Hank Greenberg

illiam Veeck Sr. became president of the Chicago Cubs when his son was three years old. By the time Bill Veeck was 10, he was working at the ballpark. He was mailing out Ladies' Day tickets at 11. As a teenager, he toiled in the stockroom and in the concession stands and with the grounds crew, and he sold popcorn and programs. By the time he neared 20, after his father died, Bill Veeck became an office boy, earning $17 a week. Within eight years, he'd become treasurer of the Cubs. He ran the commissary, worked with the ushers, manned ticket windows and ran the tryout camp for high-school players. He was in charge of park maintenance, and he

directed the planting of the ivy that still creeps up the brick walls in Wrigley Field.

All this by his 27th birthday. And then he bought the Milwaukee Brewers.

In Milwaukee, he helped clean and overhaul the entire ballpark. He shook hands until his right arm was sore, and he spoke until his voice grew hoarse. You understand by now that Veeck was blessed with a remarkable disposition, born with the ability to replenish his energies through bursts of sleep and half-hour catnaps. But that does not diminish the fact that what Veeck did, perhaps more readily and more constantly than any other baseball owner of his time, was to work. To improve his team. To improve his park. To upgrade his product.

Sometimes lost among the gaiety of his gestures, the joy of his actions, is the notion that Bill Veeck was laboring as the rest of the world slumbered. And that's the wonderful paradox that eludes so many of us in today's unflinching corporate environment: Bill Veeck was having so much *fun* while he worked that he forgot he was working. He cared so deeply for what he was doing, for the employees and fans who formed adoring circles around him, that his work—like everything else—became an unwavering passion.

"Work is life, you know, and without it, there's nothing but fear and insecurity."

John Lennon, singer/songwriter

I cannot emphasize this enough: the value of work, the importance of delving into not merely any profession, but something that stimulates you to endless depths. Here I could tell you that all that matters is hard work, that if you're spending a lifetime putting down shingling and hammering nails for eight hours a day, you'll be fulfilled. And maybe you would. Maybe that's where your satisfaction lies. But if it isn't what you want to do, then in the end, there will be a sense of loss.

Me? I would last in the shingling business for approximately four hours. That's not who I am. And the successful people I see in sports, in business, and in life, their work personifies who they are. I speak to them, or I read interviews about them, and they're asked why they do what they do, why they spend hours in pools or on practice fields or on putting greens, and all of them shrug, and then they say the same thing: the eternal mantra that governed Bill Veeck's every action.

They say, "I love what I do. I love what I do because it's fun."

And so Arnold Palmer drifts past 70, no chance of winning a tournament again, and still he plays golf every day. And Magic Johnson plays basketball in a tiny gym in Europe long after retirement. And Joe Paterno continues to coach football, and John Madden continues to broadcast football and Bill Veeck continued his attempts to dally in baseball until the day he finally passed away.

"Bill Veeck made working fun by making the environment fun," says sports mogul Marty Blake. "Every day you worked for him was glorious, and every day you looked forward to going to work."

I tell my children: Find something you love to do.

Then find a way to get paid for doing it.

Marty Blake. (Courtesy of Marty Blake)

"I loved football. I loved playing it, loved practicing it, loved talking about it and thinking about it. I even loved dreaming about it."

Dick Butkus, Hall of Fame linebacker

Larry Bird shot baskets for two hours a day during the summer. Babe Didrikson played 16 sets of tennis a day, played until she wore holes in her socks. Noah Webster spent 36 years perfecting the first edition of his dictionary. Cicero practiced speaking for 30 years to perfect his elocution. John Milton, the poet, rose at four in the morning every day while writing his epic, *Paradise Lost.* And Bill Veeck woke at five, and soaked in the bathtub while reading book after book, and by seven or eight, his day was already ascending toward a furious pace.

These people did it because they couldn't wait to work. Because work became their unflinching guide. Because they had an unwavering drive. Because they couldn't imagine doing anything else.

A study by the National Commission on Productivity revealed that only two out of every 10 employees in all occupations work to their full potential. Workplace efficiency, of course, is one of those issues that perplexes and baffles experts. But I don't think this is a complex issue. It's just that those other eight people probably aren't doing what they want to do. Or they aren't challenged by it anymore. They're bored. Or they're frustrated. And so, of course, productivity's going to slip.

Find something you love to do. Then find a way to get paid for doing it.

And then work at it. Work like you never have before. Work every day. Work like Ben Hogan, the golfer, until your hands bleed. Or work like Ken Burns, the documentarian, who spent 10 hours a day, six days a week, for two-and-a-half years, cutting his epic film, "Baseball."

"Life is not forever. Every moment of our lives, we truly need to live. That's the best we can do while we're here. Things that we love."

Dot Richardson
Olympic softball star

Don't get me wrong. I'm not advocating becoming some sort of overdriven workaholic who sacrifices his life for his career and skewers his family in the process. There is a fine line here, and it is different for everyone. What matters is that you find yourself on the right side of it.

Even when he was buried in his work, Bill Veeck never neglected his family. His wife adored him. So did his children. And because he found it, because he discovered the proper balance, he had everything he wanted.

"Shallow people believe in luck; believe in circumstances: It was somebody's name, or they happened to be there at the right time, or it was so then, and another day it would have been otherwise. Strong people believe in cause and effect."
Ralph Waldo Emerson, philosopher

William Veeck Sr. was a self-educated man. After he died, and his son dropped out of Kenyon College to work for the Cubs, Bill Veeck also became self-educated, burying himself in a veritable graduate school of baseball management and into a mountain of books. And again, I admit that we are discussing an extraordinary man here, with an uncanny constitution, but the the basic message should not be lost, the message that Veeck consistently passed along to his employees.

There is nothing owed to you.

You work for what you get. You

William Veeck Sr. (Brace Photo)

create your own breaks. The winning and losing, the success and the failure, is your own fault. Veeck had a hand in virtually everything at his ballpark, everything dealing with his ballclub. He'd walk around the park picking up trash. He'd inspect the infield grass. He'd negotiate contracts while standing in the shower and while lying in a hospital bed. "The hardest worker I've ever seen," says ex-player and broadcaster Jimmy Piersall.

He was not a believer in overnight successes. Quite simply, he spread his money so thin that he didn't have the money to invest in an overnight success. It's part of the reason why he resented a juggernaut like the New York Yankees, who were always good, who took for granted the fact that they always would be good. Veeck wanted the satisfaction of creating something good from nothing at all like he did in Cleveland,

Bill Veeck burns up the contract of Indians manager Lou Boudreau after Cleveland won the 1948 World Series. (Courtesy of Bob Broeg)

conjuring a World Champion from ashes and dust.

He always kept his commitments. When the grounds crew was short a man, he picked up a rake or a hose. He banged on a typewriter as a guest columnist at the World Series. When he retired to Easton in 1960, the *Chicago Sun-Times* offered him a spot as a guest columnist, and each week he'd provide three times as much copy as they asked for. And in case you've forgotten, this is a man who spent most of his life nagged by various infirmities, in and out of hospitals and surgeries, grinning through the agony and showing up for work despite it all.

"The heights by great men reached were not attained by sudden flight, but they, while their companions slept, were toiling upward in the night."

Henry Wadsworth Longfellow, poet

Even when he wasn't working, he was working. Those nights in the local taverns, in the Bard's Room, staying up until four in the morning talking baseball, that was business. Even as he was relaxing, he was selling, making himself seen and known and understood, subtly publicizing his product.

That, again, is the paradox of this man's life. That he never felt like he was working. That he never made it seem like work. And yet he was *always* working. Most of the time he couldn't let a conversation pass without introducing some mental conundrum as stimulation.

His employees followed him quite willingly on this dizzying quest. He stayed late, and they stayed late because they were swept in by his unwavering energy. They wanted to contribute to his box of ideas, and, of course, they were encouraged to contribute because the last thing Veeck strived to create was an office hierarchy. Or an environment stained with negativity. His employees wanted to be there when things happened, when promotions came together. They fell as deeply for this game as he had. "If you worked for Bill Veeck … You didn't ever rush out of this game and say to yourself: 'Oh, my gosh, I'm burned out; I've had all I could stand' because he allowed the sweetness not be chewed out of it," Mike Veeck once said.

"When I was a young man, I observed that nine out of 10 things I did were failures. I didn't want to be a failure, so I did 10 times more work."

George Bernard Shaw, playwright

Bill Veeck taught his son the same way his father taught him. Mike Veeck learned the business of baseball by selling White Sox ticket packages door-to-door, by sweeping floors, by cleaning the bathrooms at Comiskey Park. And at home, there was no respite. Bill Veeck designed his own sprinkler system. He planted hundreds of flowers around the periphery of the house, and the children happily joined him on "weeding day," if only because his presence transcended the tedium of the job. The children also did laundry and housework. They began most days with chores. Mary Frances once taped a note above the paper-towel holder that read, "One Will Do It."

Their father was their example. He was always willing to do it, to work, because he couldn't sit still for very long. He labored mercilessly, determined to finish the job, even if all he was working on was a desolate piece of wood.

Among Bill Veeck's plethora of interests was antique furniture. At first, he went to auctions, but then Veeck got the idea to start trolling junk places for bargains. So he found a peach-basket bottom rocking chair for $10. The chair was clinging together in disparate segments, and the finish was a mess, and Veeck vowed to scrape that chair to its original wood.

"It'll fall apart," Mary Frances said.

But Veeck scraped. He scraped with a pocket mirror until the skin on his hands was cut and torn. He scraped until he found the original finish. And today, Mary Frances still has the chair. It squeaks, but it's a prize, a testament to the value of a man who's willing to bleed just to finish a job.

"I don't think the world is as competitive today as it once was. But this is still a competitive existence. I think it's a responsibility, not an obligation, to do the best you can. I play to win. I don't like to lose. And when you win, you know you've earned it."

Chapter 15

One-Legged Man Playing Tennis

"I went to a Little League dinner with Bill once. He told the kids: 'You've heard it said that it doesn't matter if you win or lose, it's how you play the game. Well, forget that. Winning is everything.'"

Fred Brozozowski,
former White Sox investor

I submit this statement as irrefutable truth: There is no more competitive business in this nation than professional sports. It is cutthroat, it is merciless, it is based solely on the premise of winning, and I love every nauseating moment of it. Except, of course, the losing. Hate the losing. We all do, those of us who are successful or those of us who hope to be. If we don't, we're due for a self-examination. Those of us in the business of sports who lose might also be due for the unemployment line. There is no place for mercy. The day the NFL season ended in 1998, five coaches were fired within the span of an hour.

No one *enjoys* losing. At least, I hope not. There are merely some of us who hide our disgust for it more gracefully than others. And no one hid it with more panache than Bill Veeck. He was the Rodney Dangerfield of losing baseball teams. He had a joke for every defeat, for every second-division club, which meant he'd mustered an entire repertoire by the time he retired.

There was this: "I represent losers. Without us, there wouldn't be winners."

Or his well-chronicled comment to pitcher Lerrin LaGrow after he signed with the White Sox: "What do you want to do, start or relieve? We're so bad, it doesn't matter."

There were his St. Louis stories, about employees sleeping in box-office tills, about sad doubleheader crowds, about teams that couldn't hit or pitch or field or even be bothered to pretend. Bill said about his poor Brownies: "We've actually got three teams—one going, one coming, and one here."

Or this, from ex-White Sox pitcher Ken Brett: "Our

Ken Brett. (Courtesy of the Philadelphia Phillies)

1976 team was so bad that by the fifth inning, Bill Veeck was selling hot dogs to go."

So much of Veeck's career was spent among struggling teams, and so much of his legacy stems from the chaos and explosions and witticisms that illuminated the game instead of the game itself. And so the truth is lost. The truth is that one of the first things Veeck did when he arrived to run the White Sox in 1959 did not involve some gimmick or elaborate fireworks display. It was the rather bold gesture of placing billboards around the city that proclaimed, "We *will* bring a pennant to Chicago."

Mike Veeck was keenly aware of his dad's thirst to compete and win. Said Mike, "Lost in a lot of the showmanship was a tremendously sound baseball mind."

Losing tore at Veeck. He knew how this business worked. He tinkered unmercifully with his team until he'd found an acceptable roster. He hired some of his best friends as managers. He fired some of his best friends as managers. Larry Doby had a .425 record the last two months of the 1978 season with the White Sox. Still, he thought he might be re-signed by Veeck. It wasn't good enough. This is a business, after all. And you can only mask mediocrity for so long until it becomes pathetic and unacceptable.

Not to mention terribly unprofitable.

"Success in life goes only to the person who competes success-fully. A successful lawyer is someone who goes out and wins cases. A successful physician is the person who wins by saving lives and restoring others to health. There is nothing wrong with the will to win."

Knute Rockne, football coach

Bill Veeck hated the Yankees. Always. Throughout his entire career, he was unsettled by the mere contemplation of those pinstripes. It's true that he once called Yankees general manager George Weiss "a fugitive from the human race," and when Marty Appel, a Yankee employee, was talking to George Steinbrenner on the phone in the press box, relaying play-by-play of the game, Veeck sidled over and clicked the receiver, hanging up on him. Part of it was the show. Give the fans a rivalry. Create one if you have to. And part of it was that Veeck really *did* hate the Yankees because the Yankees always won and did it with such cool and unwavering precision.

So in that wake, Veeck crafted a reputation as the underdog. Here lies the explanation for his universal appeal—that people could relate with someone who'd lost before winning, whose career swerved along a bell curve of highs and lows. Because that's how most of us live. "The other owners had the financial strength," says his longtime co-author, Ed Linn, "and Bill had his physical problems. People like to root for the underdog."

But Veeck would do virtually anything to breach the gap, even if it flitted along the edges of the rules by mere millimeters. He called this "gamesmanship." Baseball is replete with gamesmanship, from coaches stealing signs to players stealing each other's bats to fans craning over the stands to interfere with fly balls. Veeck had already built moveable fences in Milwaukee that he'd shift between innings, depending on the situation. When he bought the Indians, he did the same, albeit more surreptitiously so as not to disturb the commissioner's office. So in the middle of the night, before the muscled Yankees came to town, his grounds crew would push the fence back as far as it could go. And in the middle of the night before the weak-hitting Browns arrived, he'd slide the fences 15 feet forward. He'd have his groundskeeper slope the infield depending on the proficiency of his team to bunt, and raise or lower the pitcher's mound depending on the next day's starter and water or starve the grass depending on the abilities of his infielders. He'd station someone on top of the scoreboard with a pair of binoculars to steal signs. (One White Sox pitcher, Alan Worthington, was so opposed to this practice, he actually quit the team.)

"I love my competition. If it weren't for them, I wouldn't be as good as I am."

Joe Paterno, football coach

Joe Paterno (Courtesy of Penn State Sports Information Department)

Veeck never broke the rules, of course. Just bent them to radical angles sometimes until they looked like tire irons. (The same happens in basketball, teams tightening the nets and the rims on their opponent, or removing air from the ball, or turning up the heat in the visitors locker room. Or so I've heard.)

All right. So maybe Veeck cheated once. But Bob Elson deserved it. The White Sox broadcaster had this reputation as "the world's greatest gin rummy player," and he had a rather ingratiating way of letting people know. So once in spring training, Veeck and Hank Greenberg conspired to overthrow his reign. They killed Elson at gin. Destroyed him. Left him in pieces.

What Elson didn't know, and perhaps never knew, is that Greenberg and Veeck were playing with a marked deck.

"We thrive on competition. We do it for a living, and we do it for recreation. We do it for all the things we want and just for the sheer love of competing for its own sake. Sure, let's admit it. There's an ugly side to competition. But doesn't the good outweigh the bad?"

**Harvey Mackay,
author and speaker**

We can't suppress a competitive urge. And we shouldn't. This is our nature. There is a story told by Detroit sportswriter Joe Falls about calling Joe DiMaggio on his 70th birthday. DiMaggio spoke with Falls for half-an-hour. The next spring, Falls saw Ted Williams, DiMaggio's old rival, and told

Harvey Mackay (Courtesy of Mackay Envelope Corporation)

him of the conversation, and Williams said, "When I'm 70, you call me. I'll give you an hour."

Bob Gibson, the Hall-of-Fame pitcher, continually beat his young daughter at tic-tac-toe. Ty Cobb would kick the first-base bag to move it two inches closer to second, to aid him—even in miniscule fashion— when he stole a base. Sam Walton, the founder of Wal-Mart, was once playing a vendor of his in a tennis match, and the vendor, a skilled player, hit a lazy return, and Walton halted the game and said, "If you're not going to play to win, I don't think we should continue."

Veeck competed with the same ferocity that he demanded from his teams. He'd swim three laps underwater just to outdo his children. He'd beat them at tennis. He'd beat anyone at tennis ("I'm afraid to play tennis with him," Hank Greenberg once said, "because he tries so hard to beat me.") or paddleball or he'd outlast them on the dance floor. The wooden leg was irrelevant. Like it wasn't there. And the realization that it was there only drove Veeck to hit his service return even harder. "That's why I play tennis," he once said. "One-legged men aren't supposed to play tennis."

Veeck had hired Max Patkin, who later became renowned as baseball's Clown Prince, in 1946, and shortly after, Veeck showed up in the dugout where Patkin sat before a game. This was not long after Veeck's leg had been amputated, and he was wearing his new wooden leg, adjusting to it, showing it off. He sat next to Patkin. He said, "I'll bet you $20 I can beat you from here to the outfield fence."

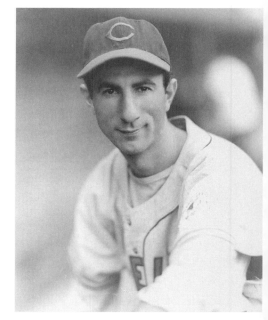

Max Patkin. (Brace Photo)

So Patkin raced Veeck.

And the man with the pristine wooden leg, who as a boy had embroiled himself in rollicking fights with neighborhood bullies, who would play poker all night to win back the pennies he lost, won the race to the outfield wall.

"Don't bother to be better than your contemporaries or predecessors. Try to be better than yourself."

William Faulkner, author

This is the benefit of competition. It is not the winning, although the winning, on the surface, is where our bliss (and in some cases, our job security) lies. But we need the competition to expand ourselves. It leads to greater focus, to a purer grain of thought. Even when we lose, we are afforded an opportunity to see inside ourselves: what's lacking, what's missing. It helps us to think more clearly, to wade through our muddled thoughts.

For example, sportswriter Bob August and Veeck were once talking about a pitcher for the Brooklyn Dodgers who had set a strikeout record for a rookie. Neither could remember the pitcher's name.

A few days later, August's phone rang. A voice said, "Karl Spooner." It was Veeck. He'd found the answer. He'd found it first.

But then, it was his directive to find anything first. To win it before someone else could. Or to roll headlong into a fight.

One afternoon, when a brawl broke out at the ballpark between two patrons who had been drinking without regard to consequences, Bill's assistant, Charlie Evranian, left the press box to break it up and found himself in a headlock. Veeck ran out and grabbed one man's mane of hair, and the man punched Veeck in the lip. Veeck punched him in the nose. They rolled down a flight of stairs. Veeck landed on top.

When the fight was over, when it had been broken apart, Veeck picked up his glasses, straightened his shirt and lumbered back to the press box. "It's tough to break the habits of a lifetime," he said.

He was 63 years old.

"Let the man who has to make his fortune in life remember this maxim: Attacking is the only secret. Dare and the world always yields; or if it beats you sometimes, dare it again, and it will succumb."

William Makepeace Thackeray, novelist

He never changed. He never backed away. Just as he charged into life, he charged into competition. No inclination to shift into reverse and let it go.

When he was decades younger, before he'd met Mary Frances, Veeck was involved in a desperate attempt to woo a young dancer who was traveling cross-country on a train. At each stop, Veeck had a basket of roses delivered to her. By the time she arrived in New York from Los Angeles, she looked like she'd opened a flower shop on the way there.

And when he was decades older, and lay in a bed at Illinois Masonic Hospital in Chicago recovering from one ailment or another, he shook the hand of a fan of his, a young college student named Tom Crigley. And what Tom Crigley remembers about that handshake, 20 years later, is the unwavering force of it, the steel-cabled grip, as if, amid the debilitation, Veeck had to empty his spirit into this lone gesture to prove that he could still clamp as hard as anyone.

"I'd like to be devious, but I can't find it in myself."

Chapter 16

The Last Honest Used-Car Salesman

"Bill Veeck was the most honest and sincere man I have ever met in professional sports. His word was gospel as far as I was concerned."

Jim Delsing, former

major league outfielder

S o we've spent dozens of pages building up Bill Veeck's reputation as an incorrigible hustler. And now it's going to be torn down. Because truthfully, Veeck wasn't much of a hustler at all. No one respects hustlers for their integrity, for the value of their word. Hustlers pawn you a Pinto with bald tires and an exploding radiator, then bask in the slickness of their sale.

Now I'm not saying Veeck couldn't have sold you that car, couldn't have talked you into it. What I'm saying is that he wouldn't because his conscience wouldn't let him, because his slickness was nothing more than an image that faded in close-up. The truth is that he paid off contracts diligently, and he rewarded players who might not have deserved it, and he was savagely honest and heroically faithful, even in the wake of his most public and glaring failure.

In 1979, after the riots of Disco Demolition Night had left the Comiskey Park field a ravaged mess, 7,000 fans tearing out heavy patches of grass and setting fires and ripping apart the batting cages between games of a twi-night doubleheader with the Tigers, Veeck stood with Tigers manager Sparky Anderson, surveying the destruction with a distant glimmer of hope.

"Sparky," Veeck said, "I know we can get this field right."

"We can't get it right," Anderson said.

"Well," Veeck said, "then we'll have to forfeit this game." We?

"Who created this mess?" Anderson asked. "You or me?"

Veeck said, "I did."

"Would you buy a used car from yourself?"

Sparky Anderson

We live in a nation that shuns accountability, which dodges the truth through technicalities and complications and the shroud of a defense lawyer and a speechwriter and a public-relations firm. And so perhaps there is a message here, that in facing the bleak circumstances that eventually forced him from baseball for good, Bill Veeck did not complicate matters with some sort of complex doublespeak—even though Disco Demolition Night wasn't even his idea, but his son Mike's, and even though I'm certain that with his gift for oratory and salesman-ship, he could have spun a favorability to the situation.

But Bill Veeck didn't want that sort of trust. He wanted the trust that spurned from humanity stripped to its barest nature. He wanted the trust that I preach to my children, the absolute trust that cultivates among families or among employees who bear an unpretentious honesty, who have never had the cause to doubt each other's word. Because one doubt collapses the whole notion of absolute trust. And Veeck didn't have the heart to obliterate that notion.

"To be honest, as this world goes, is to be one man picked out of 10,000."

William Shakespeare, playwright

A boyhood friend of the Yankees' Tony Kubek once wrote to Veeck about a 13-year-old Little Leaguer he was coaching in Maryland, and Veeck stayed in touch with the man and wound up drafting that Little Leaguer in 1976 with the White Sox. More than 20 years later, Harold Baines appears bound for the Hall of Fame.

Great hitter. Never much of a talker, Harold Baines. So consider what he said about Bill Veeck to be the equivalent of an elegant monologue, stripped of the annoying pretense.

In a single sentence, he simply declared Bill Veeck the most honest man he'd ever met in baseball.

"It would be a blatant lie for me to say that I am always honest, always honorable, always dependable," Veeck once wrote. "I'm not."

Of course not.

Harold Baines. (Courtesy of the Baltimore Orioles)

Everyone has lapses. Veeck was known to duel dishonesty with a wrath of his own. But this is the manner of the honest man, abiding ferociously by his own philosophy, expecting the same of others. And of the hundreds of people I spoke to, no one can remember Veeck reneging on his word. The first time he met you, he trusted you, he embraced you, the manner of his spirit demanding an adherence to honesty. I felt it when I pulled into that driveway the first afternoon I met him.

A whole trail of qualities are fertilized by honesty. And it all begins with a word, with your word, the promise of it, the value of it. Our word is what establishes our honesty, and our honesty produces our integrity, and our integrity is what makes us whole.

Integrity: The quality or state of being complete.

From integrity comes **trust,** and from trust comes **respect,** and from respect comes **loyalty.**

But none of that matters if people don't believe what you're saying in the first place.

"A man who lies to himself and believes his own lies becomes unable to recognize truth, either in himself or in anyone else, and he ends up losing respect for himself and for others. When he has no respect for anyone, he can no longer love, and in order to divert himself, having no love in him, he yields to his impulses, indulging in the lowest form of pleasure, and behaves, in the end, like an animal in satisfying his vices. It all comes from lying ... lying to others and lying to yourself."

Fyodor Dostoyevsky, author

Veeck told his children they could tell him anything because there wasn't anything he hadn't done in his harried youth. He yearned for an honest household, a family that wasn't fearful of the truth. No secrets.

It was the same with his players. They wanted something, they felt they deserved something, and they came to him. Although sometimes they didn't have to.

Ken Keltner was a veteran third baseman with the Indians who had been a perpetual holdout before Veeck bought the team. The first time

Veeck spoke to Keltner about a contract before the 1947 season, he offered a base amount of money, then said this, "If you have a good year, there'll be a $5,000 bonus at the finish."

"What do you mean by a good year?" Keltner asked suspiciously.

"I don't like to define a thing like that in figures," Veeck said, "but let's say if you hit .280 and bat in about 80 runs, you'll get the money."

Keltner agreed. On the final day of the season, Keltner found Veeck under the stands, and Veeck asked, "How come you haven't been up to get your bonus check?"

Keltner was hitting .257. "I haven't earned any bonus," he scoffed. "I've had a lousy year."

"In my book," Veeck said, "you had a great year. You never stopped hustling. You've earned the five grand."

The next season, 1948, the Indians won the World Series, and Keltner had one of the finest seasons of his career.

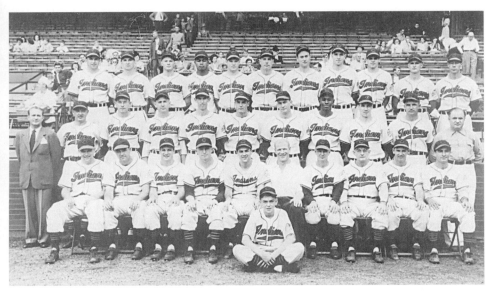

The 1948 World Champion Cleveland Indians. (Courtesy of Russell Schneider)

"There are no minor lapses of integrity."

Tom Peters
Business expert

This is not a philosophy. This is humanity. This is integrity. A survey of 1,300 senior executives revealed that more than 700 indicated the most necessary human quality for enhancing executive effectiveness is integrity. The survey did not indicate how many of the executives actually *possess* the integrity to do things like this:

Give a young player named Thad Bosley a two-year major-league contract with the White Sox because Bosley's brother was dying of Hodgkin's disease and Veeck wanted Bosley to have enough money to provide for his family. Or sign utility player Eric Soderholm to a two-year, $150,000 deal after his performance as Comeback Player of the Year with the White Sox in 1977, despite the obvious knowledge that Soderholm had a bad knee. Or give pitcher Steve Gromek back twice the amount his contract had been cut in 1947 after the Indians' majestic 1948 season.

"Treat people right," Veeck said, "and they'll treat you right."

We forget, in our haste to preserve our character, to shift responsibility, to associate blame, that in a society that shuns accountability, it is our reputation that defines us. And what weight will a reputation hold when you carry a bundle of half-truths in tow? What weight will a reputation hold when your promises are merely trite coverups? Red Auerbach, the old Boston Celtics coach, lived hard by his promises, so much that if he told a player something, and the owner of the team said he couldn't abide by it, Auerbach would pay the money from his own pocket.

Red Auerbach. (Courtesy of Boston Celtics)

Sometimes as the owner, Veeck was the one telling his players he couldn't abide by something. Yet, nearly every time the player got what he wanted. Even if it was more than he deserved.

This is not a philosophy. This is integrity. This is trust. Even now, there is an underlying current of respect for the man. People remember him as the truest of friends, as good as his undeniable word. He could argue with Dizzy Dean about a comment Dean made on the radio, and before long, they shed their harshness and hugged and were back telling stories again. And the day the White Sox clinched the American League pennant in 1959, Veeck was in Bloomington, Illinois, speaking at a Little League banquet he'd committed to long before.

"Whatever Bill would tell you," says ex-White Sox and Indian Al Smith, "he would do."

There is no indication as to how many of those 1,300 executives can claim that same sort of faithfulness from their employees.

"Integrity can be neither lost, nor concealed, nor faked, nor quenched, nor artificially come by, nor outlived nor, I believe in the long run, denied."

**Eudora Welty,
author**

Honesty is another way that Bill Veeck won you over. We've discussed the intense commitment of his employees, of his players, of his friends, the effectiveness of influence and empowerment and listening. But nothing makes an impression on a person like bald truth, like honoring shortstop Billy Hunter's contract in 1953 in St. Louis even though he was nearing bankruptcy, or being one of the few owners in baseball with the dignity to phone a player when he was going to be traded. There is nothing like a man who apologizes for his mistakes, who stands behind his friends, who accepts your word at its face, whose handshake is worth every carbon copy of a written contract.

Honesty and integrity build trust and respect, and that path leads to the one quality that Veeck himself once defined as "the greatest quality in the world."

That path leads to loyalty.

"Loyalty means not that I agree with everything you say, or that I believe you are always right. Loyalty means that I share a common ideal with you and, regardless of minor differences, we strive for it, shoulder to shoulder, confident in one another's good faith, trust, constancy and affection."

Dr. Karl Menninger, psychiatrist

The White Sox had a grass outfield and an Astroturf infield until 1976, when Veeck announced he was tearing up the Astroturf, replacing it with grass, cutting it into small squares and giving them away over a weekend. So a fan named Chuck Franenkel went down on a Sunday, and a sign hung near the entry gate, apologizing, but all of the Astroturf had been given away.

Chuck Franenkel wrote Bill Veeck a letter, said he was upset, said he wanted a piece of turf, and Veeck wrote him back, that he was sorry, that he'd see what he could do. Sure, Franenkel thought. Don't hold your breath.

Ray Meyer. (Courtesy of DePaul Department of Athletics)

A week later, a package arrived at Franenkel's house. Inside was a small square of Astroturf.

This is not a philosophy. You tell someone you're going to do something, and you carry through. And they believe you'll carry through the next time, and they'll stand by you the next time, and then you are standing shoulder to shoulder, your lives intertwined.

One more story of truth and loyalty of respect and honesty. It comes from Ray Meyer, the ex-DePaul University basketball coach who shared the Chicago spotlight with Veeck for so many years. Meyer saw Veeck at a dinner once, in 1978, a week after his reeling team was clobbered by UCLA.

"Looks like you're going to have a bad year," Veeck said.

"No, Bill," Meyer said. "We're going to be good. You watch."

March 1979. DePaul advances to the NCAA Final Four. The week after, another dinner, another encounter between Meyer and Veeck.

"Coach," Veeck said, "I won a ton of money on you."

"How did you do that?" Meyer asked.

"Well," Veeck shrugged, "you told me you had a good team."

"When I signed Larry Doby, the first Negro player in the American League, we received 20,000 letters—most of them in violent and sometimes obscene protest. Over a period of time, I answered all. In each answer, I included a paragraph congratulating them on being wise enough to have chosen parents so obviously to their liking. Thinking about it, it seems to me that all my life I have been fighting against the status quo, against the tyranny of the fossilized majority rule. I would prefer to think of it as an essential decency."

Chapter 17

The Razor Edge of Disaster

"Bill always felt conventional wisdom should be challenged. Just because the world says you have to do it a certain way, doesn't mean that's the right way. The safe way may not always be the right way."

William Brashler, writer

This might have been his legacy: the integration of major-league baseball, the shattering of the color line, the most dynamic step in a heady revolution in professional sports. Bill Veeck tried to buy the Philadelphia Phillies before he enlisted in the service in 1944, four years before Branch Rickey and Jackie Robinson in Brooklyn, four years before Veeck and Larry Doby in Cleveland, four years before the gates of segregation crashed for the final time. Veeck's idea was to buy the team and to stock it with Negro League players and to gloat quietly as the Phillies coasted to a pennant in 1944. He appeared to have a deal too. The franchise was in financial shambles. The lineup was inept. No one wanted it. As one last diplomatic gesture, Veeck informed Commissioner Kenesaw Mountain Landis of his plan. Landis thought Veeck was joking. Veeck insisted he was not. Landis notified National League Commissioner Ford Frick, and entanglements ensued, and Veeck's plan died under a mountain of bureaucracy and covert racism. Baseball, and the nation that nurtured it, took one more angry breath before embracing equality.

Kenesaw Mountain Landis. (Brace Photo)

I was seven years old when the color barrier was finally broken, years before the dawn of the civil-rights movement. Memories of a polarized society lingered. The racial barriers in our nation were fiendishly pronounced. The divide was deep. Acceptance was grudging and bitter. For Robinson, for Doby, for those who came after, enduring the unrestrained bigotry of the ignorant was their burden. Veeck once estimated that for every black customer he gained after signing Doby, he lost a white one.

"I can describe Bill Veeck in one sentence," says Negro Leagues star Buck O'Neil. "He was one of the few men I ever knew who was without any racial prejudice."

And for Veeck to make such humanitarian gestures, reaching out to Doby, shielding him from the hatred, was more than merely a flourish of generosity and spirit. It was the act of a man who could take risks and beat away his fears and stand before a divided world and speak with unwavering courage.

His ideas were consistently scorned. His thoughts were discounted. His peers dismissed him. His sweeping ideas for expansion, for free agency, only took hold after his time had passed. All this is because he was a man who transcended his time, whose legacy is considered "radical" only because his views portend a more idyllic future, because he was afraid of nothing. Certainly not of dreaming far ahead of his own age.

"The ultimate measure of a man is not where he stands in moments of comfort but where he stands at times of challenge and controversy."

Rev. Martin Luther King, Jr.

There was a part of Veeck that relished the struggle, the angry tugs of life's most desperate chances. He didn't have to join the Marine Corps in World War II. He didn't have to break away from the Cubs and buy the dilapidated Milwaukee Brewers. He didn't have to spend his career taking last, desperate chances on franchises, on players, or on cities that were in desperate need of a believer.

But he did. He took chances because life was his amusement park, his roller coaster, a mountain of risks, of success and failure, of terrible fear and charged elation. This is, after all, the way life works. Without fear, there is no elation. Without chance, there is no success. Every decision is fraught with the same anxieties, and yet those decisions are what shape our lives. If I don't go away to college at Wake Forest, if I don't play pro baseball in Miami the week after my father's death, if I don't accept the general manager's job in Spartanburg at 24, if I don't accept the Chicago Bulls' GM job at 29, where am I?

Bill Veeck, U.S. Marine Corps.
(Courtesy of Russell Schneider)

"Living is Limitless."

Martha Stewart

The blurred fear of an uncertain future accompanied every step. But there was a distant comfort, as well, in knowing that Veeck was taking broad steps long before me, on much broader stages, waging war against discrimination, against the tyranny of baseball's oafish establishment, against the conventional wisdom of his time. Whispering to Larry Doby before his first big-league appearance, "We're in this together." Doby recalled, "Nothing could have helped me more to give me determination. I knew he was behind me." Or checking out of a posh private club in Cleveland after the front desk informed him that his Jewish friend, Harry Grabiner, would not be permitted a room. Moving spring training with the Indians from Florida to Arizona to dodge the south's tyrannical discrimination. Signing an aging Satchel Paige in 1948.

Mike Veeck observed, "Nobody stood around when dad hired Larry Doby and said, 'What a great move. Gosh, you're a civil rights activist.' The majority of the people wrote nasty letters and questioned dad every step of the way."

You were around him long enough, and you felt it radiate. "Bill's fearlessness," says ex-sportswriter and broadcaster Larry Merchant, "rubbed off on people."

Veeck once told Tony LaRussa, "A man who is cautious is so timid he never savors anything completely. Don't be cautious. Just don't be injudicious."

"The worst danger we face is the danger of being paralyzed by doubts and fears. This danger is brought on by those who abandon faith and sneer at hope. It is brought on by those who spread cynicism and distrust and try to blind us to our great chance to do good for all mankind."

President Harry S. Truman

He held forth as if he feared nothing. He despised cautiousness. He fought boys twice his size while growing up and refused to quit fighting until they let go. He never lost that abandon. He attempted to move the hapless St. Louis Browns to Los Angeles, then Baltimore, in the hope of reviving an otherwise flatlined franchise where the fans would embrace them. He was a patron saint of lost causes; of players like the Philadelphia Athletics' Russ Christopher, a pitcher with a heart condition who was sickly, his face gaunt and hollow, his body buried in blankets, when Veeck visited him in a hospital bed in 1948.

Russ Christopher. (Brace Photo)

"Hey Russ," Veeck said. "Do you think you can pitch?"

Christopher's voice was a hoarse whisper. "I don't know," he said.

"Do you want to?"

"Sure," Christopher said. "I want to."

And so Veeck, then with Cleveland, bought his contract for $25,000. And Christopher, only able to pitch a couple of innings at a time because of his heart condition, had a 2.90 earned run average in 45 relief appearances as the Indians won the World Series.

These chances he took, this blatant disregard for the timidity that often accompanies chance, was what urged me to see him that summer day in Maryland. It was what fueled me in Spartanburg: his words, his comfort, our weekly conversations, concluding with his assurance that what I was doing was what I was supposed to be doing. "A fellow who dares," he'd called me long ago in his syndicated column.

I would dare to call him the same.

"Good men have the fewest fears."

Christian Nestell Bovee, philosopher

On the deck of an antiaircraft unit in the Pacific, in the midst of World War II, the lights would train on the faraway glint of a Japanese bomber. Private First Class Bill Veeck was schooled as an ammunition passer, a gunner and a searchlight operator, and those instances that the bombers appeared, he would later say, provided "the most thrilling moments I can remember" from the war.

So here was a man who extracted small pleasures even from the adrenaline of battle, even if he didn't condone it, even though he lost his leg because of it, even after it caused him a lifetime of pain. Of course it scared him. But this is the essence of Veeck's uniqueness: He could savor the rush of every emotion, even the animalistic rush of his own fear.

Life and its bell curve of emotion was to be cherished, to be maximized, to be lived to one's own standards. Conformity and timidity were wasted gestures. "Bill," says author Studs Terkel, "believed in the individual." And in turn, he fought for the individual. He spent his life delving down the thornier path, lifting the wayward and the meek, sprinkling opportunity in his wake.

In the mid-1970s, when women were banned from the press box, one of Veeck's employees, Judy Shoemaker, had come to see him. One writer became upset, wanted Shoemaker to leave, wanted to preserve the sanctity of the rules. Veeck intercepted him, explained the

Private First Class Bill Veeck. (Courtesy of Bob Broeg)

situation, and told the writer, "Sit down. Puff on your cigar. The woman is staying." And he did the same for Melissa Ludtke, one of the first female sportswriters in Chicago, after she was banned from the Bard's Room. He overruled the writers. He let her in.

There is a notion that courage is man's chief virtue because it allows his other virtues to become exposed—that courage is merely the door. Without it, life is bound by the prejudices and values of others, and one is doomed to Thoreau's timeless prophecy, that life of "quiet desperation."

How many times did Veeck put his future in jeopardy for his beliefs? How many angry letters did he answer? How many threatening phone calls did he placate? "Bill Veeck never believed that skin color or religion should prevent people from having an opportunity," civil rights leader Reverend Jesse Jackson once told me. "He was fair in his dealings with all people."

One reason Veeck's family moved to Maryland during his hiatus from baseball was because the schools were not segregated. When he learned the local movie theatre forced blacks to sit in the balcony, he was so furious he thought of moving away. Instead, he managed to have movies flown in, then showed them for free at his guesthouse. Civil rights protesters slept on his lawn during the March on Washington in 1963, and Veeck himself marched with the Rev. Martin Luther King Jr. When he was told he couldn't get a visa to visit Cuba, he chartered a plane and flew there on his own.

There was skepticism. There were enemies. He didn't care. This was his life. He was going to live it.

"Every great thing in the world balances, at all times, on the razor edge of disaster."

Thornton Wilder, author

With every promotion loomed the spectre of crashing failure. Think of Grandstand Managers Night. For an evening at Sportsman's Park in St. Louis, in an otherwise meaningless game, Veeck handed baseball's utmost power to the fans, allowing them to make the decisions, holding up red "Yes" or green "No" placards in a democratic vote, on whether to change pitchers or play the infield in or steal bases, while baseball's furious establishment raged at this "travesty of the game."

"The other owners hated my father," says Mike Veeck. Of course they did. He made fun of them by name in his books, and he battered their reliance on tradition in newspaper and magazine articles. The reason he couldn't move the Browns to Baltimore or Los Angeles was because the other owners wouldn't let him, because they attempted to bankrupt him during the 1953 season. They stuck him with an unattractive schedule, pitting him against the crosstown Cardinals—who had even changed their slogan to "A *Dignified* St. Louis Tradition," in a pointed jab at Veeck's absurdity, and were owned by the behemoth Anheuser-Busch brewing company. Their plan worked. Veeck sold, and then the owners voted to move the Browns to Baltimore without him, squeezing him out of the game.

Some time later, when Veeck was undergoing surgery, a friend of

Connie Mack (left) and Bill Veeck shake hands at Grandstand Managers Night. (Brace Photo)

his asked for a moment of silence on his behalf during an owner's meeting. Afterward, one of the owners snarled, "If you ever pay a public compliment to that guy again, you're fired."

He came back, of course. He was going to take ridiculous chances with this sport, to stretch it to its breaking point, and those who didn't appreciate him didn't have to watch. And if he failed, he failed. It wouldn't stop him from trying again.

There is the story of Veeck signing the ageless Satchel Paige midway through the 1948 season, when he was (at least) 42 years old, perhaps edging closer to 50. And Veeck was criticized mercilessly for it, for employing a publicity stunt in the midst of a pennant race. The editor of *The Sporting News,* J.G. Taylor Spink, decried Veeck for "demeaning the standards of baseball in the big circuits," accusing Veeck of signing Paige only because he was black.

Paige went 6-1 for the Indians down the stretch of a pennant race. The criticism ebbed. After every Paige victory, Veeck sent Spink a telegram with Paige's statistics, and a line that read, "DEFINITELY IN LINE FOR *THE SPORTING NEWS* AWARD AS ROOKIE OF THE YEAR."

But then, there would always be something. Veeck was imbued with such longevity and ingenuity that he caught the rest of the game

Bill Veeck signs Satchel Paige. (Courtesy of Russell Schneider)

unprepared. Even the media that adored him would sometimes fail to see the scope of his experimentation. His whole career was marred by mostly errant criticism. It's one of the reasons that his story deserves to be told again, told now, when the events of the past can be viewed with a less jaundiced eye. "He was considered radical once," says former American League President Gene Budig, "but it's now proved that he was way ahead of his time. He was criticized by the establishment. Now he's vindicated. He challenged other clubs to be new and bold."

Here was a man who dared. To him, that meant more than any criticism and more than any vindication.

"A timid person is frightened before a danger; a coward during the time; and a courageous person afterward."
Jean Paul Richter, author

Courage opens the door. We've talked in these pages of developing personality and imagination, of embracing the day and those who populate it. The first step begins here, with a deep breath, with the brashness to follow your heart, even if it seems to be sparking along senseless paths. For example, a man named Robert Manry, a copy editor for the *Cleveland Plain Dealer*, in 1965, after deciding his life had become staid and tedious, vowed to sail a 13 1/2-foot boat from Falmouth, Mass., to Falmouth, England. Seventy-eight days later, enduring loneliness and storms and sleeplessness, he arrived in England to a welcoming crowd of 40,000 people.

So far, we've discussed the cerebral form of courage, of risky decision-making. This is the essence. But there is something to be said for blunt physical courage as well, that rare and mythical nature of comic-book heroes. And in compiling anecdotes for this book, I came across something so remarkable that it seems almost fictional, like we should be drawing pictures of Bill Veeck with pen and ink. There were two stories that came in, from two separate sources, both startling testaments to the depth of Veeck's character.

There were other stories as well, stories of Veeck helping to push a car out of a ditch in the middle of winter without a coat; of Veeck, while with the Brewers, picking up a man who'd had a heart attack during the National Anthem and carrying him under the stands to a doctor. But nothing like these two.

The first came from Duane Pillette, who played for Bill Veeck from 1950-53. It was at a team swim party,

Gary Pillette, now in his 50s, might not have made it that far had it not been for Bill Veeck's bravery. (Courtesy of Duane Pillette)

another Veeckian flourish that hardly seems a possibility today. Pillette's son, Gary, was diving into the pool, hit his head on the side and sunk to the bottom.

Only one person saw what had happened. And so Bill Veeck stood and dove into the pool, flailing that wooden leg, pulling Gary Pillette from the bottom of the pool and dragging him to safety.

Gary Pillette is in his 50s now and retired from Microsoft. "Bill saved his life," Duane Pillette says.

It wasn't long after hearing Pillette's story that I talked to former Browns pitcher Tommy Byrne, who attended a family party during the 1952 All-Star break in St. Louis. Veeck and Byrne and most of the party were embroiled in a game of water polo when Byrne's wife, who was eight months pregnant, began screaming, and no one could figure what was wrong. Out went Bill, hobbling along the side of the pool to the other end, diving in and pulling Byrne's three-year-old son, John, off the bottom. "Bill saved him," Tommy Byrne says.

Here are two lives that Bill Veeck rescued with such obvious heroism that it seems almost unfathomable. Take those, and add them to the hundreds of lives that he urged forth more subtly with his public display of fearlessness and valor. The sum of it is a man who dared to live life, to save lives, to stare down hatred and bigotry and the shadow of his own mortality. And who dared to do it without a coat.

"I'm not handicapped; I'm crippled. Webster's defines handicapped as 'to place at a disadvantage.' I don't believe I am. Most important, by making no apologies to anybody at all, you are debarred from making them to yourself. You are giving yourself no out, no excuses. When you act small and helpless, you feel small and helpless."

Chapter 18

Can't Beat the Mileage

"My father always said that there is nothing so beautiful as scar tissue."

Mike Veeck

o there he was in the Continental Bank of Illinois in 1975, attempting to buy the Chicago White Sox, his golden tongue wagging away in anticipation of a half-million dollar loan from some helpless employee. And Bill Veeck stood and gestured emphatically to drive home his point, and there went his wooden leg, an explosion of springs and nuts and pinions, an unruly scattering of mechanisms across the carpet. Softly, almost unintelligibly, he asked for a pair of pliers—to put himself together. "Bionic Man I'm not," he said.

Only his body betrayed his weakness. Bill Veeck's flesh and bones were a dreadful curse, his punishment an uncomfortable melange of hospital visits, of surgeries, of sodium pentathol shots, of fuzzy hearing and inexplicable blackouts and a wooden leg that had a tendency to explode into shrapnel at the most inopportune times.

There are more stories about the wooden leg than can be included here: the leg Veeck was fitted with after losing the original in World War II, the leg he threw a postamputation party for once he'd gotten the replacement, dancing well into the night in a Cleveland ballroom with a thousand of his closest friends. Veeck had hoped his wooden leg would become a trademark of his character, an identifying mark of his color, a sort of cachet. So he built the ashtray in it, and he astounded children by stabbing a knife through it, and he painted it bronze every spring, then tanned the rest of his body to match (he used boat paint, and by the end of the summer, it often faded to green). He treated the whole issue as if it was part of his encompassing circus act.

Veeck refused to see it any other way, to give in to his own weakness, his own self-pity. This was how the simple man drowned himself. Veeck preferred to suffer in silence, betraying nothing, making light of the serious moments, of his brushes with mortality, of the time when he couldn't breathe and hopped in a cab and told the driver, "Go as fast as you can," and he poked his head out the window to force air down his throat.

His leg became a theatrical device. When his family went to the beach, he would unstrap it at the end of the water, and one of his children would run the leg back toward the beach. "We liked running up the beach with a leg," Gregory Veeck says. "It was a rite of passage."

He slammed the leg on tables for emphasis and stored it in airplane aisles for shock value. His secretary would trip over it when she walked in his office. He gave one of his old legs to a Chicago bar to put on display (The inscription: "Can't beat the mileage. Hope it fits.").

"That was the story of Bill's life," says ex-Chicago columnist John Schulian. "He realized that nothing is ever as bad as it seems."

"No matter how deep my hurt, I always smiled. I refused to be discouraged, for neither God nor man can use a discouraged person."

Mary McLeod Bethune, founder, Bethune-Cookman University

That leg must have fallen off a dozen times in public places, once when he stepped out of a cab with a *Chicago Sun-Times* reporter. Afterward, Veeck sat on the curb with a screwdriver, piecing it back together. He had a half-dozen operations on his other leg and once broke it while slipping on the men's room floor at a technical school in Chicago ("If I'd have broken the wooden leg," he said while being carted to the hospital, "I could have fixed it in shop class.") And yet he refused all help. He elbowed people who tried to help him over steep curbs. He danced and played tennis and lived his life with every semblance of normalcy and presented such a brilliant façade that the reality of his pain became almost transluscent.

It would poke through at times, in extreme moments, with close friends. He once confided to announcer Ken Coleman, the day before he was due back in the hospital for more surgery and more sodium pentathol. His eyes welled with tears. "Nobody can imagine what it's like," he said, "to get up in the

Bill Veeck and his famous wooden leg (Baseball Hall of Fame)

middle of the night to go to the bathroom. And have to crawl on the floor in pain to get there."

But he disguised these moments. He wouldn't let the pain dictate his life, even though it was present for most of his life. It began when he fell four stories from a dormitory window at Kenyon College, breaking both his legs. The pain lingered through the war, through dozens of surgeries and hospital visits, as he battled a fungus on his ear, as half a lung was removed, as he retired from baseball from complications of what he thought was a brain tumor (turned out the blackouts and numbness were caused by a chronic concussion), as the stump of his leg was sawed further and further northward. "Does a man stop smiling because he wears false teeth?" he often asked.

It got worse as he got older, as his faculties began to weaken, as his eyesight and his hearing dwindled, and his bones became brittle and unstable. He refused to recognize it, except to form the embryo of a joke. He attended employee picnics while wearing an oxygen mask. He snuck out of the hospital to go to games. He was always the last one to get in the car, holding the door for everyone else. Acknowledgement of weakness only mired him in weakness.

"Life is not an easy matter. You cannot live through it without falling into frustration and cynicism, unless you have before you a great idea which raises you above personal misery, above weakness, above all kinds of perfidy and baseness."

Leon Trotsky, political revolutionary

The formation of a pearl, author Charles Swindoll once said, begins with pain, with a grain of sand piercing the shell of an oyster, irritating its innards, the oyster's resources rushing to the spot to heal the pain with fluids that would have otherwise remained dormant. The grain of sand is covered in fluid, hardened and healed, and what remains is a pearl. It is a symbol of stress, a healed wound, a precious gem born of adversity.

We all suffer through pieces of our life, with stinging memories of our childhood or a failed marriage or a broken home or an unsatisfying job. How we handle these moments is a bellwether for how we'll handle our lives, for whether we'll build upon them or collapse underneath them. I once had lunch with Dr. Warren Wiersbe, a pastor in Chicago. I was struggling in my job at the time. He told me, "Don't waste your sufferings."

Don't waste my sufferings?

I gave it a moment. I let it settle. It didn't make sense. Now, almost 30 years later, it does.

A couple of years ago, I wrote my autobiography, *Ahead of the Game*, stripping my life to its foundation, describing it with absolute candor, the death of my father when I was 22, the birth of my mentally retarded sister, the pain of my divorce, the losses with teams that were meant to win and didn't. All of it belongs to me. All of it is how I became me, how I bettered myself, how I accepted my fate.

I thank Bill Veeck for that. He was my pearl. So

Jim Williams, Pat's dad (Author's collection)

many irritants, and all they served to do was inundate him with a deeper beauty. His wooden leg did become a trademark; an unending source of fascination and wonder. When outfielder Jim Lemon came to visit him for the first time, in the midst of their conversation, Veeck slipped off his leg, handed it to a man and told him, "Tell Charlie to take a half-inch off this. It's too long."

That story is 50 years old. Jim Lemon remembered it with startling vividness. But then, this is not the kind of line you hear twice in a lifetime.

Wally Phillips, longtime WGN Chicago radio personality, once told me, "Bill Veeck was an overcomer. He wouldn't let adversity defeat him. He had a reservoir of strength when adversity hit, that allowed him to overcome it with a triumphant spirit. He could laugh and make light of his own misfortune and always stay upbeat. I really believe Bill was a messenger. He was sent here to inspire us and encourage us to deal with our own setbacks and defeats with the same good humor."

"I honestly believe that people who are not subjected to some adversity usually end up as well-fed housedogs."
Walter Annenberg, businessman and ambassador

Maybe when a man spends his life fending off a withered body, when he's confined to hospital beds and examination rooms, he figures the only way to fight the pain is to make light of it. But Veeck did more than that. He transcended the pain. His indomitability was startling. Bill Durney's wife, Ruth, was once bustling about her apartment, trying to figure out what to send Veeck in the hospital after one of his leg operations. The doorbell rang, and Ruth answered it, and there were three-dozen long-stemmed roses, arranged in a vase.

Ruth picked off the card, opened it and read, "Just because it's a nice day. Bill Veeck."

Ten other bouquets went out that day to 10 other wives.

He called amputees in the hospital to console them ("Look at it this way," he would say. "One pair of socks will last you twice as long. And in the winter, only one foot will get cold."). He told one fan whose leg was wrapped in a heavy brace, "If I had another leg to give you, I would." He demonstrated the leg to curious children. He consoled an amateur soft-ball player who had broken his leg, slipping the wooden leg off and telling him, "Here. Use mine."

"I only fear two things," he'd say, brandishing the leg. "Fire and termites."

You couldn't speak of illness and infirmity without Veeck lightening the atmosphere. He wrote a whole chapter about it in *Veeck—As In Wreck*. Once, his leg exploded when he was covering the 1983 American League Championship Series for a Chicago newspaper, and he was wheeled onto an airplane with his wooden leg in his lap.

"Do you need a doctor?" an airline employee asked.

"All I need right now," Veeck said, "is a carpenter."

He scrambled to his own feet when he fell, no concerned queries permitted. He accepted the continued brittleness of his body with a startling nonchalance. When sportswriter Hal Lebovitz visited him in a Cleveland hospital after his leg had been amputated, Veeck was playing with a Slinky.

"I'd spend time with Bill," says *Chicago Tribune* sports columnist Bob Verdi, "and I'd come away thinking, 'Who's handicapped? Him or me?' "

———————————

"In the presence of trouble, some people grow wings; others buy crutches."

Harold W. Ruoff

———————————

I could quote a survey here, like the one that revealed that 87 percent of people felt life crises—divorce, illness, the death of a loved one—gave them a stronger sense of purpose. I could talk of Kristi Yamaguchi, the gold-medal winning figure skater who was born with twisted feet, or of Auguste Renoir, the painter whose rheumatism was so severe that he couldn't hold a brush without wincing. But this is a book about the spirit of Bill Veeck, and there is a story that belongs here, a story of proud indignation in the face of a crippling disease. It is the story of Bill Veeck's granddaughter.

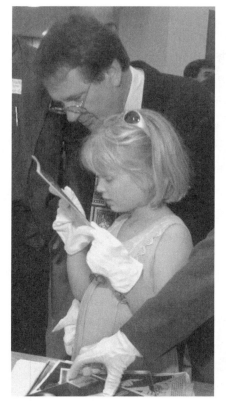

Rebecca Veeck, daughter of Mike Veeck and granddaughter of Bill Veeck, looks at photos in the library of the Baseball Hall of Fame. (AP/Wide World Photos)

As these words are written, Rebecca Veeck is seven years old. And she is going blind. She has a rare disease called retinitis pigmentosa, and there is no known cure. In the meantime, she has embarked on a nationwide tour with her father, Mike, who resigned his job as vice president of sales and promotions for the Tampa Bay Devil Rays to be with her. In November 1999, she went to the Baseball Hall of Fame, paged through photos of her grandfather and saw his plaque on the wall.

Even though Bill Veeck didn't live long enough to see his granddaughter, Mike knows he would have told her, "Everybody has something that makes them different. Have a laugh with it, make other people comfortable."

They've made light of everything, Mike and Rebecca. They began singing the name of the disease to each other at home, Mike calling out, "Ret-in-it-is," and Rebecca chiming, "Pig-men-tos-a." They mimicked running into doorways together. Odd, perhaps. Even bordering on tasteless. But this is the only way Mike Veeck knows how to deal with something like this. It's the way his father taught him. It's the way he's taught his daughter.

"I'm not scared," Rebecca says. "If I go blind, I'll deal with it."

"In nature, nothing is perfect, and everything is perfect. Trees can be contorted, bent in weird ways, and they are still beautiful."

Alice Walker, author

There is one other Veeckism that creeps to mind here, one of those self-effacingly clever phrases he cobbled together late in his life. It went like this: "I only have a leg-and-a-quarter, a lung-and-a-half, my hearing is shot, and my eyes are gone. I've given the world all the edge I'm going to give it."

Here's something else he told writer Thomas Boswell in 1981, "Suffering is overrated. It doesn't teach you anything."

I hate to bring this up now, Bill, but this is where you were wrong. You taught me everything I needed to know about coping with the inevitability of disappointment. You were a pearl. You were beautiful in suffering.

And you never even met your granddaughter.

"*Progress brings complaints. You cannot set yourself against the status quo and expect that the status quo isn't going to fight you back. The status quo, by definition, wins almost every battle; otherwise, it ain't the status quo anymore. So you pick yourself up, dig the dirt out of your ears and try again.*"

Chapter 19

You Can't Beat a Man Who Won't be Beat

"My father died on the second of January because he was the eternal optimist. He lived through the first to make sure it wasn't going to be any different."

Mike Veeck

I have acquired a rather sadistic hobby in my old age: I run marathons. Actually, some wouldn't call it running. It is more like a diligent and upbeat walk. But realizing that misery thrives on company, and being the heady salesman that I am, I've convinced my wife, Ruth, to run them with me. So in 1997, 10 days after our wedding, we ran the Boston Marathon together, Ruth and I, and at the nine-mile mark, Ruth pulled up, told me her knee was hurt, that she had to stop at a first aid station. Her parting words: "Keep going. Don't quit. I love you."

I plugged onward. For 11 miles, I shuttled along by myself, thoughts of Ruth bandying about in my weary head, of her disappointment, an impending feeling that perhaps Ruth would think she had let me down. It was at the 20-mile mark that I wheezed up Boston's deathly Heartbreak Hill, my body fading, my legs crumpling, my heart fluttering.

And then someone called my name.

And then someone called my name again. A cruel hallucination this was.

Pat Williams and his wife, Ruth, complete the 2000 Boston Marathon. (Author's collection)

I peered over my right shoulder. Ruth was waving at me, smiling. She'd had her knee treated. She had run 11 miles by herself to catch up to me. We ran the last six miles together. Before we reached the finish line, Ruth even stopped to apply her lipstick.

There are two didactic branches to this story. The first is that I might be the slowest runner in the history of the Boston Marathon. But we'll concern ourselves with that at another time. The second, of course, is that perseverance is paramount—that nothing is accomplished by stopping altogether, by melting beneath the circumstances.

I produce this story, the image of marathon running, because it is the most literal example I can evoke of man's ability to push ahead amid the daunting collar of limitations. And I explore this concept because it is one of the final lessons of Bill Veeck's life, of his enduring legacy, his unending *want,* and his efforts to buy teams and move teams and promote teams. And even when he failed miserably at all of the above, the ability to scrape the dirt off his collar and hobble onward.

"When running up a hill, it is all right to give up as many times as you wish as long as your feet keep moving."
Shoma Morita, physician

He spent his final days on the phone to Cleveland, calling Browns owner Art Modell, calling his old friend Hank Greenberg from the last of his hospital beds, mustering one final binge of effort to buy the Cleveland Indians. He'd been called by Cleveland sportswriter Hal Lebovitz, and told Lebovitz to keep it quiet so as not to hurt his chances. And then, in the midst of one last brilliant grasp at the game he loved, he succumbed quietly.

It was a perfect end. It was the end he'd foreseen in his own autobiography, trailing off *Veeck—As In Wreck* with the prophetic and often-quoted final sentences:

Sometime, somewhere, there will be a club no one really wants. And then Ole Will will come wandering along to laugh some more.
Look for me under the arc-lights boys. I'll be back.

Those words were written years before he bought the White Sox for the second time, years before he contemplated a return to Cleveland. He wouldn't let it go, see, not so easily. Pinned into a corner by his finances, he attempted to move the St. Louis Browns to Baltimore before letting them go, but the owners allowed it only after Veeck had sold the team. Before he bought the White Sox for the first time (in 1959), he attempted to buy the Indians (again) and the Detroit Tigers (where his six-million dollar bid, the largest in baseball history at the time, was turned down) and even the Ringling Brothers Circus. He dabbled in the minor leagues in Miami and explored bringing baseball to the West Coast. Before he bought the White Sox for the second time (in 1975), he ran a racetrack

(Suffolk Downs) and attempted to buy both the Washington Senators and the Baltimore Orioles. He was snubbed in favor of men with less money, with less baseball savvy, with fewer investors. He was snubbed because he was Bill Veeck. He was snubbed for reasons even he didn't understand.

And yet there he was when another team went for sale, sniffing around, gauging interest, unable to leave his interest untended. "Life is not what happens to you," says broadcaster and former sportswriter Larry Merchant. "It's what happens next. You couldn't keep Bill down. He was special that way. He was magical."

"When my back is against the wall, nothing can stop me. Whether you can or not, you hold on; that's the essential. When you're out of willpower, you call on stubbornness; that's the trick."

Henri Matisse, artist

Brian Piccolo was a freshman running back when I was a senior at Wake Forest. He roomed with Gale Sayers in Chicago and played for the Bears, and in June 1970, at the age of 27, he died of cancer. Before he did, I had the chance to visit with him. He gave me a business card. "You can't quit," is how the card was inscribed. "It's a league rule."

I carry that card in my wallet. I show it to my

Brian Piccolo. (Courtesy of Wake Forest University)

children when they begin to whine, when they tell me they can't handle the workload in advanced English or they tell me their swimming coach is abusing them (of course, that's the idea—the more laps they swim, the longer and deeper their sleep at night. But I digress.) My kids have this idea that quitting is the panacea. They're like me when I was 14, when I was playing summer-league baseball in Wilmington, Delaware, for the first time, and I sat in the backseat, my grandmother in front.

"Well," she said, as I gathered my things, "I hope it goes well."

"If it doesn't," I said, "I can always quit."

My grandmother swiveled in her seat so fast I think she contracted a mild case of whiplash. "I never want to hear that from you again," she said.

And so I haven't said it again.

"It's not that I'm so smart. It's just that I stay with problems longer."

Albert Einstein, scientist

You might know of a daytime talk-show host named Sally Jesse Raphael. Her program is certainly not high art but consider this: She was fired 23 times by radio stations before she found her niche. "The only talent," she says, "is perseverance."

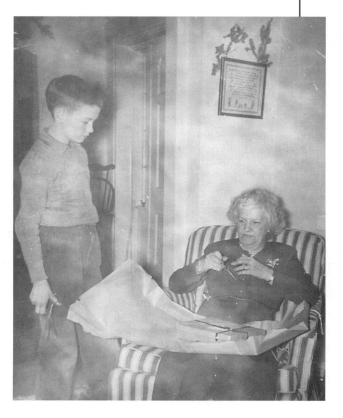

A young Pat Williams and his grandmother. (Author's collection)

This is why I enjoy speaking of failure. When I give a speech, I can tell dozens of stories of regretful errors in judgment, of the tribulations of brilliant men struggling to find their way. There is some solace in knowing that Walt Disney received a dishonorable discharge from the Navy, was told he'd never amount to anything, went bankrupt several times and was fired by a newspaper for lack of ideas. Or that Bob Dylan was once booed off the stage at his high-school talent show. Or that Woody Allen flunked a class in motion-picture production at two New York colleges. Or that Harvard University rejected young Warren Buffet's application for graduate school. Or that some of the best novelists of the modern era were deluged with rejection slips.

Or that Bill Veeck never finished college. And he bought that first ballclub in Milwaukee with just those $11 in his pocket, $10 of which he spent buying drinks at a bar across the street from the train station (the remaining dollar, he framed). And for all his fortune, for all the joy he spread, he died virtually broke. "I think that's great," Mike Veeck says.

Veeck merely traded his properties, one for another, like the stack of baseball cards he kept in his desk. He was fond of saying, after he bought the White Sox in 1975, that he traded the house in Maryland for a property in Chicago, one known to outsiders as "center field" at Comiskey Park. Because his mind was always whirring,

Bill Veeck, new owner of the Chicago White Sox, stands outside Comiskey Park, December 16, 1975. (AP/Wide World Photos)

because everything appeared before him with the gilt of opportunity, he could never stop moving, never stop buying and selling and trading, never withdraw voluntarily from the game. "Bill was like a kid with a new toy," says Rudie Schaffer, Veeck's constant baseball partner, "and once the novelty of the toy wears off, he looks for another toy. That was Bill Veeck."

Which is why he went looking for teams, why he once told a Chicago columnist that he would buy "any team that is so weak, it can't defend itself."

Once, in St. Louis, a *Sporting News* writer sat with Veeck in the press box. Veeck was leaping from his seat, shouting at the umpires, shouting at his own coach/mascot, Max Patkin, shouting at anyone who would listen.

"War to the bitter end!" Veeck cried. "Action!"

"We are made to persist. That's how we find out who we are."

Tobias Wolff, author

With Veeck, you learned to persist. Larry Doby burst through a forest of racism and prejudice with Veeck at his side. Minnie Minoso was given at-bats in 1976 and 1980 so he could become the first major-league player to appear in five decades of play. When 38-year-old Jim Bouton approached Veeck at the White Sox's spring training camp and told him he'd developed a knuckleball and wanted a tryout, Veeck peered up at him from his spot on the grass along the right-field line. He was shirtless, bronzing his body in the sunshine.

Jim Bouton owes his last fling in the majors to Bill Veeck. (Courtesy of Jim Bouton)

"All right," Veeck said. "We'll give you a uniform. See what you've got."

Bouton went to the minor leagues and flopped around for a while before landing in Atlanta, where he won a single game. And he owes that single game, that last comeback, to Veeck.

"If you have some minimal talent, bathe with regularity and aren't certifiably insane, you can survive in any field if you simply are determined to hold on."

Charles Peters, author

A necessity of perseverance is thickness of skin. It is perhaps the most easily abandoned of all the topics we've discussed here. Failure can be blatant and demoralizing. Even Veeck needed encouragement at times. A month after *USA Today* first went to press, Veeck was writing a guest column for the 1982 Cardinals vs. Brewers World Series. He was working in the right-field bleachers in St. Louis in the cold, punching the keys on a manual typewriter, giving the copy to a runner to hand to co-author Ed Linn in the pressroom to edit, then having the runner give it to *USA Today* sportswriter Rudy Martzke to punch into a computer. It was complex, and it was a hassle, and after the first two games, when the Series went to Milwaukee, Veeck called Martzke in his hotel room and said, "I quit."

"I'm thinking, 'I can't have the great Bill Veeck give up on me,' " Martzke says. So he went to Veeck's room, and he harangued as well as he could, telling Veeck he couldn't quit when he told others they shouldn't quit, appealing to his pathos.

"All right," Veeck said. "I'll stay."

And he stayed for the rest of the Series. And it became a yearly pilgrimmage, Veeck at the World Series, Veeck the sportswriter, Veeck pecking away at his typewriter in the cold.

"There comes a time in a man's life when to get where he has to go, if there are no doors or windows, he walks through a wall."

Bernard Malamud, author

All of which leads to another marathon story. This one from Mexico City, the 1968 Olympics (this has nothing to do with me, if you haven't already guessed). Darkness was unraveling, and the last of the Olympic marathon runners were straggling toward the finish line, and the stands were emptying, and finally, the wail of police cars began to pour forth. A lone runner staggered into the stadium. His name was John Stephen Akhwari, and he was from Tanzania, and his leg had been injured in a fall and was crudely bandaged and spotted with blood. He hobbled the final lap. The spectators stood and applauded vigorously.

When he had finished, someone asked why he hadn't quit. "My country did not send me 7,000 miles to start the race," he said. "They sent me 7,000 miles to finish."

Certainly, there is no shame in falling short, in finishing last, in struggling, in failing, as long as you are steaming forward in the process. It is a romantic concept—one that Veeck embraced, one that he espoused shamelessly.

His idea for the exploding scoreboard came from a play by William Saroyan called "The Time of Your Life." The whole play takes place in a saloon. It focuses on a man playing pinball, asking the bartender for nickel after nickel to play the game, falling short time and again. Just before the final curtain, he wins, and the machine explodes in a montage of ringing bells and flags flying and a rendition of "Dixie."

"Saroyan was saying something," Veeck said. "You keep tryin' and tryin', and you finally do hit a winner."

"*I believe very strongly that we are all working together for the best interests of the ballclub. I cannot see why the fact that I own some stock and they don't should have any bearing on our personal relationship.*"

Chapter 20

The Incidental Leader

"Bill Veeck was special because of his brain. He could look around the corners and see in advance, and then had the guts to pull it off. Veeck was a rare combination: the dreamer and the doer."

William Barry Furlong,

Writer

This chapter comes to you by a sort of cosmic accident. Consider it a bonus. I stumbled across the idea for it as this book was being put together, as themes were being formulated and pulled apart and then pieced back on top of one another. Yet I didn't realize what I had discovered until I nearly tripped over it.

I often lecture and speak and attend conferences on the rather immaterial notion of leadership. But then, these days, in the high-powered world of self-help, who doesn't? Leadership conferences are weekly occurrences, the invitations flooding my mailbox. I could present you with an entire library of newly minted books on leadership. From sports, we have been buffeted with the management philosophies of Joe Torre and Mike Shanahan and Lou Holtz and Dean Smith. There are books based on the theories of military leaders: Robert E. Lee, George Patton or Ulysses S. Grant. Now there are even books based on biblical figures such as *Moses on Management*. Add these to my own volumes, and you're nearly drowning in leadership philosophy.

So why didn't I see this here? Maybe because the spectre of Veeck's own modesty wouldn't allow the vision to crystallize. In all of his books, in all of the reams of newspaper articles written about him, among all the interviews I've done, I have trouble finding one mention of the word **leader** (Webster's definition: **A person or thing that (acts as guide); directing, commanding or guiding head, as of a group or activity.**). Most likely, Veeck eschewed the word for its esoteric connotation. Instead, it took my own realization, while trawling through all of this information, that a common theme had emerged.

The thing is, when I speak, I elucidate seven principles of leadership. And I've noticed that all seven of these principles unite to form a picture of the man we've spent these pages dissecting. So, to be honest, what follows is a bit of repeat. But I hope it serves as further illumination of what we've already uncovered and reveals that what we've spent the first 19 chapters exploring, essentially, is Bill Veeck on Leadership.

THE SEVEN PRINCIPLES OF LEADERSHIP
ACCORDING TO PAT WILLIAMS

1.   VISION

———————————

"Great leaders are visionaries. They have an instinct for the future ... a course to steer ...a port to seek. For persuasion, they win the consent of their people."

Arthur Schlesinger Jr., historian

"Baseball, like many other simple and primitive cults, practices the simple rites of ancestor worship. It sometimes seems to me there have been only about two rule changes affecting the game in the past fifty years. When I had the names of White Sox players printed across the backs of their uniforms in 1960—under the obviously misguided notion that the fans might want to know who they were— protests came in from every other team in the league. They weren't quite sure what they were protesting…"

Bill Veeck

As this is being written, my league, the NBA, is in the midst of a stormy feud over whether coaches should be microphoned during games and whether cameras should be permitted in locker rooms. And somewhere, Bill Veeck is regaling his audience with that husky laugh, and shrugging and asking, "What's the big deal?" Because years before, in St. Louis, he'd floated the idea of trading for shortstop Bud Blattner and miking him up to broadcast a game while playing the infield.

He was one of the first to propose interleague play, to float the idea of divisional realignment. We know about his efforts to integrate blacks into baseball. But he also formulated a way to bring female players in for tryouts, to have them compete with men's teams, to sign at least two to professional contracts. His sponsor pulled out. But Veeck remained committed. He was just a few years early.

He was the first to merchandise season tickets months in advance. In *Veeck—As In Wreck,* he was already proposing theories to speed up langorous three-hour games, still a thorny issue among baseball's purists.

Bill put it this way: "To adjust one's plans to changing conditions is not, of course, a sign of panic at all. It is a sign of balance, of intelligence, of real leadership. Freezing to an outdated situation—that is a sign of panic."

There is one Veeck innovation we haven't discussed in intimate detail here (and we won't bore you with the financial breakdown), but his theories and ideas, his deep understanding of high finance, tax laws and accounting, were the precursor to modern free agency, the outline for the dynamic of modern sports, like it or not.

"He pioneered many areas of baseball finance that are still in effect today," says Furlong.

The clearest visions are simple and easily understood. They're also attainable simply with a unanimity of resources. The clearest visions are like the ones that appeared to Bill Veeck in the midst of conversation, the ones that populated his box of ideas, the thousands of notecards that are testament to his ever-flickering and unconventional brilliance.
"Bill had incredible vision," says current baseball commissioner Bud Selig. "He was so right on so many things."

2.   COMMUNICATION SKILLS

"An understanding up front prevents a misunderstanding at the end."

Stephen Covey, author

"I have a thing about doors. If you know your people, then you don't ever have to keep the doors closed."

Bill Veeck

Here are my chicken-scratched subheadings under this category. Tell me they don't just smack of Veeck:

A.   Communicate Optimism and Hope
B.   Be a Motivator
C.   Become a Storyteller
D.   Check the Perceptions of Your Employees
E.   Be a Good Listener
F.   If You Are Not a Natural Public Speaker, Get Trained

Baltimore Orioles announcer Chuck Thompson once had the privilege of eating dinner with Veeck and Casey Stengel in Detroit. You know those psychological profile questions about who you'd invite to the "ultimate dinner party"? Well, this would have been a strong candidate for any baseball zealot. The whole night, the two men spoke in code, using no proper names:

"The big left-hander …"

"The blonde kid who got in trouble …"

"The goofy guy from Iowa …"

Amazing. In a world of communication breakdown, Veeck, the man of a thousand speeches, could even deliver his point in unique and primitive tongues.

3.   PEOPLE SKILLS

Casey Stengel. (Courtesy of New York Yankees)

"The most important single ingredient in the formula of success is knowing how to get along with people."

President Theodore Roosevelt

"The only way to know what the people want is to ask them. Besides, I enjoy talking baseball with people. I especially enjoy talking to people while I'm watching a ballgame."

Bill Veeck

In receiving hundreds of testimonies from fans while compiling this book, I've found that most follow a similar pattern. Veeck befriended them, unsolicited, in the stands, or at a bar, or he moved them from the bleachers to the box seats, no questions asked, or he responded to their request or complaint with twice the energy the query had generated. Sure, the volume of the stories is remarkable. But the consistency is what's astounding. He talked to kids for their junior-high reports. He issued press passes to single-watt college radio stations. He found tickets to World Series games for complete strangers.

Avi Poster was in high school when he and a buddy, Jack Jacobson, took their dates to a White Sox game. As they walked to their car after the game, they passed through a dark tunnel and were roughed up by some neighborhood thugs. The next day, Jack called the Sox, got Bill Veeck on the phone and lodged his complaint. That afternoon, Rudie Schaeffer held the stepladder while Bill clambered up to change the light bulbs in the tunnel. Avi and his friend were informed by Bill and invited back to another game.

Chicagoan John Walsh remembers, "I was in the third grade at Seven Holy Founders School. I was walking to school and a man saw me and asked where I was going (his car had broken down and was in the repair shop). He asked if he could walk me to school. I said yes. Then he asked me if I liked baseball. I said yes. Then he asked me if I liked the White Sox. I didn't know it was Bill Veeck, but at school the teachers knew who he was. Later in the morning the teachers showed me the newspaper with Bill's picture. So, that's how I met Bill Veeck, and I've never forgotten it."

When John Suralski was lugging cables and hauling equipment as a gopher for Chicago's WGN television, Veeck invited Suralski and his co-workers up to the Bard's Room for a meal. Everyone else was dressed up, and Veeck hauled his beleaguered and underdressed workers to the front of the line.

"You're good enough to work with me," he said, "then you're good enough to eat with me."

Says sportswriter Jerry Izenberg, "He was one of the few executives anywhere who actually knew what people wanted."

What they wanted, quite simply, was to *feel* wanted. And once they felt that, a burgeoning trust, they could be led, hand-in-hand, toward the same wondrous vision.

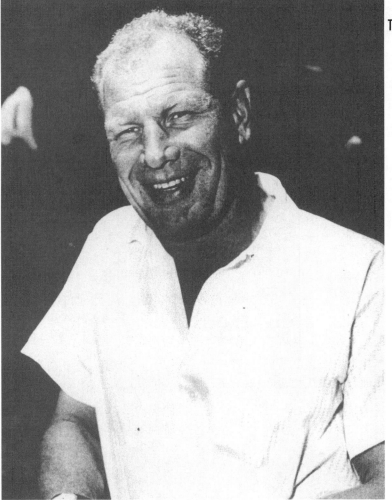

Bill Veeck was a man of character. (AP/Wide World Photos)

4. CHARACTER

"People buy into the leader before they buy into the leader's vision."

John Maxwell,
Speaker and Author

"There are times when people do things just because they want to do them. Maybe the only thing in it for me is a nice feeling inside."

Bill Veeck

This was the man holding to his word. This was Larry Doby ennobling him with his trust, insisting that Veeck was one of the few men who did not bend his character to conform to the situation. This was Veeck balancing humility and unmistakable confidence, unyielding in pursuit of his ideals.

This was Veeck staying in a Milwaukee hospital with an outfielder named Hal Peck, sitting by his bedside for an entire night, talking with his wife, dabbling ointment on Peck's blistering leg after Peck had accidentally shot himself in the foot while trying to exterminate some rats in his hen house. Or Veeck sitting up all night in a Cleveland hospital with Jim Hegan's wife, Clare, six months pregnant, until Hegan could arrive from Boston to be with her. It's Veeck hiring and paying for a private nurse to stay with her until she left the hospital. It's someone who concerned himself for days when he passed by a stranded motorist while riding in a cab and didn't have the time to stop and help.

"One word to describe Bill Veeck?" Clare Hegan asks. "Kind."

5.   COMPETENCE

"Leaders are made, not born. They are made by hard effort, which is the price all of us must pay to achieve any goal that is worthwhile."

Vince Lombardi, coach

"I grew up in the atmosphere of a ballpark. I've raked the diamond, painted seats, counted money, sold hot dogs. Now I'm doing what I most want to do—run a ballclub."

Bill Veeck

Phil Cavaretta signed with the Cubs in 1935. He walked into Phil Wrigley's office, and there was this boy, emptying wastebaskets, running errands as if he'd been plugged into a socket. Veeck had just begun with the Cubs a couple of years before, as a young office boy making a few dollars a week. Cavaretta remembered the boy, his efforts, his inescapable energy. He still remembered seeing him 65 years later.

The one thing no one can deny of Veeck is that he earned his place in baseball. He was obsessed with self-improvement, with personal growth, with ascending an infinite learning curve, through reading, through writing, through intense conversation, through late nights and early mornings.

So many of the young people I meet today are in a hurry to ascend, to move forward, to push ahead toward something with a glossier profile. I was the same way in Spartanburg. But what matters more is utilizing every angle of a situation, working hard and building a reputation. The opportunities will come. Veeck owned three different major league clubs in four different spans, when most of his colleagues didn't want him around at all. And by the time he got to each, his employees had an ever-thickening tome of respect on which to build.

6.   BOLDNESS

"Boldness has genius, power and magic in it."
Johann Goethe,
author

"I believe in fireworks, both figuratively and literally. I have learned the business value of a good, rousing feud. After all, the men in the other uniform are the enemy."
Bill Veeck

Here are some quotes from rival owners shortly after Eddie Gaedel batted for the St. Louis Browns (anonymous, of course):

"Veeck is making a farce out of baseball, and it's got to stop."

"Can you imagine what this disgraceful performance will do to baseball? Why, in a couple of years, it might reduce our game to wrestling."

Eddie Gaedel's obituary made the front page of *The New York Times*. His jersey is part of a display at the Baseball Hall of Fame. It was one of the first things Bill Veeck's granddaughter saw on her cross-country trip during her battle with blindness.

I'll repeat what I've said before: This is not to advocate foolish and uncalculated risk. This is merely to say that chance is the only path toward advancement, and that bold strokes are the only way to take what you are owed.

Veeck and his employee, Dick Hackett, were delivering World Series tickets to New York restauranteur Toots Shor in Chicago in 1959, and Shor tossed a wad of crumpled bills onto the table, telling Hackett, "Help yourself." Hackett took the money for the tickets, picking through a tangle of bills. And then Veeck pulled a wadded $20 bill from the stack, handed it to Hackett, and told him, "Toots forgot to tip you."

7.   BE A SERVANT

"If we do not lay out ourselves in the service of mankind, whom should we serve?"

**Abigail Adams,
former First Lady**

"I have to be on the giving, not the receiving, end. If you give me a woolen muffler, I've got to send you back a herd of sheep. I'm not bragging or complaining or looking for any psychological interpretations. I'm stating a fact. That's the way I am, and that's the way I always have been."

Bill Veeck

Bill Veeck frequently sat with the fans in the grandstand. (AP/Wide World Photos)

Two things that always seemed to startle people—the complexity of Veeck's thoughts and the simplicity of his nature. What I did not expect was a man who would throw himself into peril for the benefit of a complete stranger, who could not hide his compassion and his willingness and his amorous satisfaction with life.

One night in the '60s, Bill invited me to hear him speak at a banquet in Darlington, South Carolina. Bill insisted that I stay over that night in his room. He ordered a roll away bed that he slept in and demanded that I have the "big bed."

Have I told you about the suntan oil? It seems Veeck had this preoccupation with the nature of tanning products. Seems that in his last years, while sitting in the centerfield bleachers at Wrigley Field, the sun beating on his leathery skin, Veeck would dole out suntan oil like he used to hand out Ladies' Day tickets. He would bring a bag, would carry a half dozen types of sunscreen, would counsel people on their skin type, on the level of protection they needed and would squeeze it in their hands. There are stories of Veeck, his grizzled face covered in a wide-brimmed straw hat, rubbing suntan oil on astounded strangers' backs in the Wrigley Field bleachers. As if they can hardly comprehend that this man who led them to so much joy for so many years, who had such a deafening effect on their National Pastime, would spend even a moment to shield them from danger.

"Bill Veeck and Pat Williams...
what a winning exacta this is!"
–Larry King

Marketing
YOUR DREAMS

Business and Life Lessons from Bill Veeck
BASEBALL'S MARKETING GENIUS

"I'm for the dreamer. The only really important things in history have been started by the dreamers. They never know what can't be done. I have wandered through life on the philosophy that if you wish for something to happen and do everything possible to make it happen and convince yourself that it's going to happen—who knows?—it may happen."

PAT WILLIAMS
WITH MICHAEL WEINREB

A Word of Tribute by Roger Kahn and Foreward by Mike Lupica

Epilogue

If You Don't Have
a Dream . . .

"All our dreams can come true if we have the courage to pursue them."

Walt Disney

And so what remains is a dream. You should see it by now, should have a grip on it, however tenuous, however clouded. That's the message of the previous 20 chapters. That's the finale. Don't let pragmatism and cynicism dull the vision. Veeck was scrambling on his death bed to buy a baseball team.

It was all that Veeck could have asked for on his epitaph: for men to dream like him, to tarry about in deference to their visions, to believe and to push forth in spite of the skepticism and the doubt.

Lorn Brown. (Courtesy of Lorn Brown)

Veeck was a facilitator. There was a man in Evansville, Indiana, a longtime broadcaster, a friend of White Sox announcer Lorn Brown, who had been doing play-by-play of minor-league baseball and college sports for years. The man had a dream. He wanted to broadcast a major-league baseball game. And so Brown told Veeck, and Veeck called the man, and the next thing he knew, Veeck was flying him to Chicago to broadcast a weekend series.

He hated to see a dream pass without fulfillment. Why do you think he was always taking desperate chances with people, and why do you think he was buying playoff tickets for the fan he'd never met, and why do you think he spent hours talking to high schoolers for their reports? He was a facilitator. He wanted people to succeed. He wanted to see them push ahead. When Larry Whiteside was a struggling baseball writer in Milwaukee in the 1970s, he went to Bill Veeck. "Bill always took the time," says Whiteside, now a prominent sportswriter with the *Boston Globe*.

Jerry Tatar's father was once a farmhand for the White Sox, and in 1977, Tatar wrote Bill Veeck and asked him what the White Sox could do to honor his father. Veeck called back, told Jerry Tatar he could treat his father to dinner for four in the Bard's Room before a game and to four box seats. And he'd let him throw out the first pitch. It was a typically generous Veeckian flourish.

Eventually, Mike Veeck worked through the details with Tatar, and Tatar pulled him aside, asked him how much he owed for the tickets, for the seats, for the honor.

And this is what Mike Veeck said, "I can't put a price on a man's dream."

All of which calls to mind a lyric from the musical "South Pacific;" one of those lines that adhered somewhere in my brain when I first saw the show in the late 1940s and hasn't let go since.

"If you ain't got a dream," the lyric goes, "how you gonna have a dream come true?"

"All great men and women are dreamers. Some, however, allow their dreams to die. You should nurse your dreams and protect them through bad times and tough times; to the sunshine and light which will always come."

President Woodrow Wilson

I hope you were dreaming while you read this book. (Not *sleeping* and dreaming, of course.) I hope you were ensconced in the idle daydreams that we allow ourselves to indulge in, until we suddenly reach the age when it seems as if we're wasting time in the recesses of our mind.

Well, we're not.

Dreams are not merely a respite but a commodity. Let them go, and you might as well give up. There is work involved in the fulfillment, and there is a persistence required, but that's to be expected. Just trust me when I tell you it can be done.

Of course, it helps to have an example, someone to follow, someone to emulate. Larry Lucchino, president of the San Diego Padres, never met Veeck, yet told me that he thinks about Veeck every day, that his marketing philosophy is filtered through Veeck's vision. Dave Dombrowski, president of the Florida Marlins, was a disciple of Veeck's from the Bard's Room in Chicago. And one of the letters Veeck received after Eddie Gaedel batted in St. Louis came from a boy in McCook, Nebraska.

The letter asked for a tryout with the Browns. Veeck wrote back, told the boy he was too young, but that he would be guaranteed a tryout when he finished high school. And for the next couple of years, the boy wrote Veeck, offering suggestions, lineup shifts, until Veeck invited the boy and his father to St. Louis for a Browns vs. Yankees series.

Gene Budig, from McCook, Nebraska, later became president of the American League. And he and his wife named their daughter Mary Frances after Veeck's wife.

Roland Hemond, now with the Arizona Diamondbacks said in *ESPN Magazine*, "At Comiskey, we had a showerhead in the bleachers that the fans loved, If it weren't for that showerhead, we wouldn't have our pool here (at Bank One Ballpark). Our VP of marketing, Scott Brubaker, was raised in the Chicago area. When he mentioned that showerhead to the press, a pool company called about putting one in."

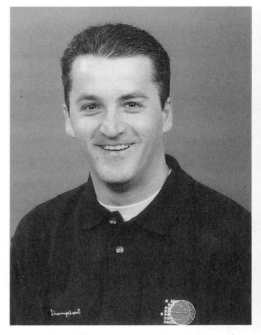

Steve Giles. (Courtesy of the Orlando Magic)

A former employee of ours with the Orlando Magic, Stephen Giles, first read *Veeck—As In Wreck* in a sports marketing class at Georgia Southern University. He found himself referring to Veeck's views, to his philosophies, time and again. He had never met Veeck, and yet he carried away a piece of the man, kept it with him like a rabbit's foot. "He emphasized that it was all right to dream," Giles says, "as long as you did everything in your power to make those dreams come true."

"I've dreamt, in my life, dreams that have stayed with me, ever after, and changed my ideas; they've gone through and through me, like wine through water, and altered the color of my mind."

Emily Bronte, author

He had a way of nudging you. And before you knew it, you were clamoring after what you wanted in a way you never had before. It was what he did best. He was a facilitator. He pushed people, whether it was consciously or merely a product of his generosity. Two successful executives wrote and told me how Veeck had motivated them simply by giving what was then their employer, a tiny AM radio station in suburban Chicago, press credentials for the White Sox games.

Steve Weaver was working in public relations for an indoor soccer team in St. Louis when he stumbled across *Veeck—As In Wreck* at the library. He finished it in two days, wrote Veeck in Chicago and told him how much he'd enjoyed the book. Veeck wrote back, said, "Look me up when you're in Chicago."

So Weaver left St. Louis. Drove straight to Chicago. Walked into Bill Veeck's office.

"Why are you here?" Veeck asked.

Weaver showed him the letter he'd sent.

"Yes," Veeck said. "But why are you here?"

"I came to see you," Weaver said.

Weaver stayed for three days. He saw the idea box on Veeck's desk. Veeck told him the franchise lay in that box. Seven days later, a package came for Weaver. In it was a box containing a blank set of 3 x 5 cards. "Start your box," Veeck had written. "Let's trade cards."

Weaver is a broadcaster in Portland, Oregon, and he still has the box, and he still fills it with ideas.

Our dreams die only if we let them. And there is no reason to let them.

"A man is not old until regrets take the place of dreams."
John Barrymore, actor

I recently caught Bob Feller in a major-league baseball alumni game. Let's just say that, at 81, Feller doesn't have much juice left in that right arm. I could have caught his pitches barehanded. And yet I've never

Bob Feller (on mound) and Pat Williams (catching) teamed up in an old-timers game. (Author's collection)

seen a man so relish his time on the mound—as if he were still young, as if this was still Cleveland in 1948, Bill Veeck's Cleveland, and this was September and the pennant was still in doubt.

I enjoyed that moment. I enjoyed it because I don't believe in age. I stopped counting long ago. But then, we should all be like Satchel Paige, who never even started counting, and had no intention of letting go of anything. In 1965, Bill helped me sneak Satchel into town to pitch an

In 1965, the great Satchel Paige (left) pitched an exhibition game against Pat Williams' Spartanburg team. (Author's collection)

exhibition against our Spartanburg team. It was a hit. Only problem was, Satchel didn't want to leave town after that. He signed a photo for me, and it still hangs in my office. He wrote, "Best wishes from Satchel Paige, who would love to play here in Spartanburg."

Best I can figure, he was about 60 at the time.

In 1990, the late actor Walter Matthau was asked by a reporter if he was approaching retirement. Matthau replied sharply, "That word is alien to my vocabulary. Retire to what? I'm doing the work I like."

I once met a man at a convention who told me of his grandfather, a custodian at his church, who refused to retire when he was 65, who worked until he was 85, when he fell from the roof of his house and broke his shoulder.

The man couldn't raise his arm above shoulder level. He told the therapist he'd like to wax cars as his therapy. He waxed cars until he was 100, when he grew tired of it. Then he took flying lessons, and then, at 102, he began woodworking, building footstools, until he died, two days before his 105th birthday.

Our dreams die only if we let them.

Grandma Moses was painting at 101, and Picasso was painting at 90, and Bach was composing at 85, and I just hit 60 myself, yet continue to convince my body (sometimes unsuccessfully) that I am still the same teenager who dreamed of playing major-league baseball, the same tentative young man who once rumbled in his car along the gravel driveway of an estate called Tranquility, with nothing but a vague premonition of what my life might become.

"If you have built castles in the air, your work need not be lost. That is where they should be."

Henry David Thoreau, philosopher

As I hope you've noticed by now, this is a story that revels in its optimism. Understand that it is merely an attempt to reflect the dynamic impact of the most uplifting man I've known, a man whose dreams were so vivid that they sometimes startled the world around him. And it's why I leave you here, in the midst of your own dreams. All I can tell you, while in pursuit of your dreams, is to believe, to live, to hope, to enjoy yourself, to work, to risk, to persevere and to love. That's not so hard, is it?

But remember the reward. The reward is that your impact will last beyond yourself. The reward was there at Veeck's funeral, when Minnie Minoso, who once batted for Veeck's White Sox at the age of 57, the epitome of every dream this rubbery-faced and kinky-haired man had ever facilitated, showed up at the Church of St. Thomas the Apostle wearing a White Sox cap, a uniform, and baseball shoes.

When the funeral ended, Minoso went to his car, tugged on the door, and realized he'd locked himself out. He called for help. Fans started calling back with advice. Eventually, a nun emerged with a coat hanger, and Minoso jockeyed with the hanger, fiddling with the window until the lock popped open. He leapt into his car, signed a few autographs, and

Minnie Minoso was one of Bill Veeck's favorite players. (SPI archives)

sped away, tires squealing. Outside the church, the people wondered to themselves what Bill Veeck might have done; what he might have said. Outside the church, the people smiled.

Soon after the funeral, Mary Frances was digging through the house when she discovered a note. They'd always written to each other for more than three decades; notes of love and sentimentality and humor. Seems he'd written this one while waiting to be taken to the hospital for the last time.

On one side he'd expressed the depth of his love for Mary Frances. On the other, he'd written, "Tell everyone it has been lots of fun."

Afterword

by Michael Weinreb

I knew of the midget. Of course I knew of the midget. I had seen the photo-
graph of a chubby-cheeked Eddie Gaedel, of the catcher kneeling and the
umpire hunched over behind him. I had seen the midget's shrunken jersey
hanging in the Hall of Fame, and I heard mention of the flamboyant man who
claimed this moment as his legacy. But it was more than 20 years before my
birth when Eddie Gaedel batted in St. Louis, and by the time I took on this project, the
Browns were a musty piece of history, *Veeck—As In Wreck* was available only by special
order, and Veeck himself had been dead for 13 years.

And so I had concerns, writing a motivational book about a man I had never
met, a man who is known to my generation only through a legacy of photographs and
hand-me-down stories. What was the relevance, and what was the importance, and what
would be the impact of a decades-old story on my generation, a nation of unforgiving
media-saturated skeptics?

By now, you have read everything that has been written by and about these two
unquenchable men, Pat Williams and Bill Veeck. And I hope the words have a burnish of
truth to them because the truth is that I believe them myself.

Maybe it's merely a sliver, but I would like to think that I share a kindred notion
with the hundreds of others, executives, ex-players, fans, who contributed comments and
anecdotes and tributes for this project. All of us own a piece of this man. Sometimes, it
was merely a single moment in a long life, a phone conversation, a handshake, a dab of

suntan lotion, but there is a radiance to those stories that assures you it was more than that.

Veeck assuaged their fears. Veeck imbued them with confidence. Veeck freed them, helped them reach places they might not have found alone. Forgive me if that sounds ridiculously upbeat, but that's the nature of this man. Inhibitions were foreign to him. His presence, even on paper, even years after his death, is gloriously liberating.

And perhaps that's the value of men like Veeck—that they're able to filter through the debilitations of society, to illuminate what we might have set aside in an attempt to rationalize our own failures. And to do it without stripping away their sense of humor, their compassion, their unqualified zest for people.

So this is my Bill Veeck story. This is how he's changed me. Now I find myself quoting him to friends, using his philosophy as a template, asking myself, "How would Veeck handle this?" as I reconsider the direction of my career in journalism, as I head to Boston University this fall to attend a graduate program in fiction writing. "He was the first to convince me I was a writer," says Mark Kram, "not just a sportswriter."

It's possible, in some ethereal way, that he did the same for me. And someday, in the baseball Valhalla he once described in *Veeck—As In Wreck*, I hope to meet him. But there is no hurry. The day awaits.

I would like to extend my thanks to my family—to Bill Eichenberger, Larry Pantages, Greg Couch, Jim Derendal and Jim Banks, for helping me to become a writer; and to my friends Steve Recker, Ryan Jones, Damian Dobrosielski, B.J. Reyes, Kevin Gorman, David Giffels and Chuck Klosterman.

Special thanks to Terry Pluto, for his always pertinent advice and for affording me the opportunity to write this book, and to Pat Williams, the most enthusiastic co-author I will ever have, not only for inflicting my mailman with a hernia, but also for his unwavering patience and endless encouragement.

MICHAEL WEINREB
AKRON, OHIO
MAY 2000

Appendices

Bibliography

Alexander, Charles C., *Rogers Hornsby* (New York: Henry Holt and Company, 1995)

Allen, Lee, *The Hot Stove League* (New York: A.S. Barnes & Company, 1955)

Allen, Maury, *All Roads Lead to October* (New York: St. Martin's Press, 2000)

Boudreau, Lou, *Covering All the Bases* (Champaign, IL: Sagamore Publishing, 1993)

Broeg, Bob, *Memories of a Hall of Fame Sportswriter* (Champaign, IL, Sagamore Publishing, 1995)

Caray, Harry, *Holy Cow!* (New York: Villard Books, 1989)

Charlton, Jim, *The Who, What, When, Where, Why and How of Baseball* (New York: Barnes and Noble, 1999)

Condon, Dave, *The Go-Go Chicago White Sox* (New York: Coward-McCann, Inc., 1960)

Creamer, Robert W., *Stengel – His Life and Times* (New York: Simon and Schuster, 1984)

Dickson, Paul, *Baseball's Greatest Quotations* (New York: Harper Perennial, 1991)

Eskenazi, Gerald, *Bill Veeck: A Baseball Legend* (New York: McGraw-Hill Book Company, 1988)

Feller, Bob, *Now Pitching Bob Feller* (New York: HarperPerennial, 1990, 1991)

Feller, Bob, *Strikeout Story* (New York: A.S. Barnes & Company, 1947)

Fitzgerald, Ed, *The American League* (New York: A.S. Barnes & Company, 1952)

Golenbock, Peter, *The Spirit of St. Louis* (New York: Avon Books, Inc., 2000)

Gossage, Richard "Goose", *The Goose is Loose* (New York: Ballantine Books, 2000)

Greenberg, Hank with Ira Berkow, *Hank Greenberg: The Story of My Life* (New York: Times Books, 1989)

Helyar, John, *Lords of the Realm* (New York: Villard Books, 1994)

Herzog, Brad, *The Sports 100* (New York: MacMillan, 1995)

Hornsby, Rogers, *My Kind of Baseball* (New York: David McKay Company, Inc. 1953)

Kahn, Roger, *A Season in the Sun* (New York: Harper & Row Publishers, 1977)

Kaiser, David, *Epic Season* (Amherst, Mass.: University of Massachusetts Press, 1998)

Karlen, Neal, *Slouching Toward Fargo* (New York: Avon Books, 1999)

Kuhn, Bowie, *Hardball* (Lincoln, NE: University of Nebraska Press, 1987, 1997)

Lewis, Franklin, *The Cleveland Indians* (New York: G.P. Putnam's Sons, 1949)

Lieb, Frederick G., *The Baseball Story* (New York: G.P. Putnam's Sons, 1950)

Lowenfish, Lee, *The Imperfect Diamond* (New York: DaCapo Press, Inc., 1980)

MacPhail, Lee, *My Nine Innings* (Westport, CT: Meckler Books, 1989)

Marshall, William, *Baseball's Pivotal Era, 1945-1951* (Lexington, KY: The University Press of Kentucky, 1999)

Martin, Don, *Team Think* (New York: Dutton Publishing, 1993)

Meany, Tom, *There've Been Some Changes in the World of Sports* (New York: Thomas Nelson & Sons, 1962)

Miller, James Edward, *The Baseball Business* (Chapel Hill, NC: The University of North Carolina Press, 1990)

Miller, Marvin, *A Whole Different Ball Game* (New York: A Birch Lane Press Book, 1991)

Minoso, Minnie, *Just Call Me Minnie* (Champaign, IL.: Sagamore Publishing, 1994)

O'Connell, Kevin, *City of Champions* (South Euclid, OH: Green Road Press, 1997)

Okrent, Daniel and Lewine, Harris, *The Ultimate Baseball Book* (Boston: Houghton Mifflin, 1991)

Okrent, Daniel and Wulf, Steve, *Baseball Anecdotes* (New York: Harper & Row, 1989)

Paige, Satchel and David Lipman, *Maybe I'll Pitch Forever* (New York: Doubleday, 1962)

Patkin, Max and Stan Hochman, *The Clown Prince of Baseball* (Waco, TX: WRS Publishers, 1994)

Peary, Danny, *We Played the Game* (New York: Hyperion, 1994)

Pepe, Phil, *Talkin' Baseball* (New York: Ballantine Books, 1998)

Petterchak, Janice and Jack Brickhouse, *A Voice for All Seasons* (Chicago, IL: Contemporary Books, 1996)

Phalen, Rick, *A Bittersweet Journey* (Tampa, FL: McGregor Publishing, 2000)

Pietrusza, David, *Baseball – The Biographical Encyclopedia* (Kingston, NY: Total Sports Illustrated, 2000)

Pietrusza, David, *Judge and Jury, The Life and Times of Judge Kenesaw Mountain Landis* (South Bend, IN: Diamond Communications, Inc., 1998)

Pluto, Terry, *Our Tribe* (New York: Simon & Schuster, 1999)

Pluto, Terry, *The Curse of Rocky Colavito* (New York: Simon & Schuster, 1994)

Reidenbaugh, Lowell, *Cooperstown – Where the Legends Live Forever* (New York: Gramercy Books, 1999)

Ribowsky, Mark, *Don't Look Back – Satchel Paige in the Shadows of Baseball* (New York: Simon & Schuster, 1994)

Schneider, Russell, *The Boys of the Summer of '48* (Champaign, IL: Sports Publishing, Inc. 1998)

Singletary, Wes, and Al Lopez, *The Life of Baseball's El Senior* (Jefferson, NC: McFarland & Co. Publishers, 1999)

Smith, Curt, *The Storytellers* (New York: MacMillan, 1995)

Smith, Curt, *Voices of the Game* (New York: Simon & Schuster, 1987, 1992)

Smith, Peter, *Onward!* (New York: Scribner, 2000)

Stone, Steve, *Teach Yourself to Win* (Chicago, IL: Bonus Books, Inc., 1991)

Strock, James M., *Reagan on Leadership* (Rocklin, CAL: Forum, 1998)

Sugar, Bert Randolph, *Hit the Sign and Win a Free Suit of Clothes from Harry Finklestein* (Chicago, IL: Contemporary Books, 1978)

Thompson, Chuck, *Ain't the Beer Cold* (South Bend, IN: Diamond Communications, Inc., 1996)

Torry, Jack, *Endless Summers* (South Bend, IN: Diamond Communications, Inc. 1996)

Tygiel, Jules, *Baseball's Great Experiment* (New York: Oxford University Press, 1983, 1997)

Vandenberg, Bob, *'59 Summer of the Sox* (Champaign, IL: Sports Publishing, Inc., 1999)

Vandenberg, Bob, *Minnie and the Mick* (South Bend, IN: Diamond Communications, Inc., 1996)

Vandenberg, Bob, *Sox: From Lane and Fain to Zisk and Fisk* (Chicago, IL: Chicago Review Press, 1982)

Veeck, Bill with Linn, Ed, *The Hustler's Handbook* (New York: G.P. Putnam's Sons, 1965)

Veeck, Bill with Linn, Ed, *Thirty Tons a Day* (New York: The Viking Press, 1972)

Veeck, Bill with Linn, Ed, V*eeck—As In Wreck* (New York: G.P. Putnam's Sons, 1962, 1986)

Wallace, Joseph, *Baseball – 100 Classic Moments in the History of the Game* (New York: Dorling Kindersley, 2000)

Ward, Geoffrey C. and Burns, Ken, *Baseball – An Illustrated History* (New York: Alfred A Knopf, 1994)

Williams, Pat with Bill Lyon, *We Owed You One* (Wilmington, DE: TriMark, 1983)

Williams, Pat with Jerry B. Jenkins, *The Gingerbread Man* (Philadelphia: Holman Publishers, 1974)

Williams, Pat with Jim Denney, *Ahead of the Game* (Grand Rapids, MI: Fleming H. Revell, 1999)

Williams, Pat with Jim Denney, *Go For the Magic* (Nashville, TN: Thomas Nelson, 1995)

Williams, Pat with Jim Denney, *The Magic of Teamwork* (Nashville, TN: Thomas Nelson, 1997)

Williams, Pat with Larry Guest, *Making Magic* (Orlando, FL: Sentinel Communications, Inc., 1989)

Wolfe, Rich and George Castle, *I Remember Harry Caray* (Champaign, IL: Sports Publishing, Inc., 1998)

Young, A.S. "Doc", *Great Negro Baseball Stars* (New York: A.S. Barnes & Company, 1953)

In Appreciation . . .

I have been researching this book for over 40 years. During those years, I corresponded with close to 700 people who all provided a unique view of Bill Veeck. A few of the people I've listed did not know Bill personally but were still kind enough to take the time to respond to me anyway. I'm grateful to all of these special people and apologize if I omitted anyone's name. The contributors are listed by category.

I want to extend special thanks to the following organizations who really extended themselves in providing me with articles and photographs related to Bill Veeck's life:

Baseball America (Alan Simpson and Will Lingo)

Baseball Weekly (Paul White)

Brace Photos (George and Mary Brace)

National Baseball Hall of Fame and Museum (Jeff Idelson, Jim Gates, Rich Gannon, Bruce Markusen, Eric Enders and Staff)

Society for American Baseball Research—SABR (Ted Hathaway)

Sports Illustrated (Rob Fleder)

The Sporting News (John Rawlings, Sean Deveney, Peter Newcomb and Steve Geitschier)

Baseball Scouts

Hugh Alexander

Ellis Clary (deceased)

Jocko Collins

Nick Kamzic

Ed Liberatore

Wes Livengood (deceased)

Mrs. Wes Livingston

Fred McAllister

Gary Nickels

Art Parrack (deceased)

Harry Postove (deceased)

Art Stewart

Ollie Vanek (deceased)

Broadcasters and Producers

Mel Allen (deceased)

Eddie Andelman

Richie Ashburn (deceased)

Vince Bagley

Red Barber (deceased)

Bud Blattner

Jack Brickhouse (deceased)

Heywood Hale Broun

Lorn Brown

Jack Buck

Bill Campbell

Chip Caray

Harry Caray (deceased)

Skip Caray

Ken Coleman

Bud Collins

Beano Cook

Chet Coppock

Howard Cosell (deceased)

Steve Dahl

Jeff Davis

Jim Durham

Randy Eccles

Bob Elson (deceased)

Dick Enberg

Pete Franklin

Peter Gammons

Joe Garagiola

Marty Glickman

Curt Gowdy

Dave Greenwalt

Jerry Gross

Milo Hamilton

Ken "Hawk" Harrelson

Arne Harris

Ernie Harwell

Sonny Hirsch (deceased)

Pat Hughes

Dave Kaplan

Jim Karvellas

Larry King

Gene Kirby

Mike Leideman

Roy Leonard

Vince Lloyd

Denny Matthews

Tim McCarver

Jim McKay

Sean McManus
Red Mottlow
Bill Mazer
John Mengelt
Jon Miller
Jeannie Morris
Johnny Morris
Brent Musburger
Brad Palmer
Jim Paschke
Wally Phillips
Bob Prince (deceased)
Ed Randall
Jay Randolph
Jack Rosenberg
Byrum Saam (deceased)
Dick Schaap

Vin Scully
Ken Solarz
Fran Spielman
Bill Stern (deceased)
Chuck Swirsky
Joe Tait
Jack Taylor
Chris Thomas
Chuck Thompson
Bob Uecker
Tim VanWagoner
Steve Weaver
Tim Weigel
Chris Wheeler
Warner Wolf
Bob Wolff

Educators

Roger Noll
Ben Ockner

Bill Sutton
Andrew Zimbalist

Family and Friends of Bill Veeck

Jean Breithaupt
Keith Buralli
Phil Frye (deceased)

Jimmy Gallios
Scott Jones
Nick Kladis

Former Employees/Partners/ Associates of Bill Veeck

Elise Allen

Bob Bertucci

Roger Bossard

Fred Brozozowski

Milton Cross

Aaron Cushman

David Dombrowski

Bill Durney (deceased)

Mrs. Bill Durney

Charlie Evranian

Nancy Faust

Bob Fishel (deceased)

David Frye

Peter Frye

Bea Furlong

Tess Glatzhofer

Hank Greenberg (deceased)

Dick Hackett

G. Leo Hughes (deceased)

Evelyn Johnson

George Koch

Fred Krehbiel

R. E. Littlehohn (deceased)

Jeffrey Loebel

John McCartney

Gary Mowder

Max Patkin (deceased)

Howard Pizer

Roy Rivas

Jean Robbins

Glenn Rosenbaum

David Schaffer

Rudie Schaffer

Herm Schneider

Judy Shoemaker

Chuck Shriver

Ken Solomon

Tom Weinberg

Former Players and Wives

Luis Aparacio

Harold Baines

Frank Baumann

Yogi Berra

Ron Blomberg

Bob Boone

Ray Boone

Thad Bosley

Jim Bouton

Jim Brosnan

Ken Brett

Tommy Byrne

Mrs. Tommy Byrne (Sue)

Bob Cain (deceased)

Mrs. Bob Cain (Judy)

Phil Cavaretta

Clint Courtney (deceased)

Jim Delsing

Joe DeMaestri

Billy DeMars

Bucky Dent

Dom DiMaggio

Larry Doby

Moe Drabowsky

Ryne Duren

Jim Dyck (deceased)

Harry Eisenstat

Del Ennis (deceased)

Sammy Esposito

Ed Farmer

Bob Feller

Mrs. Nellie Fox (Joanne)

Stan Galle

Oscar Gamble

Ralph Garr

Ned Garver

Joe Ginsberg

Rich "Goose" Gossage

Otto Graham

Steve Gromek

Johnny Groth

Mel Harder

Jim Hegan (deceased0

Mrs. Jim Hegan (Clare)

Mike Hegan

Mrs. Elston Howard (Arlene)

Billy Hunter

Monte Irvin

Don Johnson (deceased)

Judy Johnson (deceased)

Lamar Johnson

Jim Kaat

Russ Kemmerer

Bob Kennedy

Tony Kubek

Whitey Kurowski (deceased)

Lerrin LaGrow

Jim Landis

Chet Lemon

Jim Lemon

Don Lenhardt

Danny Litwhiler

Frank Mancuso

Babe Martin

Len Merullo

Ed Mickelson

Gene Michael

Minnie Minoso

Les Moss

Hal Naragon

Buck O'Neil

Andy Pafko

Satchel Paige (deceased)

Billy Pierce

Jimmy Piersall

Duane Pillette

Ted "Double-Duty" Radcliff

Robin Roberts

Eddie Robinson

Rich Rollins

Al Rosen

Ron Santo

Herb Score

Andy Seminick

Bob Shaw

Roy Sievers

Moose Skowron

Al Smith

Eric Soderholm

Jim Spencer

Mike Squires

Steve Stone

Dizzy Trout (deceased)

Steve Trout

Virgil Trucks

Mickey Vernon

Al Widmar

Del Wilbur

Del Wilbur Jr.

Stan Williams

Ted Williams

Ken Wood

Wilbur Wood

Allan Worthington

Early Wynn (deceased)

Gus Zernial

Richie Zisk

Managers and Coaches

Sparky Anderson

Ray Berres

Lou Boudreau

Bobby Bragan

Vic Bubas

Leo Durocher (deceased)

Dallas Green

Don Gutteridge

Don Kessinger

Tony La Russa

Tommy Lasorda

Bob Lemon (deceased)

Jim Leyland

Al Lopez

Marty Marion

Jim Marshall

Jack McKeon

Charlie Metro

Ray Meyer

Russ Nixon

Paul Richards (deceased)

Bill Rigney

Don Shula

Jack Stallings

Casey Stengel (deceased)

Chuck Tanner

Zack Taylor (deceased)

Public Relations/Publicity Executives

Bob Allen

Marty Appel

Brian Bartow

Ben Bentley

Rick Cerrone

Haskell Cohen (deceased)

Benjamin de la Fuente

Bob DiBiaso

Joel Glass

Bob Ibach

Cliff Kachline

Richard Levin

Christine Mankowski

Alex Martins

Brian McIntyre

Tim Mead

Harvey Pollack

Scott Reifert

Rich Rice

Bob Rosenberg

Marsh Samuel

Larry Shenk

Amber Simon

Ed Smason

Bill Stetka

Jason Zillo

Dave Zinkoff

Sports Executives

Ernie Accorsi

Dick Armstrong

Buzzie Bavasi

Peter Bavasi

Gary Bettman

Stormy Bidwell

Marty Blake

Jim Bowden

Bob Brown

Dr. Gene Budig

Bob Carpenter (deceased)

Ruly Carpenter

Frank Cashen

A.B. "Happy" Chandler (deceased)

Jerry Colangelo

Ned Colletti

Blake Cullen

Harry Dalton

Bing Devine

William DeWitt Sr. (deceased)

Bill DeWitt Jr.

Andy Dolich

Frank Dolson

Richard Dozer

Milt Drier

Ruth Dryjanski

Eddie Einhorn

Dan Evans

Don Fehr

Howard Fox

Rob Gallis

Bill Giles

Stephen Giles

Pat Gillick

Lou Gorman

Eddie Gottlieb (deceased)

Jack Gould

Steve Greenberg

Calvin Griffith (deceased)

George Halas (deceased)

Barry Halper

John Harrington

Roland Hemond

Jerry Hoffberger (deceased)

Bob Howsam

Max Jacobs

Stan Kasten

Ben Kerner

Dick Klein

Irv Kosloff (deceased)

Jerry Krause

Larry Lucchino

Andy MacPhail

Larry MacPhail (deceased)

Lee MacPhail

Mike McClure

Andy McKenna

Dr. John McMullen

Doug Melvin

Gene Michael

Marvin Miller

Art Modell

Dick Moss

Dick O'Connell

Peter O'Malley

Gabe Paul (deceased)

Gabe Paul Jr.

Hank Peters

Bob Quinn

John Quinn (deceased)

Jerry Reinsdorf

Arthur Richman

Herk Robinson

Dave Rosenfield

Terry Ryan

Jerry Sachs

Abe Saperstein (deceased)

Ron Schueler

Allan H. "Bud" Selig

Bill Smith

Tal Smith

Jon Spoelstra

Dr. Charles Steinberg

Jon Steinmiller

David Stern

Lee Stern

Syd Thrift

Jim Toomey

Mike Veeck

Fay Vincent

Roger Wexelberg

Phil Wrigley (deceased)

Sportswriters

Maury Allen

Dave Anderson

Bob August

Lacy J. Banks

Gordon Beard

Furman Bisher

Bob Blanchard

Hal Bodley

Thomas Boswell

Bob Broeg

Bob Burns (deceased)

Roger Brown

Jimmy Burns (deceased)

John Carmichael (deceased)

Al Cartwright

Murray Chass

Bill Christine

Dave Condon (deceased)

Mike Conklin

Bill Conlin

Frank Deford

Mike Downey

Dick Dozer (deceased)

Joe Durso

Jerry Eizenberg

Jim Enright (deceased)

Joe Falls

David Feschuk

Ron Firmite

Ed Fitzgerald

Red Foley

William Barry Furlong

Mary Garber

Joe Gilmartin

Bill Gleason

Joe Goddard

Bill Granger

Jerry Greene

Jack Griffin (deceased)

Larry Guest

Sid Hartman

Mark Heisler

Philip Hersch

Mickey Herskowitz

Stan Hochman

Bob Holbrook

Jerome Holtzman

Ken Hornack

Stan Isaacs

Melissa Isaacson

David Israel

Phil Jackman

Steve Jacobson

Bill Jauss

Roger Kahn

Ray Kelly (deceased)

Dave Kindred

Moss Klein

Leonard Koppett

Mark Kram

Dave Krider

John Kuenster

Sam Lacy

Jack Lang

George Langford

Ring Lardner, Jr.

Hal Lebovitz

Allen Lewis

Bernie Linsicome

Jim Litke

Bill Livingston

Bob Logan

Doug Looney

John Lowe

Mike Lupica

Bill Lyon

Will McDonough

Bill Madden

Bob Maisel

Bob Marcus

Rudy Martzke

Peter May

Jackie MacMullan

George McClelland

Tom Meany (deceased)

Larry Merchant

Bernie Miklasz

Fred Mitchell

Joe Mooshil

Leigh Montville

Malcom Moran

Jim Mullen

Mark Mulvoy

Ed Munzel

Jim Murray (deceased)

Skip Myslenski

Ross Newhan

Ken Nigro

Phil Pepe

George Plimpton

Terry Pluto

Ed Pope

Shirley Povich (deceased)

Bob Oates

Ed Prell (deceased)

Ron Rapoport

Rick Reilly

Tracy Ringolsby

Cooper Rollow

Ed Rooney

Steve Rosenbloom

Bob Ryan

Bus Saidt (deceased)

Brian Schmitz

Russell Schneider

John Schulian

Blackie Sherrod

Terry Smith (son of Red Smith)

Wendell Smith (deceased)

Ray Sons

Watson Spoelstra (deceased)

Jayson Stark

John Steadman

Eddie Storin

Bert Randolph Sugar

Paul Sullivan

Rick Talley (deceased)

Rick Telander

Les Timms

Dave Van Dyck

George Vass

George Vecsey

Bob Verdi

Mark Whicker

Russ White

Larry Whiteside

Bob Wolfley

Steve Wulf

Bob Young

Matt Zabitka

Vick Ziegel

Paul Zimmerman

Writers, Authors, Publishers, and Editors

Renuka Andrew
Roger Angell
Ira Berkow
Asher J. Birnbaum
Bill Brashler
Jimmy Breslin
Terry Cannon
George Castle
David Claerbaut
Bob Creamer
Gerald Eskenazi
Allan Goldstein
Peter Golenbock
Ron Green
Bob Greene
David Halbertstam
Eldon Ham
W.C. Heinz
Kenan Heise
John Helyar

Hank Hersh
Donald Honig
David M. Jordan
Pat Jordan
Irv Kupcinet
Roland Lazenby
Ed Linn (deceased)
Lee Lowenfish
Jeff Neuman
Kevin O'Connell
Daniel Okrent
George Plimpton
Doug Raymond
Larry Ritter
Ray Robinson
Mike Royko
Studs Terkel
John Underwood
Rick Wolff

Chicago Area Fans

Richard Ahrendt
Larry Axelrood
Peter Baker
Dr. Tom Baldwin
Lee Balterman
Dale Barnes
Fred Batko
Jack Beermann
Paul Bird

Tony Borcich
Bob Budler
John Burke
Don Burns
Mike Chagdes
Wayne Chinn
Tom Crigley
Alan Crown
Jeff Davis

Bill Fagiano

Chuck Farnenkel

Mike Finch

Frank Flanagan

Bob Formanski

Marc Friedman

Neal Friedman

Allan Goldin

Ron Grahl

Carmela Hartigan

Bill Hoagland

John Hoermann

Rev. Jesse Jackson

Jack Jacobson

Roger Johnson

Ted Karavidas

Jim Kauss

Jim Kigewski

Mike Kristan

Harriett Layfield

Jay Leon

Jeff Loman

Don Lynch

Pat McCallig

Mike McCarney

Dr. William McCarthy

Tim Moehl

Kevin Newman

Ed Nichols

Bob Panek

Evans Papanikolaou

Emil Peterson

Don Petritis

Bill Pokrajac

Avi Poster

Jerry Pritikin

Tony Radinski

Bert Rappaport

Paul Rosenbaum

Jim Ross

Jack Ruddy

John Ruddy

Tony Rudecki

Keith Shay

Richard Smith

Bob Strunck

Mike Sullivan

John Suralski

Jerry Tatar

Page Townsley

Greg Viti

Ray Vollacker

Tim Voss

John Walsh

Jim Warden

Paul Weininger

Bob Whitney

Norb Wojtanowski

Cleveland Fans

Ed Bieri

Chuck Pasternak

Jim Prohaska

Norton Rose

Bob White

St. Louis Fans

Bill Borst

Irv Fisher

Gene French

Lou Gualdoni

Charlie Hughes

Bill Miller

Tom Raber

Dr. Rodney Wead

Milwaukee Fans

Dr. Paul Bank

Mort Comisar

Ken Klein

Jerry Mendelsohn

Ron Meredith

Barbara Mueller

Carlton Roffa

Jack Rogers

Dick Schultz

Ed Smith

John Stern

Tim "Shoe" Sullivan

Miscellaneous Fans

Gil Asbrook – Scottsdale, AZ

Jack Barns – Sarastoa, FL

Carol Beeler – Orlando, FL

John Bernhart

Jim Brahe – Orlando, FL

Terry Cashman – New York

Ted Cobb – New York

Bill Connell – Boston, MA

Ruth Cornelison – Wilmington, DE

Karen Couch – Texas

Sean Deveney

Rob Dewey – Virginia Beach, VA

Rudy Drnek

Cal Goldberg – Boston, CT

Dave Harpham

Phil Hochberg – Washington, D.C.

Ken Hussar – Lancaster, PA

Steve Hyde – Wilmington, DE

Randy Johnson – Alabama

Roger Johnson

Dave Kaplan - New Jersey

Tom Lambke, Phoenix, AZ

Harvey MacKay – Minneapolis, MN

Jeff McCauley – Utah

Michael Marlewski

Harry, Jeanette and Kevin Meisel – Orlando, FL

Dick Miller – Austin, TX

George Mitrovich – San Diego, CA

Bill Ossher – Phoenix, AZ

Charlie Owen – Maryland

Jeff Parsons

Bob Reich

Jack Robarts – Boston, CT

Don Roth – Lynbrook, NY

Mort Schanerman – NY

Dick Smith – Arlington, VA

Jay Strack – Orlando, FL

Paul Verschoor – Phoenix, AZ

Craig White

Ken Wilson – Los Angeles, CA

Tom Wolf – Los Angeles, CA

Hugh Wyatt – Baltimore, MD

If you would like to contact Pat Williams directly, please call him on his direct line at (407) 916-2404 or e-mail him at pwilliams@rdvsports.com. Mail can be sent to the following address:

Pat Williams
c/o RDV Sports
8701 Maitland Summit Boulevard
Orlando, FL 32810

If you would like to contact Pat Williams regarding speaking engagements, please contact his assistant, Melinda Ethington. She can be reached at the above address or at her direct number at (407) 916-2454. Requests can also be faxed to (407) 916-2986 or e-mailed to methington@rdvsports.com.

We would love to hear from you. Please send your comments about this book to Pat Williams at the above address or in care of our publisher at the address below. Thank you.

Mike Pearson
Sports Publishing, Inc.
804 N. Neil St., Suite 100
Champaign, IL 61820
http://www.SportsPublishingInc.com